*National Insecurity and Human Rights*

# National Insecurity and Human Rights

*Democracies Debate Counterterrorism*

*Edited by*
ALISON BRYSK *and* GERSHON SHAFIR

*Global, Area, and International Archive*
*University of California Press*
BERKELEY   LOS ANGELES   LONDON

The Global, Area, and International Archive (GAIA) is an initiative of
International and Area Studies, University of California, Berkeley, in
partnership with the University of California Press, the California
Digital Library, and international research programs across the UC
system. GAIA volumes, which are published in both print and open-
access digital editions, represent the best traditions of regional studies,
reconfigured through fresh global, transnational, and thematic
perspectives.

University of California Press, one of the most distinguished university
presses in the United States, enriches lives around the world by
advancing scholarship in the humanities, social sciences, and natural
sciences. Its activities are supported by the UC Press Foundation and by
philanthropic contributions from individuals and institutions. For more
information, visit www.ucpress.edu.

University of California Press
Berkeley and Los Angeles, California

University of California Press, Ltd.
London, England



Library of Congress Cataloging-in-Publication Data

National insecurity and human rights : democracies debate
counterterrorism / edited by Alison Brysk and Gershon Shafir.
    p.      cm. — (Global, area, and international archive)
    Includes bibliographical references and index.
    ISBN-13: 978-0-520-09860-2 (pbk. : alk. paper)
      1. Civil rights—Case studies.    2. Human rights—Case studies.
    3. Terrorism—Prevention.    4. International law—Case studies.
    I. Brysk, Alison, 1960– II. Shafir, Gershon.
    JC585.N37   2007
    363.325'17—dc22                                          2007018438

Manufactured in the United States of America

16   15   14   13   12   11   10   09   08   07
10   9   8   7   6   5   4   3   2   1

The paper used in this publication meets the minimum requirements of
ANSI/NISO Z39.48–1992 (R 1997) (Permanence of Paper).

# Contents

*To those who stand for rights in the face of fear—
especially Miriam and Vivienne.*

# Acknowledgments

We undertook this project as concerned scholars and citizens who saw the international abuses and logic of conflict we had each studied for decades in other regions suddenly echoed in our own society. We were also inspired by responses to these legal abuses from global civil society, in this case the perspectives of our academic colleagues from various democracies who cast a critical eye on the decline of U.S. behavior and norms, challenging us to explain what went wrong. As American civil society finally begins to question the conduct of the post–September 11 "war on terror," and concerned publics in other democracies debate counterterror measures inspired or encouraged by the United States, we hope to contribute a comparative analysis that shows that (state) crime does not pay—and reminds us that human rights is the basis for a just *and* effective foreign policy.

A key intellectual catalyst for this project came from Alison Brysk's participation in the Transatlantic Dialogue on Human Rights (2004–5), organized by the University of Minnesota's David Weissbrodt, the University of Essex's Kevin Boyle, Morten Kjaerum of the Danish Human Rights Institute, and J. Paul Martin of Columbia University, and supported by Marco Stoffel of the Third Millennium Foundation. All of the participants in these Copenhagen and New York sessions helped to shape the agenda for this project, and contributed greatly to our knowledge of the issues.

This volume grows directly from a conference held in February 2006 at UC San Diego and UC Irvine. That conference was attended by all of the contributors, as well as Frank Buijs (University of Amsterdam, Netherlands). Their willingness to travel long distances on short notice, draft incisive analyses of emerging issues on tight deadlines, and engage in days of thoughtful, constructive dialogue give this volume whatever virtues it may possess.

We are extremely grateful to a collection of institutions that sponsored the conference, whose flexibility recognized the policy relevance of the topic. They include UCSD's Dean of Social Sciences Paul Drake and Sociology Department, and UCI's Citizen Peace-building Program, Center for Unconventional Security, Center for Global Peace and Conflict Studies, Dean of Research William Parker, Center for the Scientific Study of Ethics, and Political Science Department.

We were also blessed with the enthusiastic and multifaceted support of an extraordinary team of graduate assistants: Helia Jazayeri, Daniel Wehrenfennig, and Joseph Klett. Helia's identification of literature and participants, Daniel's logistical wizardry and contribution to Chapter 10, and Joseph's work on a comprehensive timeline of events were essential and much appreciated.

Finally, a special note of thanks to Nathan MacBrien and UC Press, who showed unusually early and consistent support for the project. Nathan's vision and encouragement, as well as GAIA as a home for wide diffusion of new work in international studies, transformed a reverie into a reality.

# 1 Human Rights and National Insecurity

Alison Brysk

Human rights is the first casualty of unconventional war. Even in liberal democracies, perceptions of national insecurity can rapidly destroy citizen support for international law and democratic values, such as the rule of law and tolerance. Political leaders and defense establishments arrogate the right to determine national interest and security threat, undermining democratic checks and balances and creating a politics of fear. When terrorist violence is framed as a war—an uncontrollable, external, absolute threat to existence and identity—it disrupts the democratic functioning and global ties of target societies. Terrorism has succeeded in destroying democracy when a national security state, without the knowledge or consent of its citizens, tortures and kills detainees, runs secret prisons, kidnaps foreign nationals and deports them to third countries to be abused, imprisons asylum seekers, spies on its citizens, and impedes freedoms of movement, association, and expression on the basis of religion and national origin.

But some democracies do better than others, even in the face of overwhelming threats. How can liberal democracies cope liberally? We can learn from comparing experiences and exploring alternatives from the United States, United Kingdom, Israel, Spain, Canada, and Germany. We find that counterterror policies reflect a state's history of threat and consequent institutional toolkit, the construction of its national interest, and the public's perception of the threat to that interest. Since similarly situated target states advance different counterterror policies, to safeguard rights in the face of threat we must analyze the influence of differing rights values, legal regimes, incorporation of international norms, and legitimacy base for the exercise of authority. If we can rethink national security so it is not a fixed defense of borders by any means necessary, but an evolving mode of protection for citizens from both external and institutional violence, human rights become neither a trade-off nor a luxury. Rather, they constitute an integral part of a sustainable defense of the citizenry and the democratic political community.

This book considers the responses to security threat in policies regarding the use of torture, detention, and civil liberties in the "best-case scenarios" of developed liberal democracies: the United States, United Kingdom, Israel, Spain, Canada, and Germany.[1] Beyond comparing distinctive responses, as members of the Western alliance and partners in multilateral endeavors, many of our cases mutually influence policies, from the importation of the "Israeli model" to the United States, to U.S. pressure on Canada. These cases also display different phases of response to historical waves of terror. The general trend shows that lessons learned from a previous phase eventually improve responses that protect rights. Like Art and Richardson's (2006) wide-ranging study of prior democratic experiences with combating terrorist threats, we conclude that democracy is actually the best basis for a long-term response.

## FROM 9/11 TO ABU GHRAIB: IS THE CURE WORSE THAN THE DISEASE?

The now-infamous photos from Iraq's Abu Ghraib prison—hooded, manacled detainees subjected to torture and degradation at the hands of smiling U.S. guards—were a veritable shot heard 'round the world representing the loss of human rights standards by a country founded on rule of law that had invaded Iraq to establish democracy. While members of the George W. Bush administration attempted to paint the behavior at Abu Ghraib as an isolated incident, the scandal quickly became intertwined with related revelations: extensive violations and indefinite detention at Guantanamo, dozens of detainee deaths at U.S.-controlled facilities in Afghanistan and Iraq, at least 100 illicit extraditions ("renditions") to outsource the torture of detainees to abusive allies in the "war on terror," thousands of undocumented and indefinite detentions within the United States, prolonged imprisonment and/or summary deportation of immigrants and asylum seekers, and widespread loss of civil rights under the Patriot Act and related changes in domestic security policies and practices. Although the United States had not been immune to historical abuses against dissidents and racial and ethnic minorities, or to war crimes abroad, the extent, systematic design, and justification of human rights violations following 9/11 was unprecedented (Ratner and Ray 2004; Mayer 2005a, 2005b; Sidel 2004). Furthermore, the extensive record of memos and debates within the Bush administration, as well as military investigations, show that these abuses were the result of systematic policies, not the excesses of pathological individuals.

The 9/11 attacks—the catalyst for new U.S. counterterror policies—unleashed a dynamic of escalating unconventional war described as a newly necessary response to the threat of globalized terror networks. Yet that response bears comparison to historic and comparative patterns of abusive counterinsurgency, from Algeria to Argentina. The approximately 3,000 Americans who were tragically and reprehensibly murdered at the World Trade Center and the Pentagon have not been honored by the similar numbers brutalized in Guantanamo, Abu Ghraib, Afghan battlefields, and third-country renditions—nor by the now estimated 150,000 Iraqi civilians killed since the U.S. invasion. There is no credible evidence that post-9/11 policies have improved the security of American citizens or prevented further attacks (Benjamin and Simon 2004), and indeed a lack of intelligence coordination and multilateral support—which the 9/11 investigations suggest increased U.S. vulnerability—has only been exacerbated by the new national security state (9/11 Public Discourse Project 2005; Pfaff 2005). Of 417 suspects charged in terror-related investigations, only 39 have been convicted—most of lesser charges (Shane and Bergman 2006). The only country where attacks arguably have been forestalled, the United Kingdom, has followed a distinctive model incorporating much greater accountability to the rule of law (albeit not absent abuses). At this point, it seems fair to say that the cure has been worse than the disease (Hersh 2004).

At the same time, a historic weakness of U.S. security policy and scholarship has been a reluctance to consider relevant comparative experience. That is the goal of this volume. This gap is especially ironic since national security by definition must occur within an international context of interaction with allies, enemies, and border-crossing flows and forces. Cross-national comparisons reveal a broader set of potential responses to national insecurity that can often provide a more justifiable mode of protection for citizens.

The case studies in this book analyze the determinants, incidence, and implications of counterterror policy in terms of human rights, complementing several recent theoretical and global examinations (Wilson, ed., 2005; Roth and Worden 2005). We find that counterterror policies are determined by the construction of national security, struggles between legal regimes and the politics of fear, and the international context.

## THE CONSTRUCTION OF NATIONAL SECURITY

Historical experience plays a dynamic role in the construction of national security, as states learn and institutionalize different modal responses to the trauma of war, previous terrorist threat, shifting national and regional boundaries, and alliances (Katzenstein 2003). For example, whereas the

United States faced 9/11 with a relative dearth of recent security doctrine and an emerging default unilateralism, Germany had absorbed a systematic reconstitution of its identity following defeat in World War II, previous democratic response to a more manageable terrorist threat during the 1970s, and a strong normative and institutional commitment to European regional security. Such baseline experiences are renegotiated by national elites when new threats emerge, by reference to broader constructions of national security by their own publics, security forces, experts, and the international community.

Does national security mean the protection of borders, citizens, or government? As authorities face a variety of internal and external threats to public order, a critical question in their response will be, security *for whom?* This, in turn, depends on whether the state is conceived as a territorial, ethnic, democratic, or cosmopolitan political community. Each of these conceptions dictates a corresponding orientation to national security: sovereignty for territory, nationalism for ethnic membership, citizenship rights for democratic domestic community, and international law for global community.

Perception of the source of threat is also crucial, that is, security *from what?* Is the use of violence by nonstate actors constructed as a war (local, global, or metaphorical), crime, social conflict—or even a state of nature? National defense will depend upon who is being defended from what. Security from conventional war dictates military means, typically partially restrained through the Hague and Geneva Conventions, whereas unconventional war downplays interstate laws of war and multilateral alliances. In contrast, control of criminal violence is usually subsumed in democratic legal systems, although it may be less subject to international monitoring and standards. The view of terrorism as an expression of social conflict reflecting comprehensible grievances (albeit not necessarily justifiable) has not been widely accepted by the cases in our study, but would theoretically articulate with global initiatives of developmentalism, humanitarian intervention, and/or conflict prevention in source areas—something resembling a human security perspective.

Furthermore, all of these types of states and national defense concepts are *most* at risk for systematic violations of rights when challengers are defined as "evildoers" beyond the scope of human community. When terrorists are inscribed as part of a state of nature—a transhistorical plague, or "enemies of humanity," as pirates once were—they forfeit even the rights of enemies or criminals. Since terrorists reject the distinction between soldiers and civilians by definition, the stage is set for the state to respond in kind. National security ideology can predispose or exacerbate obedient enactment of total suppression, when counterinsurgency is predicated on eradicating the identity and existence of the Other, not just controlling the illicit use of violence. Although legitimate war and policing commonly resort to the dehumanization of their target group, counterterror policies against an unmarked threat that crosses both identity boundaries and state borders are especially prone to this political imaginary, as a psychological defense against radical uncertainty.

What do these constructions of national insecurity mean for universal standards of individual human dignity? Territorial states defending their sovereignty against unconventional war, such as the United States, may quickly trade their internal democratic commitments against external threat; human rights stop at the water's edge. Ethnic states like Spain will also face severe challenges, but will be more successful at maintaining rights standards when challengers are defined as internal criminals subject to domestic standards rather than external ethnic enemies. Further along the spectrum, states with cosmopolitan identities like Germany or strong citizenship regimes such as Britain should be more responsive to universal norms. Although all states reflect some shifting blend of security identities and threat perceptions, we can identify dominant characteristics and link them to rights outcomes. However, all liberal democracies now face the additional challenge of a post-neoliberal securitization of state identity, in which the shrinking welfare state reinscribes its role as a guardian of public order. But when security *from unconventional threat* overwhelms public deliberation and the rule of law, national insecurity becomes a recipe for human rights abuse.

## "DIRTY WAR" ON DEMOCRACY: THE POLITICS OF FEAR

All social systems include some rule-governed coercive responses to unauthorized violence. But when states' monopoly of coercion is challenged by domestic or transnational wielders of violence, rather than by competing militaries, some leaders argue and citizens come to believe that conventional defense cannot protect them. The politics of fear includes the construction of threats as total and unknowable, enemies as subhuman Others, and the use of force as a healthy and necessary assertion of identity that overrides the rights of potential enemies. In times of national insecurity, paternalistic elites manipulate primal fears to answer the question, *security by whom?* by narrowing decision making into the executive branch of government, and even within an individual executive.

Under conditions of national insecurity, security elites often invoke "states of exception" to suspend the rule of law, which may also include derogations of international commitments. They argue that individual rights to liberty are trumped by the collective right to security—and fearful publics often support such arguments. "Necessity," they claim, knows no law. Democratic institutions that check executive and military power are denigrated, courts evaded, and opposition parties co-opted. And when security threats are constructed as total war, the need for intelligence becomes the overwhelming logic of counterinsurgency, all of which shifts military doctrine and institutional forms toward military dominance, executive privilege, the use of special forces, and the unchecked power of intelligence agencies.

The unpredictability of terror heightens its disruptive impact, especially in open societies whose functioning depends on high levels of flow of people, production, and communication across borders, as Richard Falk's chapter in this volume makes clear. National insecurity as radical uncertainty pushes state policies toward three distinct but linked distortions of democracy and the rule of law: state terror, the use of torture, and outsourcing of the state's "legitimate monopoly on coercion." State terror is the adoption of unaccountable unofficial structures and tactics by state agents that shadow the official national security state, "fighting fire with fire" through the creation or redeployment of special forces, and practices such as targeted assassination. These forces use torture, which eventually spreads through regular military and police units in the speculative belief that it can yield information on the hidden enemy—even though that belief has proven ineffective and even counterproductive in the larger political struggle. In a related vein, states seek to escape from accountability for the indiscriminate and illegitimate use of force in counterterror by creating grey zones of governance: quasi-autonomous units like paramilitaries and private security contractors, offshore and clandestine detention centers, and closed military tribunals (Lelyveld 2005).

Although these developments have occurred in somewhat parallel fashion across threatened democracies, the ideology and practices of national insecurity have been accepted more readily in some cases than in others. For example, U.S. security deliberations revealed in the Guantanamo and Abu Ghraib investigations show that presidential directives, Justice Department memos, and military commanders consistently argued for the permissibility of coercive interrogation in terms of intelligence gathering and systematically created parallel zones and units of state violence (Danner 2005; Margulies 2006). By contrast, Britain's Law Lords ruled against indefinite detention, and even after the July 2005 London bombings the British Parliament debated and modified a proposed extension of the period of preventative detention.

This variation in policies can be mapped against variation in prior legal regimes, which are reinforced or reconstructed in response to terror. *Unitary* legal regimes such as Germany's apply uniform legal standards derived from universal norms to all members of the political community, backed by ample processes of judicial review. Legal regimes such as Britain's depart from the same standard but permit rule-bound *derogations* from international standards and transparent modifications of domestic norms. Conflicted polities like Israel often host *differential* legal regimes in which universal standards and legal recourse apply to only one part of the population. The most anomalous and disturbing trend has been the move by the United States away from a regime similar to Britain's and toward the construction of a systematic parallel zone of illegality, a *grey zone* of state action not subject to legal standards but operating alongside a standard liberal democratic regime. This grey zone is replete with military tribunals, unregistered detentions, and other features characteristic of authoritarian dictatorships.

## THE INTERNATIONAL CONTEXT

Despite the hegemonic ambitions of the United States and the nationalist character of other targets of terror, no nation really acts alone in constructing national security. The globalized threat of transnational terror networks is matched by the international norms of human rights and the necessity of multilateral cooperation. Counterterror policies are not just comparable but are constructed across states by relations of power and influence. In a collaborative vein in which multilateral cooperation has pulled human rights performance up, the European Union has pressed member states to set human rights as a standard for common response. At the opposite end of the spectrum, the United States, as a global hegemon, has pushed allies toward a lowest common denominator of total-war counterinsurgency tactics. For example, the United States has successfully pressured traditionally respectful countries like Sweden and Canada to participate in illegal and abusive renditions of their citizens to torture zones.

International power, law, and cooperation push and pull counterterror policies, but we find the overriding framework is the way in which international factors affect domestic perceptions of national interest and legal regimes. Thus, Germany's investment in a European notion of national interest and legality overcomes the imperatives of security cooperation with the United States. Britain's human rights record with respect to counterterrorism reflects a balancing act between a U.S.-influenced interpretation of national insecurity and the European Court's conditioning of domestic legal regimes. In Spain, the combination of direct threat and lessons learned from domestic legal deviations produced a reaction against U.S. influence and a rewriting of national interest in more rights-respectful terms.

## THE GOAL: HUMAN RIGHTS AS HUMAN SECURITY

What does it mean to respect human rights in security policies? Human rights constitute a set of universal norms that limit the use of legitimate force in order to preserve human dignity: the physical security and freedom from fear that are our birthright. Counterterror policies involve the state's use of coercion to control violence by nonstate actors, and thus intrinsically involve potential threats to the freedom and bodily integrity of subjects of state power. A rough international consensus on minimal basic rights of the person is codified in the collective overlapping norms of the Universal Declaration of Human Rights, the International Covenant on Civil and Political Rights (ICCPR), the Geneva Conventions, the Convention on Genocide, and the Convention against Torture. These international legal instruments, along with emerging global jurisprudence, stipulate that legitimate national defense must not involve unregulated assassination, torture, systematic targeting of civilians, covert or indefinite detention, cruel and inhumane punishment or prison conditions, or systematic suppression of identity (Forsythe 2000). It is against this benchmark that the United Nations Human Rights Commission condemned U.S. counterterror policy in Guantanamo as a violation of articles 7, 9, 10, 14, and 18 of the ICCPR, as well as articles 1, 3, 12, 13, and 16 of the Convention against Torture—both core standards the United States has endorsed and promoted abroad (United Nations, Economic and Social Council, Commission on Human Rights, 2006).

While international law is both an expression and a legitimation of human rights norms, the case for universal human rights rests on a deeper range of philosophical foundations. Numerous religious and moral traditions that predate and transcend national identities assert human rights as an absolute defense of human dignity and equal moral worth (although religious conceptions often exclude nonbelievers) (Ishay 2004). If these traditions or their modernized successors are accepted as the goal of political community, their version of human rights would be a national value not generally subject to trade-offs or political calculus.

In the liberal democratic model of the modern state, human rights is also written into the constitution of the body politic—albeit in a more contingent way. The social contract that legitimates the state's monopoly on coercion is premised on the rule of law. Liberal states provide not only order but governance—predictable, accountable access to a system of bounded social control. The state's right to rule and broad basis of participation are the protection of individual integrity and liberty (Orend 2002).

But human rights is also justified on pragmatic grounds that mix freely with cosmopolitan, absolute, and liberal foundations. Human rights are not just right—they are argued to produce more peaceful, stable, democratic, developed, or sustainable societies. The apogee of this position is represented by the book *In Our Own Interest,* by William Schulz, the president of Amnesty International USA (Schulz 2001). Schulz's book is a brief for the promotion of human rights as the prudent pursuit of long-term national interest that links human rights to global goods as diverse as public health, beneficial trade patterns, and environmental preservation.

These bases for human rights stand in a variety of relationships to national security and human security. If security itself is conceived as a universal individual right, the foundation of counterterror would be the protection of the individual from both external threats and state violence. Human rights expand the social contract of citizenship, in which the state guarantees both order and justice in return for collective allegiance, to a universal claim. But under conventional constructions of security, that claim too often collides with the state's enforcement of internal authority and national defense. A broader notion of national security that includes the state's responsibility to provide security *for its citizens* implies more rights, not less (Wilson 2005).

## ACADEMIC CONSTRUCTIONS OF NATIONAL SECURITY

Academic and legal constructions of national security have both interpreted and influenced counterterror policy. The paradox of a *democratic* national security state is that while specific counterterror policies may not be known or challenged, the overall national security ideology is potentially subject to civil society debate and usually submitted to some form of legislative and/or judicial review. In the United States the White House, Pentagon, and Department of Justice sought legal opinions on the status of POWs and legitimate methods of interrogation prior to drafting policy, while the German Parliament has received studies and recommendations from the German Human Rights Institute. In some cases, mainly in Europe, academic critique has supported a mobilized and transnationalized civil society, while the debate among U.S. academics has been more oriented to domestic standards and government action. Social scientists and legal scholars have reflected a representative range of positions on the potential for a trade-off between human rights and security.

The *realist* position epitomized by U.S. government legal analysts such as John Choon Yoo was laid out in academic terms—prior to 9/11—by Frank Biggio. Adopting the statist perspective associated with *Realpolitik*, this school advises the untrammeled pursuit of national interest and sovereignty as the right and duty of democratic leaders. Since terrorism is represented as a total threat to the existence of democratic societies, unilateral and preemptive actions are justified as a defense both of the hegemon and of the stability of the world order. Such perspectives are usually coupled with a reading of terrorism as war, an assertion that the threat is unprecedented, and a description of strategic scenarios in which intelligence is paramount to the survival of the political order. Biggio specifically argues that acts of terrorism should be considered acts of war under international law, and that terrorists forfeit both national and humanitarian protection as "enemies of mankind" meriting universal prosecution by any means necessary. "Although acts such as military strikes against terrorist camps, kidnapping terrorist leaders, or assassinating terrorist leaders may be illegal under international law, moral justification could make them tolerable and allow for emergence into customary international law" (Biggio 2002: 38).

In direct contrast to this position, *civil libertarian* legal scholars and human rights advocates argue for the applicability of international law and the supremacy of international human rights over national interest. For example, U.S. legal scholars demonstrate the incompatibility of U.S. use of military tribunals with the U.S. Constitution and international treaties (Wallace and Kreisel 2003; Fitzpatrick 2003). European legal scholars also tend to concentrate on the compatibility between counterterror policies and international law (such as the special issue of the *European Journal of International Law* 15[5], 2004), with special attention to the European states' multilevel regional as well as global institutional commitments (Warbrick 2004). Legal scholars show that U.S. counterterror policies embody discrimination among ethnic and religious groups, between citizens and noncitizens, among citizens of various foreign countries, and against refugees (Roberts 2004; also see Goldstone 2005).

While civil libertarian scholars do not usually address the political context of national security policy like their realist peers, human rights advocates like

Amnesty International's Paul Hoffman and Human Rights Watch explicitly argue for the pragmatic as well as the principled role of human rights standards in counterterrorism. After pointing out the contravention of universal norms by coercive interrogation, preventative detention, profiling, and renditions, these authors also argue that they are ineffective responses to terror that undermine international cooperation and erode public support (Hoffman 2004, Human Rights Watch 2003, 2004b). The comparative legal scholar Kim Scheppele provides an incisive and comprehensive argument for the sociological value of constitutionality and international law in the face of "states of exception" (Scheppele 2004). For normative as well as prudential reasons, many civil libertarians argue for an absolute respect for human rights. However, some variance is possible through derogations: many international human rights norms (notably the ICCPR) already countenance a sliding scale of unbreachable core human rights of bodily integrity, surrounded by a penumbra of civil liberties that may be suspended temporarily in true emergencies—subject to international and judicial review (also see Howard Adelman's chapter in this volume).

But the novel scholarly position in the post-9/11 world is the cluster of historically liberal analysts who accept the logic of a trade-off between human rights and the new security threat, and struggle to reconcile the norms and processes of democracy with the selective derogation of *core* universal standards. The civil liberties attorney Alan Dershowitz has argued for the permissibility of the isolated and supervised use of torture to gain intelligence in situations of imminent threat to public security (Dershowitz 2002). Others argue for an unregulated trade-off (Posner 2005). However, many analysts have questioned the plausibility, logic, and historical evidence of the oft-cited scenario of a "ticking bomb" that can be defused by information revealed through torture (Luban 2006).

Similarly, the Harvard law professor and former Deputy Attorney General Philip Heymann concludes that preventative detention may be justified albeit unpopular, and that "outsourcing" is justified:

> The United States can reap the benefits of these activities, forbidden by international human rights conventions . . . if we attempt to export the counterterrorism costs of extensive searches, electronic surveillance, coercive interrogation, and limitations on association, detention, and speech. Each of these measures, controlled or forbidden by the United States Constitution, are likely to be promising ways of obtaining needed information about terrorists' plans and of otherwise preventing terrorist initiatives. (Heymann 2002: 454)

Heymann organized a Harvard conference in 2004, in conjunction with the Department of Justice, for experts to design democratic mechanisms of control for the suspension of guarantees and the use of coercive measures.

Michael Ignatieff's *The Lesser Evil* offers the most extensive development of the position he labels a middle course between a pure civil libertarian position and a totally pragmatic trade-off of human rights to national security. Although eschewing torture, illegal detention, and unlawful assassination, he nevertheless argues that "necessity may require us to take actions in defense of democracy which will stray from democracy's own foundational commitment to dignity" (Ignatieff 2004: 8). Thus, Ignatieff relies on democratic *process*—such as public debate, judicial review, and sunset clauses—to determine the appropriateness of measures that may violate international or even constitutional standards. Although he does not specify a package of acceptable policies, at various times Ignatieff refers to government adoption of emergency powers, forms of coercive interrogation short of torture, nondiscriminatory preventative detention, and suspensions of civil liberties such as free speech and assembly. He goes on to state that "judicial responses to the problem of terror . . . are no substitute for military operations when terrorists possess bases, training camps, and heavy weapons" (Ignatieff 2004: 20). Although Ignatieff subsequently modified the acceptable equations for the trade-off in the wake of revelations of U.S. abuses, his calculus remains utilitarian (Ignatieff 2005). In contrast to his fellow post-liberals, who argue that trade-offs are required because the threat of terror is unprecedented, Ignatieff bases his conclusions on an extensive comparative and historical study of previous counterterror experiences, including several of the cases presented in this volume (Northern Ireland, Israel, and Germany). We contest his conclusions in the course of this book.

Critics of the post-liberal position (including this author) insist on the indivisibility of human rights and contend that the selective rejection of some rights leads ineluctably to the violation of core boundaries of torture, murder, and inhumane imprisonment. The slippery slope from select cases of legally mandated coercive interrogation to widespread use of torture can be seen in Israel, while the abuse of preventative detention and its link to inhumane imprisonment and torture is evident in Guantanamo and Abu Ghraib (Mayer 2005a, 2005b). Populism is no substitute for democratic legal boundaries: public debate on the suppression of violent challengers will not necessarily deter majorities from democratically endorsing violations of the rights of Others, as several of these authors have recognized in previous writings (Sullivan 2005). Ignatieff and Heymann's versions of a sliding-scale rule of law adjusted for the level of security threat simply displace the derogation of human rights standards to an unbounded process subject to the same dangers as the Weimar Republic's Nuremberg Laws, and unaccountable to international norms. As Wilson avers, "lesser evil advocates have been wildly overconfident about the probity of government and the ability of democratic institutions to monitor closely the boundary between coercion and torture. The evidence points to the contrary view." (Wilson 2005: 20). Simply put, human rights undergird democracy.

After criticizing many of the hidden assumptions of the argument for trade-offs, David Luban concludes that the abstract question of trading someone else's liberty for our own unverifiable claims of collective security is the wrong question. Luban reminds us that concrete experiences of the history of rights restrictions in the name of national security teach us that the ultimate impact is both more personal and more universal. Thus, he contends that the real question is, "How much of your own protection against bureaucratic errors or malice by the government—errors or malice that could land you in jail—are you willing to sacrifice in return for minute increments in security?" (Luban 2005: 256).

Like all academic research on complex and consequential policy debates, our first task is to frame the debate on human rights in hard times by asking the right questions. We can transcend the false trade-off of human rights for national security if we ask, *"security for whom?" "security from what?,"* and *"security by whom?"* It is a sign of the interconnectedness of both the global threat to democracies from terror and the global project of human rights that we have come together as scholars from half a dozen countries to bring comparative perspectives and information to this international debate. Our conclusion is that national security requires human security, and that global human security must be based in global human rights.

# 2  Encroaching on the Rule of Law

*Post-9/11 Policies within the United States*

Richard Falk

There are several distinguishing features of the American response to the 9/11 attacks that should be considered in evaluating post-9/11 U.S. governmental encroachments on the rule of law. These contextual elements suggest that comparisons with the counterterrorist practices of other countries need to take account of the specificities of the American situation that make it a case apart. Distinctive elements help us understand the course taken by the Bush administration after 9/11 that would remain incomprehensible if viewed purely from a counterterrorist perspective.

Most prominent among these elements was a preexisting neoconservative blueprint for a more interventionary American foreign policy, especially in the Middle East. Also important was the role of the United States as the one and only *global* state, with strategic interests and military deployments spread around the entirety of the globe. In this respect considerations other than counterterrorism became so influential in shaping the American response to 9/11 as to overwhelm the manifest security concerns raised by even terrorist threats of unprecedented magnitude. Adding to the confusion is the continuing attempt of the Bush administration to validate policy by insisting upon a counterterrorist rationale even though other explanations are far more convincing. The official justifications for the Iraq policy by the Bush White House can be contrasted with the judgment of critics that undisclosed motivations are the best explanation of the policies being pursued, which is one way of showing why it is misleading to take counterterrorist justifications at face value.[1]

Such considerations greatly complicate comparisons with the counterterrorist approaches adopted by other countries, which were by and large narrowly and straightforwardly focused on addressing the terrorist threat.

It is my contention that the United States government, at least after the Afghanistan war, was pursuing several different and incompatible strategic goals under the rubric of "counterterrorism." And furthermore, that its leadership, whether consciously or not, jeopardized counterterrorist goals so as to pursue a far wider world-order design involving grand strategic goals associated with regional supremacy in the Middle East, security with respect to regional energy supplies and pricing, long-range Israeli security, and the containment of political Islam.

At the same time, because American society was mobilized and propagandized around an essentially counterterrorist agenda, the steps taken to impair the human rights of citizens and others do resemble the circumstances of other countries, especially Israel, whose governments felt that the very survival of the country was being threatened a few years ago by the severity of the terrorist threat. Beyond this, the nature of al Qaeda and the threats it poses are both elusive in nature and changing through time, and although real, have been manipulated by American leaders so as to obscure the pursuit of more controversial strategic goals. For this reason it is difficult to tell whether there exists an authentic basis for concern about the alleged vulnerability of American society to terrorist attacks of a magnitude similar to or greater than that of 9/11.

Comparisons with the responses of other governments to major terrorist incidents may be helpful, especially the questionable functionality of the immediate American decision to treat its post-9/11 counterterrorist campaign as a species of warfare (as in the term "war on terror"), rather than as a challenge calling for enhanced law enforcement, reinforced as necessary by paramilitary operations. It seems likely that many of the worst excesses of governmental abuse in the United States might have been avoided if the response to the attacks had been described as massive crimes to be addressed by law and order mechanisms appropriate for a counterterrorist response. The international legal framework applicable to war is premised on armed conflict between sovereign states, and is not entirely suitable to govern interactions in conflicts involving nonstate actors.

While favoring an approach rooted in criminal law, reliance on law and order techniques would not necessarily avoid abusive behavior, and would likely raise of its own human rights and related concerns. The serious abuses of governmental authority by Britain, France, Germany, and Israel in the treatment of terrorist suspects by national police and intelligence forces suggest that security pressures seem almost always to erode human rights even if "war" is not declared. The United States, perhaps because of its geographic position, history, and self-righteous political culture, is more inclined than other states to resort to unrestrained behavior once it finds itself at war. This is especially so if the war was initiated by the adversary, is not against a foreign state, and the opponent has been officially depicted as "evil."[2]

It is also true that the spectacular character of the 9/11 attacks, as well as their transnational locus and the inflammatory language of Osama bin Laden, made the American response by way of war seem more appropriate than in other countries, with the possible exception of Israel, which faced a Palestinian war of liberation that pursued its goals by traumatizing tactics, including a wave of suicide bombings aimed at the civilian heartland of Israeli society. For these reasons, also, it is necessary to condition comparisons with respect to counterterrorist policies by reference to the national context of the United States, reinforced by the unique circumstances surrounding the 9/11 events.

Yet although we need to treat American counterterrorism as *sui generis*, comparisons can be instructive and useful for the future. For instance, the March 11, 2004, Madrid train bombings contributed to a repudiation of Spanish participation in the Iraq war, embodied in a widely popular slogan, "no to war, no to terrorism." Such an option has not been put on the table by the United States, even by the Democratic party, because the Iraq war's strategic stakes have been regarded by the entire American political mainstream as so far justifying the commitment even as it becomes plain that it diverts resources and energies from the more efficient pursuit of counterterrorist objectives. As of the end of 2006, the rising costs of the American occupation of Iraq may be approaching a tipping point that will swing the policy in the direction of phased withdrawal. Yet this is by no means assured. Israel's summer 2006 war in Lebanon demonstrated the volatility of political life in the region, as well as reminding the world of the persisting Israeli-American strategic commitment to reconfigure the politics of the region.[3] The currently escalating confrontation with Iran could easily produce a new cycle of political violence, with extremely dangerous regional, even global, implications.

The chapter is divided into two main parts. The first section identifies several areas of American distinctiveness as relevant for understanding both the United States' particular approach to counterterrorism and as the foundation for comparison with the policies adopted by other likeminded countries faced with terrorist threats. The second section discusses some of the inroads on human rights as fallout from the intensity of the counterterrorist campaign.

## GENERAL CONSIDERATIONS
### The Pre-9/11 Atmosphere

It is misleading to associate the totality of pressures on American freedoms as following from 9/11. In direct response to the 1995 bombing of the Alfred P. Murrah Federal Building in Oklahoma City, the Clinton administration responded by enacting in 1996 the Anti-Terror and Effective Death Penalty Act. In many ways this pre-9/11 law anticipated the looseness of definitions associated with Bush-era criminalization, especially of what constitutes "terrorism," as well as the comprehensiveness of governmental authority so widely criticized and ardently defended. This controversy has continued, surrounding the enactment and implementation of the Patriot Act, which was renewed in 2006 amid a much sharper debate than in 2001 when Congress acted as a virtual rubber stamp. The new legislation retains most of the features of the earlier version of the Patriot Act, although a few minor modifications are sensitive to civil liberties (Mertus 2005: 320).

There was in 1995 little criticism of a governmental response that seemed unconcerned about the menace posed by purely domestic sources of the extremist violence (the work of right-wing militias) directed at important civilian and governmental targets. In retrospect, it seems odd that although a federal office building was the target of Oklahoma City bombing, there was immediately fashioned a counterterrorist response directed at purely *international* sources of terrorism. What still seems surprising is the apparent unconcern in Washington with continuing threats of political violence stemming from American right-wing militias, as well as the preoccupation even in the 1990s with terrorist threats emanating from Arab countries in the Islamic world. In this respect, the American legal system was predisposed to erode rule-of-law constraints on enforcement activities prior to 9/11, especially if the abandonment of individual rights involved Islamic suspects who were foreign nationals. In contrast, the British government's response to the July 7, 2005, London bombings—which involved young Islamic extremists who were born and raised in Britain—focused on the domestic locus of the main terrorist threat now confronting the country.

Perhaps more to the point in the U.S. context is the long period of the Cold War, during which—directly and indirectly, especially under CIA auspices, and in the course of a series of Third World interventions—many abuses were committed in a manner that prefigures the patterns of abuse that have been revealed since 9/11.[4] The Cold War atmosphere of conflict waged on the global stage provided a strategic rationale for the adoption of tactics inconsistent with international humanitarian law, a dynamic that reached its climax in the course of more than a decade of warfare in Indo-china.[5] With a logic rather parallel to the current counterterrorist discourse, think tanks in the United States during the 1960s and 1970s were working on aspects of security policy emphasizing the specific challenges of what was then being described as "counterinsurgency warfare." As in Iraq these days, during the Vietnam War it was often impossible for American firepower to distinguish enemy soldiers from the civilian population. There were at the time elaborate justifications put forward for coercively separating the population from insurgents by relocation in strategic hamlets, and the like. This perspective led to the adoption of legally and morally dubious practices such as the Phoenix Program of large-scale civilian assassination. The systematic interrogation of captured enemy combatants was followed by many criminal practices, including the notorious act of throwing Viet Cong suspects from helicopters to terrify other prisoners to divulge information. As in the war on terror, the Vietnam War showed the limitations of military superiority when the stakes of conflict involve the *political* future of an occupied country that mounts a strong nationalist backlash. The frustrations of such a stymied war effort contributed a strong incentive by the United States to abandon the laws of war so as either to gain information about their Vietnamese adversary or to ignore the distinction between civilian and combatant because the information needed to confine firepower to military targets was unavailable. There, too, the enemy was accused of deliberately intermingling weapons and combatants with the civilian population. It is instructive, and somewhat discouraging, to look back to the Vietnam War to gain insight into the encroachments on international humanitarian law that have been associated with the war on terror.

## The Primacy of Geopolitics

In decisive respects the geopolitical tail has been wagging the counterterrorist dog during the Bush presidency. The domestic intensification of a politics of fear and anger seems mainly associated with mobilizing American society to support a much more militant and controversial global security strategy that had been articulated and advocated by prominent neoconservatives well before George W. Bush was elected president in 2000. Chief among those advocating such a strategy was the Project for a New American Century (PNAC), a think tank co-founded by William Kristol and Robert Kagan. Its report released in September 2000, *Rebuilding America's Defenses*, is notable for its recognition that the political climate in the United States at the time would not be conducive to an aggressive geopolitics unless "a new Pearl Harbor" awakened the American people to the dangers (and opportunities) of the post-cold war world.[6] Significantly the neoconservative world-view prior to 9/11 was not at all preoccupied with the threats posed by international terrorism, but its attention was primarily focused on so-called rogue states, especially Iraq and Iran, and to a lesser extent China, which were seen as posing obstacles to the favored course of American global grand strategy.

The contention here is that the 9/11 attacks provided the political cover needed to launch a militant foreign policy, which was based on grandiose global security goals. A previously reluctant American society was effectively mobilized for a generalized "war on terror" that, despite its label, was used by the Bush presidency as a mandate to pursue a neoconservative grand strategy that accorded priority to the political restructuring of the Middle East, starting with Iraq, but with an eye on Iran as its culminating goal.

Counterterrorism was part of the policy mix, to be sure, especially in the immediate response to 9/11 in the form of the Afghanistan war. An exaggerated and misdirected response to global terrorism was effective in giving the Bush presidency a blank check for several years in foreign and domestic policy, the prevailing rationale being that it was permissible for the U.S. government to do whatever it took to make America and Americans as secure as possible. In the years after 9/11, color-coded alerts and government warnings about imminent attacks were seemingly manipulated to sustain anxiety levels, creating a mood of aroused collective fear from time to time. These tactics helped build bipartisan Congressional and media support for intrusions on the privacy and liberties of Americans in general, and Muslim male residents in particular. At the same time, liberal opposition to such governmental tactics was marginalized through a skillful playing of the "security" card by the Bush leadership. As public opinion began turning against the Iraq policy in 2005, this security card became less effective, particularly as coupled with Bush's declining popularity as a leader. This change in political mood certainly reflected the public's growing sense of failure in Iraq, but it also resulted from such seemingly unrelated issues as the inept governmental response to Hurricane Katrina and the rising cost of gas.

## *Lawyers in Government*

It needs to be appreciated that the structure of legal argument and its normative architecture is such that it is always possible for a seasoned lawyer to present a logically coherent legal argument to support a preferred political course of action. Government lawyers generally view their professional role, especially in the context of foreign policy or national security, to be one of facilitating official policies rather than positing restraints, although this was a contested point prior to the George W. Bush presidency.[7] This use of lawyers and legal analysis to lend an aura of legality is nothing new, but it has been carried to the outer limits of plausibility, or beyond, during the Bush presidency. This vocational orientation toward facilitating political initiatives has been reinforced by recruiting neoconservative legal specialists known to share the policy agenda of the political leadership. Most neoconservatives have a highly skeptical attitude about whether international law should even be treated as real law. This skepticism is not very far removed from standard realist thinking that affirms the primacy of national security in foreign policy settings. In addition to this skepticism about law, neoconservatives favor a strong executive, and believe that a wartime president possesses virtually unlimited constitutional authority with respect to national security policy.[8]

This attitude is further reinforced by America's imperial geopolitics, which simultaneously enforces legal standards rigorously against adversaries while exempting itself. Such patterns of legal exceptionalism are particularly flagrant in the setting of international criminal accountability (for instance, prosecuting Saddam Hussein as a war criminal, while insisting on impunity for American officials) and the implementation of the treaty regime governing nonproliferation of nuclear weaponry.[9]

## The Magnitude of 9/11

The European terrorist incidents, however traumatic and cruel in their impacts, were minor in comparison with the 9/11 attacks, which were spectacular events of an unprecedented symbolic and substantive magnitude. The World Trade Center and the Pentagon were the prime symbols of American power, economic and military, and by striking them so effectively in a manner suitable for TV, the terrorists shockingly and undeniably established America's vulnerability. Beyond this, the real-time image of the plane crashing into the WTC tower created an unforgettable image of the attack that was repeated over and over for tens of millions of TV watchers. This extraordinary visualization of the attacks was given further gruesome resonance in the form of immediate eyewitness accounts offered by survivors and victims of the many human tragedies associated with the event. And finally, the early identification of al Qaeda and its telegenic and charismatic leader, Osama bin Laden, as responsible for the attacks undoubtedly helped to ensure that the memories of the 9/11 experience would be lodged deep in the political imagination of the American people and their leaders.

Cumulatively, this was a terrorist event unlike any other, and it seemed to make the American recourse to "war" an appropriate, even inevitable, response, foreclosing the "law enforcement" option, or some intermediate response, that had been relied upon by other countries faced with major and sustained terrorist challenges to their home security.[10] Public opinion, including as expressed at the United Nations, seemed to underscore this dual reality: 9/11 was a terrorist incident of unprecedented ferocity, and recourse to war, at least against Afghanistan, seemed both unavoidable and justifiable. Such a response also was congruent with the extremist language of bin Laden, who had previously declared a war without limits against all Americans, indeed against Jews and Christians everywhere (described as "crusaders"). President Bush made effective use of this understanding of 9/11 to rally the country around a response based on declaring and waging war on a global scale against terrorism in general in which foreign countries were denied the option of neutrality. There was also a widespread American fear that 9/11 could be soon replicated, perhaps causing even greater harm and havoc, a prospect given credible backing by bin Laden's menacing rhetoric and statements, as well as by the sheer daring of the 9/11 plan, with its multiple hijackings and suicide tactics. Bush constantly invoked this prospect of further attacks in subsequent months and years to claim the need for a variety of extraordinary powers for the government, especially for the executive branch. After 9/11 Bush repeatedly asserted that the dangers of nuclear weapons technology falling into the hands of anti-American terrorist groups posed the greatest of all threats to national and global security. Furthermore, it was not reasonable to wait until such a threat materialized in the form of an attack, or even involved the acquisition of capabilities that could be used to mount an attack at some future time. Rather, such a threat needed to be dealt with *preemptively,* not reactively. Bush continuously argued that this situation created truly apocalyptic dangers that had to be reduced to the extent possible.

Such fears laid the foundations for dramatic doctrinal moves by the U.S. government, including a claimed right to engage in preventive wars at times and in places of its own choosing. This doctrine was given a somewhat less provocative and misleading label by association with the right to wage *preemptive* wars, that is, initiating a war in the face of an *imminent* and severe threat.[11] Again, this distinctively American fusing of counterterrorism with the dangers associated with the proliferation of weapons of mass destruction, especially nuclear weapons, provided the essential rationale for the Iraq war, which even at the time proved convincing only to the American public and a few foreign governments. No other country, again with the possible exception of Israel, insisted that the WMD threat was so closely interwoven with the terrorist challenge.[12] Bin Laden's statements and al Qaeda's moves to acquire WMD lent some credence to the concern, but its application to Iraq in 2003 seemed farfetched, even if the Baghdad regime were to be found to possess some kind of WMD arsenal. The American concern with WMD and proliferation is, at most, tangentially related to counterterrorism. Instead, these issues are mainly associated with its pre-9/11 grand strategy, which included as a main feature a counter-proliferation approach to regional security in the Middle East. If the WMD/terrorist interface had been a genuine major worry of the Bush administration, then one would have expected that it would have concentrated on Pakistan, the country where it seems most likely that nuclear weapons may find their way into terrorist hands.[13]

In this period, as well, there were elaborate legalistic efforts made to cut corners in view of the special security demands attributed to this new kind of warfare, in which the enemy lacks a true home base and remains hidden until an attack is launched. Bush administration lawyers argued that normally applicable international rules governing the treatment of foreign fighters should be cast aside, that suspects (most of whom were, it turns out, completely innocent of terrorist connections) were "evil" and "bad guys," and that the need to obtain information from detainees justified the use of much more coercive forms interrogation.[14] A principal rhetorical device in lowering the threshold of resistance to torture was a manipulative reliance on the so-called ticking bomb scenario to explain recourse to inhumane forms of interrogation whenever a suspect may possibly have information useful to a counterterror investigation. By this logic, almost anyone detained could possibly be hiding some key information, and thus become a suitable subject for the harshest forms of interrogation.[15] Experience at Guantanamo and Abu Ghraib confirms the view that abstract justifications for abusive treatment to deal with exceptional instances of potential jeopardy (threats of weapons of mass destruction directed at heavily populated targets) are converted into implicit permission to engage in abusive behavior on a routine and comprehensive basis.

There were from the outset muted concerns from moderates and principled persons inside and outside government about Bush's posture of globalizing counterterrorism as a global war on terror. Limitations could have been introduced in relation to the particular identity of the terrorists or the geographic locus of the political violence, but in the anxious and patriotic atmosphere that prevailed after 9/11 there was an atmosphere of uncritical receptivity to all official pronouncements across the American political spectrum. Such a broad undertaking was without precedent in the history of counterterrorism. Bush never limited counterterrorist war to al Qaeda, and thus all forms of nonstate political violence came to be considered as beneath the umbrella of counterterrorism being raised above the entire planet. Such an undertaking encouraged various embattled leaders of governments around the world to claim that their struggles against self-determination movements were part of this wider global war on terror.

By moving American counterterrorist policy so rapidly, massively, and unconditionally from neglect to a war footing, it became far easier for the government to insist upon and acquire extraordinary authority to act as it saw fit, inside and outside the country, without encountering any serious legal or moral objections. At first, in public space, only civil-society organizations such as the American Civil Liberties Union and the National Lawyers Guild expressed strong opposition to security measures involving dramatic intrusions on privacy or unrestricted authority to detain and deny due process rights to terrorist suspects. It was only much later, when the abusive conditions of detention at Guantanamo became better known, and especially after the Abu Ghraib pictures found their way into magazines and onto TV, that the government found itself under serious pressure to justify its actions and modify its policies. The government's response was to take umbrage, denying all allegations of officially sanctioned torture, and ordering a series of formal inquiries into the allegations. The resulting reports placed most of the blame for the worst outrages on the unauthorized and improper behavior of deviant, low-level military personnel, some of whom have been subsequently prosecuted for dereliction of duty. In effect, the top civilian and military policy makers responded to the pressure by scapegoating those at lower levels of the military/civilian hierarchy, while insisting on impunity for themselves.

The main point here is that the peculiarly traumatizing character of the 9/11 attacks, unlike terrorist experience elsewhere and previously, made the adoption by the United States of this dysfunctional war modality an almost foregone, politically unchallenged conclusion. The dysfunctionality of this response only started to become apparent to most Americans, including opposition political figures, several years later, in the deep *aftermath* of the Iraq invasion. By this point the costs of changing the course of American foreign policy had become very high, although the costs of failing to change seemed even higher. By then, also, the defining steps taken to erode the rule of law had been put into practice. The dysfunction in relation to addressing the terrorist threat associated with 9/11 is significantly different from the dysfunction arising from a reliance on inter-state war as an instrument of grand strategy, closely connected with the project of American global dominance.

## External Location of Threats and Grievances

Unlike most political struggles involving nonstate actors, the locus of the threat that materialized on 9/11 cannot be easily situated in geographic space, nor can the grievances of the attackers be clearly identified. Also, for reasons suggested earlier, the priority given to remove the threat is uncertain due to overlapping, yet distinct and somewhat contradictory, geopolitical objectives. At the same time, this vagueness encourages a variety of anxieties about attack from within and without that made the American public willing to accept most measures taken in the name of lessening the risk of successful future attacks. More than five years later the Bush administration contends that the absence of subsequent attacks is due to this tightening of control over people and activities in the United States, making curtailments of liberties seem worthwhile.

The focus on minimizing the terrorist threat was combined with the perception of the terrorists as evil extremists. This perception discourages any moves to defuse the conflict by addressing, or even perceiving, the *root causes* of terrorist violence. There appears to be an attitude among the American leadership that all efforts to explain or understand the motives of the attackers or to account for the high levels of support enjoyed around the world for extremist anti-American politics are misguided, signaling weakness or a lack of resolve. Such efforts are alleged to divert attention from the only path to restored security, namely, the extermination of the threat. The former British Conservative Prime Minister, John Major, strongly disagreed in 2005 at a small gathering of invited guests in London. In the context of the Northern Ireland conflict, Major described how important it became for him while in government to understand that counterterrorism measures to thwart the IRA would only be successful over time if supplemented by efforts to deal responsibly with the root causes of the terrorism that had afflicted Northern Ireland for decades. Major said he found it crucial to acknowledge and remove these roots while doing his best to implement policies based on prevention and enforcement. Major contrasted this approach with his impression of the U.S. leadership's strategy for al Qaeda after 9/11.[16] In other words, Major argued that counterterrorism cannot succeed in the end if conceived exclusively as the killing and capture of terrorists. There must be a complementary *political* strategy that recognizes and responds to grievances.

The U.S. government has refused to consider the root causes of the 9/11 attacks for several reasons. To do so would challenge various aspects of the American engagement with and presence in the Middle East, including unconditional support for Israel in the conflict with the Palestinians over the future of historic Palestine. It would also raise serious doubts about the wisdom of the American deployment of military forces in areas close to sacred Islamic sites, as well as question continued support for corrupt and oppressive governments throughout the Arab world.[17] This unwillingness to look at root causes also means that any serious dissent questioning the American response to 9/11 will be automatically looked upon as evidence of disloyalty and a lack of patriotism, which has intimidated voices in opposition. This intimidation has been reinforced by mainstream media in the United States, especially by talk show hosts, who monitor the narrow parameters of permissible counterterrorist debate.

There is always some resistance to examining the grievances that might have provoked terrorism, as doing so may be seen as an expression of weakness or as giving incentives to terrorists to inflict more harm. In the American case after 9/11 this resistance was particularly strong because the Bush presidency immediately adopted such a self-righteous position by its insistence on the unprovoked and barbarous character of the attacks. It described the conflict in the metapolitical language of good and evil. As has been argued, it is reasonable to suspect that the Bush leadership wanted the terrorist threat to persist so as to provide necessary cover for going forward with the neoconservative project for global domination, which was much more controversial than counterterrorism. These pressures, while not entirely expressive of unique American circumstances, have not existed to nearly the same extent in other countries facing serious terrorist threats that were in some respects as formidable as what the United States faced after 9/11.

## Counter-Proliferation

The United States has incorporated into its broad counterterrorist approach a heavy emphasis on counter-proliferation in relation to countries seen as hostile to its view of future world order. As the Iraq war illustrates, and the threat of a use of force to destroy Iran's nuclear program confirms, the implementation of counter-proliferation policy has become a pretext for nondefensive wars that cannot be justified under the UN Charter or international law. It is claimed that preventing such proliferation is integral to prevailing in the war on terror, but the two sets of goals seem to be mainly divergent. As with counterterrorism, the primary American goal seems to be associated with reshaping the strategic environment of the world to accord with goals of American dominance. This wider set of global objectives complicates still further comparisons of American counterterrorist operations with those undertaken by other countries, and may help to explain the escalating implications of declaring "war" rather than relying on enhanced law enforcement.

Of course, conceptually there is a potential link between the terrorist threat and the proliferation of nuclear weaponry. If a country with nuclear weapons is prepared to risk its own annihilation or to transfer such weaponry to nonstate actors prepared to attack with nuclear weapons, then the danger exists. At the same time, the effort to preclude acquisition may increase the incentives to obtain such weapons, as once possessed, there is a diminished motivation to rely on force to contain a threat. If the perspective on proliferation is pushed back to the mid-1990s, it would seem rather clear that Pakistan was the most dangerous of the threshold countries, and yet when Pakistan tested and then acquired such weapons in 1998, there were no alarmist reactions.

## Creeping Authoritarianism

As suggested, all countries tend to weaken their respect for the rule of law and liberties in wartime. What is ominous in this regard with respect to the global war on terror is the combination of its intangibility and the unlikelihood of an ending through either victory or diplomacy. Unless the objectives are scaled back and concretely specified this "war" could persist indefinitely.[18] The various elements present create a further vulnerability, not only to renewed attacks at some future point, but also to further tightening of governmental control within the United States in response to a real or imagined increased sense of danger. In the event of another spectacular terrorist incident the citizenry would likely demand, and certainly would accept, a curtailment of its liberty. In other words, the security syndrome shaped after 9/11 prepares the way for radical future steps toward the weakening of constitutional governance. In this sense, consideration needs to be directed not only at the erosion of the rule of law that has followed from 9/11, but the degree to which the politics of fear creates the potential for much deeper inroads arising from either a polarization of opinion in American society or the belief by the leadership that the relative openness of a democratic society aggravates the security threat.

A foretaste of this dark set of possibilities emerged in the course of the intense 2006 debate on immigration policy, with its call for more tightly guarded borders, even including the construction of 700 miles of security fences along the Mexican border and reports of government contracts to build large domestic detention centers that would be available in times of crisis. Again the issue of counterterrorism is linked somewhat loosely to a variety of social issues associated with illegal entry to obtain employment. Whatever else, so long as the war on terror continues, there will be continuous pressures on democratic liberties and human rights, with the omnipresent danger that if matters take a turn for the worse, there will be a further tightening of the screws on the home front.

Other countries have experienced serious inroads in relation to standards to liberal legality due to prolonged counterterror campaigns. Among these are Britain (with respect to the IRA), France (in relation to the FLN), and Israel (especially, in relation to the occupation of Palestinian territories since 1967, but even more so during the wave of suicide bombings across the "green line" since the mid-1990s). In each of these instances, the struggle eroded constitutional protections for suspected militants, but also for the civilian population as a whole, both those seeking change and those being protected. With the possible exception of a severe threat to public order in France at the end of the Algerian War in 1962, the counterterrorist policies adopted never threatened the political stability of the country as deeply as have recent American developments. Because these American developments are likely to continue for years, if not decades, almost regardless of the orientation of the elected leadership, the danger to political democracy seems particularly severe. This severity also arises from the extent to which security preoccupations during the Cold War already endowed the U.S. government with vast powers.

This discouraging assessment is reinforced by some shortcomings of American political culture, including the impulse to hide the extent to which the success of the terrorist attacks on 9/11 resulted from bureaucratic incompetence or worse. This resistance to transparency is compounded by the extent that the global domination project is deceptively folded within the counterterrorist campaign. These deceptions of the citizenry naturally incline government officials to use secrecy, disinformation, and suppressive techniques to avoid exposing the full reality at issue. These factors, or some variation thereof, may have also been present in other settings involving counterterrorist agendas, but the special nature of the American relationship to world order makes the stakes higher. The magnitude of the 9/11 attacks and the perceptions of catastrophic possible future attacks should be taken into account when making comparisons with the counterterrorist programs and responses of other countries, but no less important in the search for optimal policy options.

## ERODING THE RULE OF LAW AFTER 9/11

Against the background of the preceding discussion, it is possible to identify the most serious encroachments on the domain of human rights that have been attributed to the distinctive security concerns arising from the 9/11 attacks and the counterterrorist war pursued in response. The lines of justifying argument relied upon by the U.S. government fall into three broad categories: (1) 9/11 changed everything, rendering obsolete some prior legal constraints, and making the costs of future breaches of security unacceptable; (2) the urgency of obtaining information relevant to counterterror goals provides valid grounds for engaging in more coercive forms of detention and interrogation; and (3) there are valid legal arguments that presidential powers are virtually unchallengeable in wartime and that prohibitions on "torture" and "inhumane treatment" can be evaded by clever interpretation.

## Inter arma silent leges *(In Times of War the Law Is Silent)*

It is certainly the case that throughout American history, including during the American Civil War, crucial standards of legal protection of individual rights have been weakened, if not altogether abandoned.[19] Ideas of military necessity and an atmosphere of present danger to national security have been given precedence over restraints on the normal use of governmental power. During World War II the internment of Japanese residents, including U.S. citizens, involved imposing a harsh collective punishment that was later the subject of regret, apology, and even symbolic reparations for the wrong inflicted. A U.S. Supreme Court majority upheld the internment in decisions that remain controversial.[20] As O'Donnell puts it, "once again, the deafening cry of 'military necessity' drowned out a plea to honor America's commitment to civil liberties and the rule of law" (2005: 271).

Unless there is executive sensitivity to civil liberties, human rights and the rule of law, it is unlikely that *judicial* protection during wartime will be very effective except in extreme instances of abuse where the security justifications seem frivolous. For one thing, there is a judicial reluctance to invalidate government policy in the face of uncertain knowledge as to the level of risk involved, especially when the executive branch purports to have superior secret knowledge that is not shared and an atmosphere of national emergency exists. For example, with respect to the denial of habeas corpus to a U.S. citizen, Yaser Esam Hamdi, held without charges and incommunicado in a naval prison as an enemy combatant, the lower court said, "the federal courts have many strengths, but the conduct of combat operations has been left to others. The executive is best prepared to exercise the military judgment attending the capture of alleged combatants."[21] For another, the president is charged constitutionally with authority and responsibility as commander-in-chief with respect to the conduct of war. And finally, this tradition of deference took shape *prior* to the development in the latter half of the twentieth century of procedures of accountability with respect to evolving standards governing the conduct of states during a war. It remains the case that steps taken by governments during war to implement internal security policies continue to be given a very broad "margin of appreciation," but as even a conservative United Supreme Court has increasingly shown, there are some limits to this deference that neoconservative legal advisers to the government have overstepped. How these limits eventually will be specified has not yet been established, as such recent legislation as the Military Commissions Act of 2006 (which contains fundamental challenges to normal standards of due process) has not yet been tested in the courts. Perhaps most disturbing is the power of the president to declare even an American citizen to be an "enemy combatant." The enemy combatant designation strips the person of many rights, including habeas corpus to challenge detention, and subjects her or him to both detention of unlimited duration and to possible criminal prosecution that could result in a death sentence to be carried out in the context of a military commission that grants defendants only limited rights.

This susceptibility of the rule of law to erosion in wartime is accentuated by the extent to which political leaders and their main advisers adhere to a *realist* view of foreign policy that tends to marginalize considerations of legality and morality, or, even more so, if the dominant climate of opinion is characterized by an *evangelical* approach to foreign policy as has been mainly the case during the Bush administration since 9/11. In this regard, whatever facilitates a war effort deemed "defensive," "just," and "sacred," is regarded as *legitimate,* and it is the job of government lawyers to provide a *legal* rationale. The Bush corps of government lawyers has carried this process to such extremes as to cause opposition from Pentagon legal specialists, who are fearful of the bad consequences for military professionalism and leverage in relation to violation of the rights of American military personnel who claim abuse overseas in future wars (Hajjar 2005).

In addition, the length of this war makes emergency measures less likely to be treated as temporary expedients. Once legislation is integrated into bureaucratic practice it becomes particularly difficult to get rid of. A disturbing feature of the main counterterrorist legislative measures, including the reenacting Patriot Act and the Military Commissions Act of 2006, is the absence of sunset provisions.

## The War on Terror Validates Otherwise Illegal Policies

The whole nature of *this* war is alleged to validate the sidelining of prior legal guidelines, especially international humanitarian law as embodied in the Geneva Conventions.[22] In effect, the traditional law of war, including treating captured combatants as "prisoners of war," was based on the reciprocal standards of behavior agreed upon as governing international wars between sovereign states.[23] But if the "enemy" is an invisible nonstate actor that can be anywhere and whose "soldiers" are not wearing military uniforms, then legal duties designed for governments are contended to be inapplicable. And beyond this, the nature of such a conflict in which the enemy has shown the capacity to inflict severe harm and has displayed an ingenuity with respect to tactics that include suicidal commitments, places a premium on "prevention," which creates special pressures to obtain what the Pentagon calls "actionable intelligence." As President Bush put it in a 2006 speech, "The security of our nation and the lives of our citizens depend on our ability to learn what these terrorists know."[24] It is this logic that has been used to justify "enemy combatant" classifications and "coercive interrogation" methods that critics regard as torture. Such a characterization is strenuously denied by those who have provided legal and political accounts of American detention practices on behalf of the government.[25] In the same speech cited above, Bush indicated reliance by the CIA on "an alternative set of procedures" to conduct interrogations of important suspects, but declined to specify what these were. Other sources confirm that such procedures would constitute prohibited methods under the Torture Convention, a valid treaty binding on the U.S. government.

The practices and policies generated by this rationale of a different type of war, with a concept of military necessity that cannot be easily reconciled with international humanitarian law abroad or civil liberties at home, seems to account for many of the erosions of the rule of law. Indefinite detention without charges is validated because those being held are supposed to be, or at least might turn out to be, extremist adherents of a jihadist outlook. The administration claims that such individuals would likely bolster the ranks of terrorist groups if released; at the same time, there is not enough evidence to bring criminal charges that would stand up even in the favorable setting of the military commissions decreed shortly after 9/11 by presidential proclamation to prosecute detainees who are not American citizens. Those commissions were invalidated by the Supreme Court in its 5–3 ruling in *Hamdan v. Rumsfeld* as improperly authorized by the executive branch. In 2006 Congress brought the military commissions into compliance with the Hamdan ruling by legislative enactment, but this law contains most of the abridgements of rights that were in the original executive decree: secret proceedings, admissibility of evidence based on coerced testimony, denial of right of habeas corpus, absence of any right of appeal, no right to cross-examine hostile witnesses, and no right of access to evidence used to support charges.

The unreasonableness of these practices and policies can be reliably assessed even without complete access to the realities. Most impartial reports suggest a dragnet used to hold persons in detention, with many being held without rights within and without America, most of whom are neither threats nor responsible for past wrongdoing nor possess vital information. The claim made that there are exceptional circumstances that justify suspending normal legal constraints can be rejected for two main reasons: once exceptions are allowed, abuses invariably pile up far beyond the initial claim of justification; and the existence of exceptional circumstances ("the ticking bomb") are so rare and contrived as to be irrelevant to the construction of general rules for behavior (Luban 2006).

## The Lesser of Evils

There has been considerable overlapping argumentation given by "liberal hawks" who seek to preserve an atmosphere of decency in the midst of the counterterror campaigns while accommodating to varying degrees the pressure to rely on unacceptable methods to acquire information or to detain. Rather than follow the neoconservatives down the path of limitless presidential authority to set policy, even in secret, and avoid any accountability, this balancing of competing values (decency, rule of law, human rights versus security, strong state) tries to avoid the worst, shifting the burden of persuasion back onto those claiming exceptional powers.[26] One approach in the context of torture is to make the prohibition absolute, but allow a defense of necessity as mitigating subsequent responsibility in the event of a *demonstrated* exceptional set of circumstances. Another approach is to allow a judge to issue a warrant authorizing torture in response to a governmental argument made in secret.

## An Imperial Commander-in-Chief

The neoconservative outlook is supposedly deferential to a strict reading of the constitution, but is at the same time contemptuous of international law or to laws that have been legislatively enacted or judicially interpreted to reflect liberal values.[27] In advancing this viewpoint (which recently is being vigorously challenged by Congress and in the courts), a central argument involves the powers claimed for the executive branch, and specifically the presidency, with respect to prosecuting the war against terrorism. The standard view had been that an American president is always accountable to applicable law, including during wartime. Since 9/11 John Yoo in particular has been associated with an extreme construction of the constitution that gives the president truly unrestricted and unaccountable powers over any undertaking that arises from carrying on the war (Yoo 2005; Cole 2005).

Of course, the expansion of presidential powers during wartime and an accompanying domestic controversy is far from unprecedented. The issue last seriously gained public attention in the latter stages of the Vietnam War when books with the titles "Arrogance of Power" and "The Imperial Presidency" were written by prominent American citizens (respectively, Fulbright 1967; Schlesinger 1973). At the time, President Nixon was accused of misleading Congress and the public, engaging in warfare without a declaration of war by Congress, maintaining unwarranted secrecy, engaging in surveillance without proper authorization, and planning detention centers and the like for domestic opponents of the war.

Nixon actually compiled "enemies list" of antiwar activists. What is different in the Bush presidency, aside from a Congress and media that has been so far generally supportive, is the elaborate efforts to validate these excessive claims of presidential power as beyond the reach of the rule of law, and as part of a deliberate effort to push the governing process of the country toward the far right for as long as possible. And as mentioned earlier, the uncertain duration of the war means that measures adopted to meet a present emergency are likely to remain operative indefinitely.

### Failures to Uphold International Legal Standards

An integral part of the rule of law within the United States in the early twenty-first century is the obligation to uphold *internally* applicable international standards, whether in the form of duly ratified international treaties or of norms of customary international law. These standards apply especially to the treatment of persons captured abroad and held in detention as "enemy combatants" or as unspecified suspects in some manner related to terrorism. The most comprehensive and authoritative discussion of these issues is to be found in the report of the UN Commission on Human Rights, "Situation of Detainees at Guantanamo Bay," which is extremely critical of U.S. detention policies and recommends closing the facilities, as well as providing compensation to victims of torture and cruel, inhuman or degrading treatment as prohibited in Article 14 of the Convention against Torture.[28] Guantanamo Bay is situated on Cuban territory leased on a long-term basis by the United States. It was apparently deliberately chosen as a major site for detention of captured suspects precisely because it was thought to be beyond the reach of American courts and not subject to rule-of-law constraints.

## Wiretapping without a Warrant

One controversial practice has been the recent disclosure that the president has been wiretapping without warrants communications between Americans and overseas contacts who are suspected of being connected with al Qaeda in some way. Such wiretapping appears to violate an explicit legislative procedure that covers all reasonable surveillance needs as specified in the Foreign Intelligence Surveillance Act (FISA). The statute also allows warrantless wiretaps to be ordered by the executive, but only for the first fifteen days of a war. Otherwise, judicial approval must be obtained, not an onerous burden, as the FISA court has consistently and without delay approved of security claims made by the executive branch when it seek permission to wiretap without obtaining a warrant. In effect, the claim on behalf of this domestic spying program is based primarily on the implied powers of the president as commander-in-chief, and secondarily on a strained reading of Congress's 2001 statute krown as the Authorization for the Use of Military Force (AUMF) against al Qaeda.[29] A letter to Congress signed by a distinguished group of constitutional law specialists in the United States reached the conclusion that the spying program is violating the clear intent of Congress.[30]

## Military Commissions

As described above, shortly after 9/11, President Bush authorized by executive decree the establishment of military commissions to prosecute "enemy combatants" for alleged terrorist activities. This legal maneuver was obviously designed to circumvent both the protective provisions of the Geneva Conventions, the backbone of international humanitarian law, and to avoid scrutiny by the American judicial system. There are many objections to this procedure from the perspective of human rights: the judges of the military commissions are handpicked military officers, the accused person has no rights to act in defense or even tc attend hearings, there are no rules of evidence, and no right of judicial review. The commission is empowered to impose a death sentence, and the only review is an appeal to the president, or if he decides, to the secretary of defense. The legal status of these military commissions has yet to be clarified. As has been mentioned, the Supreme Court decided in the *Hamdan* case that the president violated the separation of powers by setting up the commissions without Congressional authorization and in a manner inconsistent with Articles 3 and 4 of the Third Geneva Convention on the Treatment of Prisoners of War.[31] Clearly the reliance on commissions, as well as locating the site of detention outside of the territorial limits of the United States, reflects the dual position of the Bush administration: to treat those alleged to be associated with terrorism as engaged in "war," and thus not entitled to judicial protection; and then treating the war as being of such a special character that it is not within the domain of the Geneva Conventions, or more generally, international humanitarian law. The underlying issue is whether the president has inherent powers arising from his role as commander-in-chief in wartime or delegated powers deriving from the AUMF in 2001.[32] Additional legal questions in the case include whether a detainee can be constitutionally denied rights of habeas corpus to assess judicially the legality of confinement and treatment (as Congress has attempted in the Detainee Treatment Act) and whether the provisions of the Geneva Conventions can be enforced in an American court.

After a considerable struggle in Congress in which several leading Republican senators broke ranks with the president, the Military Commissions Act of 2006 was passed by both houses and signed by the president. Whether its controversial provisions, which will be tested in courts, will survive judicial scrutiny is difficult to predict. If they do, it will mean that the U.S. Government has authoritatively adopted an approach to detainees who are not citizens that cannot be reconciled with international legal norms and procedures.

### The 2001 Patriot Act, Reauthorized 2006

The most extensive domestic impact on human rights arising from the counterterror priority after 9/11 took the form of the very comprehensive legislation known as USA Patriot Act, initially adopted after virtually no debate in late 2001, and reauthorized and altered in March 2006 after considerable controversy in the media and Congress. This legislation consolidated preexisting governmental law enforcement authority scattered in many laws, but also added to this authority in controversial ways that have aroused opposition from the American Civil Liberties Union and other human rights groups. The Patriot Act is very long, covering in its initial enactment 341 pages.

Among its most controversial features is the adoption of a vague definition of "domestic terrorism" that could be used to criminalize activity normally associated with peaceful opposition to government policy. According to section 802, domestic terrorism include activities that "(A) involve acts dangerous to human life that are a violation of the criminal laws of the U.S. or of any state, that (B) appear to be intended (i) to intimidate or coerce a civilian population, (ii) to influence the policy of a government by intimidation or coercion, or (iii) to affect the conduct of a government by mass destruction, assassination, or kidnapping, and (C) occur primarily within the territorial jurisdiction of the U.S." There is a parallel crime of international terrorism, which is defined in terms identical to that of domestic terrorism, except that its locus transcends national boundaries. This sweeping conception of terrorism is linked to the establishment of a new uniformed police force under the authority of the Department of Homeland Security that allows the arrest of demonstrators at "special events of national significance," and along with expanded arresting authority of the Secret Service, allows felony charges against demonstrators who breach security perimeters with penalties of up to ten years in prison.

The 2006 Act renews the controversial "sneak and peak" provision that empowers the government to gather information from a variety of sources: intercepts of telephone and Internet communications, access to medical and tax records, and scrutiny of book purchases and library borrowings. There are various provisions exempting some of these surveillance and search procedures from the requirement of a prior warrant or of notification to the target of investigation and suspicion. The judge issuing the warrant may allow the delay in notification under a variety of circumstances when there exists a risk of "endangering the life or physical safety of an individual; flight from prosecution; destruction of or tampering with evidence; intimidation of potential witnesses; or otherwise seriously jeopardizing an investigation or unduly delaying a trial." These procedures are handled by the Foreign Intelligence Surveillance Court instead of a normal federal or state court, which has a record of deference to governmental requests. And the basis for granting requests is based on a claim of "reasonable cause" rather than the more restrictive "probable cause." There are some measures in the 2006 version of the Patriot Act that allow challenges to "gag orders" and place some burdens on government agents making requests for intrusions on privacy. For instance, FBI agents who want to search bookstore or library records must now gain explicit permission from one of three designated high government officials.

In essence, the Patriot Act gives to the government wide powers with a serious potential of abuse that has alarmed civil libertarians, especially as this authority has been applied to immigrant suspects detained secretly without charges for long periods of time. The statutory language, which has not been judicially tested as yet, relies on very broad definitions of prohibited activity that could be interpreted to intimidate, and even punish, normal political action. Such legislation would have been impossible to enact in the absence of the post-9/11 climate of fear and anger, an atmosphere that has been sustained by periodic alarms uttered by high officials. The linking of counterterrorism with the war on terror has been relied upon by the Bush administration and the courts to defer to governmental claims that rely on a national security rationale.

The threat to civil liberties, human rights, and the rule of law associated with developments since 9/11 is complicated by the outlook of the Bush presidency and the deliberate confusion drawn between counterterrorism and a broader foreign policy agenda unlikely to generate domestic support unless fused in the public mind with counterterrorism. It is also clear that an authoritarian tendency—partly a dormant predisposition of neoconservative leadership and partly a response to the traumatic attacks of 9/11—has been activated. This conjuncture has resulted in a series of controversial intrusions on rights, quite unhelpful with respect to genuine counterterror goals of achieving security without disrupting the democratic fabric of society. In the instance of torture and reliance on cruel, inhuman, and degrading treatment of various categories of detainees the debate about utility has not been completely settled, although there is certainly no firm evidence that such abuse produce sufficient reliable and strategically useful information to offset the harm done.

The fact that the renewal of the Patriot Act received far more legislative scrutiny than did its initial adoption exhibited both the waning of automatic Congressional approval of whatever the executive branch claims to be helpful for counterterrorism, as well as the overall weakening of the Bush presidency. The situation remains fluid. Renewed terrorist incidents of any magnitude in the United States would undoubtedly reinforce the disposition to enhance governmental enforcement authority at the expense of human rights, while evidence of governmental abuse and the further withering away of al Qaeda might produce a push toward restoring normalcy with respect to the rights of individuals. If associated extremist groups do not perpetrate major terrorist attacks, especially in the United States, it might well be a tipping point for the legislative, and possibly the judicial, branch, producing enhanced protection of individual rights and moving to uphold the integrity of the rule of law.

# 3  The United States

*Protecting Human Dignity in an Era of Insecurity*
David P. Forsythe

This chapter argues that the George W. Bush administration after 9/11 (1) has engaged in intentional abuse of prisoners in connection with its "war" on terrorism; (2) has failed to limit this abuse to the minimal and genuine requirements of defending the life of the democratic United States; (3) has unwisely sought to minimize any review of its sweeping policies, whether by international or national actors; and (4) has failed in a major way to minimize the negatives inherent in its policy of coercive interrogation, with detrimental effects overall on U.S. national security.

## THE REALITY OF THE BUSH POLICY

From the beginning of the U.S. war on terrorism, President Bush and his closest advisers (and their lawyers)—Vice President Dick Cheney (and his principal lawyer David Addington), Secretary of Defense Donald Rumsfeld, and Legal Counsel Alberto Gonzales—opted for abusive interrogation over humane interrogation. They were backstopped by lawyers principally in the Justice Department (including John Yoo). State Department officials and those from the National Security Council, including even NSC Adviser Condoleezza Rice, were apparently shunted aside early in deliberations. So were many uniformed lawyers in the Department of Defense. All of the lawyers centrally involved were civilian political appointees.[1] These lawyers may have engaged in the unethical practice of advising their clients how to violate the law.[2]

The Bush administration, declaring a metaphorical "war" implying that the usual legal restraints, and checks and balances, did not apply, abused many enemy detainees. This was presaged by Cheney's statement of September 12, 2001: "We also have to work, though, sort of the dark side, if you wish. We've got to spend time in the shadows . . . so it's going to be vital for us to use any means at our disposal, basically, to achieve our objectives" (Human Rights Watch 2005a: 9). Cofer Black, formerly of the CIA, told Congress: "After 9/11, the gloves came off" (ibid.). The administration's view of national security stressed short-term concerns about actionable intelligence and taking certain persons out of circulation—meaning detaining them indefinitely outside of any legal system. That view of national security did not stress longer-term considerations such as maintaining popular support in foreign countries (particularly European and Islamic nations) or squaring administration policies with other announced objectives (like promoting the rule of law, human rights, and democracy).

This inner circle, none with significant military service, deemed coercive interrogation necessary to the national interest—to prevent another attack on the homeland, and later to get actionable intelligence for places like Afghanistan and Iraq. Partly driving the process was a righteous indignation that the virtuous United States had been attacked by terrorists with no morals who fought a total war involving attacks on innocent civilians (Mann 2004: 297 and passim).

## VITIATING LEGAL RESTRAINT

The first step in the process was to vitiate law that might interfere with coercive interrogation, as well as to give legal cover to U.S. officials engaged in abuse (see especially Greenberg and Dratel 2005; Danner 2005). This involved first the assertion that international humanitarian law (IHL), principally the Geneva Conventions of August 12, 1949 (GCs), designed primarily to protect victims of war, did not pertain to anyone held at the U.S. naval base at Guantanamo Bay, Cuba, itself chosen as a holding and interrogation center from late 2001 (with the first prisoners arriving in January 2002) in the hopes that U.S. courts would not assert jurisdiction over events there—it being leased from Cuba in perpetuity.[3] This assertion sought to deny those fighting for the Taliban government of Afghanistan, as well as for al Qaeda, and any others detained by reason of the multifaceted armed conflict in that country, the legal protections of IHL.[4] This U.S. view clearly contradicts the plain meaning of the GCs, which apply to all situations of armed conflict. The widespread nonrecognition of the Taliban government makes no difference. Particularly GCs III and IV apply in whole or in part after U.S. attacks commenced, with III pertaining to combatants and IV to civilians. The issue is not simply who is a Prisoner of War (POW) under GC III, for even those who not qualify as a POW, or privileged combatant, but who are detained in connection to armed conflict, retain various degrees of protected status under IHL.[5] Even illegal or irregular combatants merit certain minimal protections. The Bush administration also refused to allow an independent body to make determinations about such legal status, as called for by GC III.[6] Rather, the administration labeled all prisoners at Guantanamo "enemy combatants," a term not used in IHL but drawn from U.S. national experience to deal harshly with some irregular fighters.[7]

Second, the Bush team sought to redefine provisions of the UN Convention against Torture and Other Cruel, Inhuman, or Degrading Treatment so as to make that treaty, which is legally applicable in both peace and war, meaningless. The prohibition on intentional infliction of severe pain, whether physical or mental, for example, was said to mean that short of something like organ failure, torture did not exist. Or, as a second example, that same wording was held to mean that if an interrogator did not intend to cause severe pain, the existence of such pain would not block the abuse (Greenberg and Dratel 2005). While eventually these erroneous positions were rescinded when made public and criticized, the original objective was patently clear. The official attitude toward this treaty against torture and degrading treatment was that it had no intrinsic meaning: it only meant whatever the government said.[8]

Third, memos were written arguing that in times of war, the president under the doctrine of unified command had unlimited authority to protect the nation, and that even national laws did not necessarily always apply (Greenberg and Dratel 2005). More than any other President, George W. Bush used signing statements to indicate that rather than vetoing the legislation in question, he might not apply all or part of the statute he was signing. The wisdom and legal validity of such statements was the subject of much debate.

Fourth, the decision was taken to "disappear" certain persons. That is, U.S. authorities held them in secret places but did not acknowledge detaining them, thus preventing in a practical sense any law applying to them. According to the *Washington Post*, some of these ghost detainees were held in eight locations abroad, with two locales said to be in Eastern Europe.[9] A fax originating from Egyptian sources was intercepted by the Swiss which seemed to confirm the existence of these European "black sites" near the Black Sea.[10] The Bush team displayed exceptional control over the information pertaining to such persons.[11] President Bush finally acknowledged these sites in September 2006 but refused to give full specifics.

Fifth, certain persons were "rendered" to foreign jurisdictions like Egypt known for harsh interrogation practices, under the fig leaf that assurances had been obtained regarding the prohibition of improper interrogation.[12] Apparently the Bush administration accelerated, rather than initiated, this policy, which prevented U.S. courts from exercising any jurisdiction under U.S. law.[13]

Various changes or additions to some of these early positions occurred over time. In Iraq after the invasion of March 2003, the Bush administration agreed that an international armed conflict, and then occupation, existed, to which IHL applied. In June 2006, the U.S. Supreme Court decided that Common Article 3 from the 1949 Geneva Conventions, covering nonstate actors and others in internal war, applied to detainees at Guantanamo since it had become a minimum humanitarian standard in all armed conflicts.[14] The immediate focus of the court was U.S. military commissions for trying some Guantanamo prisoners, and whether these commissions met the standards of due process called for in Common Article 3. By implication, Common Article 3's wording about broader treatment of those detainees, including interrogation techniques, also applied. That article prohibited at all times and everywhere torture and cruel, inhuman, and degrading treatment (Pictet 1960: 27 and passim). At the time of writing the United States had responded to the Supreme Court's judgment in *Hamdan v. Rumsfeld* with new legislation pertaining to both interrogation and trial in military commissions, but controversy continued and the new law had not yet been tested in U.S. courts.

## INSTITUTING COERCIVE INTERROGATION

The initial flow of information from Guantanamo under Brigadier General Rick Baccus and Major General Michael Dunleavey was deemed by Rumsfeld to be insufficient, so Major General Geoffrey Miller was dispatched to change things. Miller implemented a harsh regime, ensuring that Military Police units, like Military Intelligence, were tough on prisoners.[15] A list of different categories of interrogation techniques pertaining to U.S. military personnel was issued, modified, and reissued by Rumsfeld (Greenberg and Dratel 2005). These instructions did not necessarily cover interrogations by the Central Intelligence Agency (CIA), the Federal Bureau of Investigation (FBI), or private security firms. There were reports that intelligence agents from certain foreign governments were also part of Guantanamo interrogations. For the United States, the primary purpose of Guantanamo was first intelligence gathering, and then just as a holding facility. Initially the question of legal prosecutions was marginal in Washington, until public advocacy suits brought U.S. courts into the fray.

Certainly during 2002–4 at Guantanamo a number of prisoners were abused. This we know from a report by the International Committee of the Red Cross (ICRC) that was leaked probably by dissidents within the U.S. executive, from released FBI memos obtained under the Freedom of Information Act, and from a U.S. translator and also a chaplain who wrote books about their experiences there.[16] Eventually there were also claims by released prisoners.[17]

Some prisoners were sexually and religiously taunted and humiliated. They were restrained in painful positions. They were subjected to extremes of heat and cold. They were subjected to loud music or other noises, as well as to flashing lights. They were kept in isolation for long periods. They were force-fed liquids, then made to urinate on themselves. They were also made to defecate on themselves. They were intimidated by military police dogs. In short, there were given the "torture lite" treatment, which, more or less, the Israelis had practiced against Palestinian detainees for considerable time in the Middle East, and which the British had used for a time against members of the Irish Provisional Authority in Northern Ireland.[18] The process was such that both FBI agents and CIA agents sought to distance themselves from it, lest they be held legally responsible for it. The CIA might have been doing something similar in other places, but the agency did not want to be tagged for the abuses at Guantanamo.[19]

In addition, some prisoners were physically beaten and otherwise abused by U.S. Military Police in actions that did not seem to be approved by Military Intelligence or higher authorities.[20] Later, there was the issue of U.S. forced feeding of Guantanamo inmates on hunger strikes. Confronting charges of brutal forced feeding, the detaining authority maintained that restraint systems and techniques were humane.

In Iraq from spring 2003, the U.S. invading forces found themselves with large numbers of detainees and also a persistent and violent insurgency against their presence. The poor management of prisoner affairs was part of a bungled occupation.[21] In that situation General Miller was transferred from Guantanamo to Iraq in August to systematize and improve the quest for intelligence. One U.S. report accurately said that the U.S. treatment of Iraqi prisoners "migrated" from Guantanamo.[22] Certain prisoners were hidden from the visits of the ICRC and kept in darkened isolation in an effort to break them into giving more information. As usual, abuse also occurred by troops in the field at the point of capture, especially by U.S. Special Operations Forces that are trained to act outside the bounds of conventional warfare. This abuse was such that the CIA distanced itself from it.[23] The U.S. Central Command for Iraq, headed by Lt.-General Ricardo Sanchez, was never staffed and organized properly, which allowed the egregious abuses of Iraqi detainees that became infamous in 2004 with the release of unauthorized photographs of humiliating treatment. Lt.-General Sanchez also explicitly authorized certain abusive techniques, as well as pressing subordinates for more actionable intelligence from prisoners.[24] In Iraq some of the prisoner abuse proved fatal, unlike Guantanamo as far as we know.

In Afghanistan from 2001, there were persistent reports of prisoner abuse.[25] As in Iraq so in Afghanistan, some of the abuse proved fatal. Eventually the U.S. military reported investigations into some thirty deaths while in U.S. custody in both Iraq and Afghanistan. In 2006 Human Rights First claimed that ninety-eight prisoners had died while in U.S. custody in Afghanistan and Iraq.[26] Released prisoners described the same sorts of confinement in painful positions and other techniques used at Guantanamo.[27] Various press reports confirmed the accuracy of these and other charges.[28]

All of this coercive interrogation constituted a violation of IHL and also of the UN Convention against Torture—both of which prohibit degrading treatment, or torture lite, as well as torture heavy. It violated the Uniform Code of Military Justice, which itself was based on IHL. And it probably violated various tenets of U.S. constitutional law, particularly the Eighth Amendment prohibiting cruel and unusual punishment, although U.S. courts had not so ruled at the time of writing.[29]

## COVERING RHETORIC, REACTIVE POLICIES

Early on, President Bush sought to provide reassuring rhetoric about the treatment of enemy detainees, but it was patently meaningless. He said that such prisoners would be treated humanely, in keeping with the principles of the Geneva Conventions, but only in so far as "military necessity" permitted.[30] So obviously humane treatment could be overridden on the basis of what U.S. leaders might say to be military necessity.[31]

Other administration statements over time reiterated the theme of humane treatment that ruled out torture. But aside from withdrawing the more extreme assertions about the definition of torture,[32] the administration refused to say exactly what constituted torture, or that torture lite was off limits.[33] Bush officials simply refused to address the fact that torture lite in the form of degrading treatment was also prohibited by international law. At times administration spokespersons simply avoided the truth, as when the Pentagon denied abuse at Guantanamo, saying detainees were treated humanely and properly, even when the reliable ICRC and other overwhelming evidence clearly indicated otherwise.[34] When in 2005 it became clear that abuse was part of the interrogation of the presumed twentieth hijacker, Mohamed al-Kahtani of Saudi Arabia, Rumsfeld did not deny the nature of the process but rather said that the process was closely monitored by specialists.[35] So the argument was that the process of coercive interrogation existed but was limited and controlled. Since it was presumably torture lite instead of torture heavy, apparently it was legitimate. It was also presumably legitimate because it was yielding life-saving information, or so it was said.

Still further, the process of "disappearing persons," or turning them into "ghost detainees," continued, as well as the policy of "rendering" persons to interrogators in places like Uzbekistan and Egypt. It should be noted that during the armed conflict and occupation of Iraq, the transfer of detainees out of the area is a clear violation of IHL. One can understand the nature of interrogation in places like Egypt by looking at the State Department's annual human rights reports, which find repeatedly that torture and other abuse of prisoners is systematic in those states. There would be no point in having such policies if prisoners were to be treated humanely, in conformity with legal obligations. A legal and fully humane approach would not require "disappearance" or "rendition." It is in the context of "disappearances" that there have been reports of "water boarding," or making a prisoner think he will drown for his refusal to say what interrogators want. This certainly would qualify as torture heavy.[36]

At Guantanamo and in Afghanistan and Iraq, the U.S. military brought criminal proceedings against a variety of individuals in connection with prisoner abuse.[37] Most of those charged were distinctly toward the bottom of the military hierarchy. There were some administrative sanctions, including of some higher officers. One brigadier general in the Army Reserve, Janis Karpinski, nominally in charge of the infamous Abu Ghraib prison in Iraq, was demoted.[38] Also sanctioned was Colonel Thomas Pappas, despite his statement that he was pressured by superiors to get tougher with detainees in Iraq.[39] When the policy of coercive interrogation went out of bounds, then the United States sometimes brought charges or levied sanctions against its own military personnel. Punishments were usually light (Human Rights Watch 2005a). One does not know for sure the role and fate of private interrogators under contract, or agents of the CIA and FBI.

At the same time, the administration made sure that the spotlight of inquiry did not proceed very far up the chain of command. After the photos surfaced regarding abuse at Abu Ghraib, several investigations were commissioned, mostly about Iraq. The military inquiries appear to have been carefully structured to fragment foci and to avoid review of the Office of the

Secretary of Defense, and of course of the White House. The one "independent" panel, made up of former members of the national security establishment like James Schlesinger, former secretary of defense, did find personal and institutional responsibility for prisoner abuse at high levels, but refused to name names (see also Strasser 2004). The follow-on report by Vice Admiral Albert Church III remained classified. A released summary cleared all high-ranking military officials in Iraq of any responsibility for abuse of prisoners.[40] Members of the Schlesinger panel did not vigorously protest.

No one beyond General Karpinski and Colonel Thomas Pappas was held responsible for any sins of omission or neglect regarding Iraq. No high officer was held responsible for the conscious hiding of prisoners or keeping them in inhumane conditions. General Miller, a major player regarding both Guantanamo and prisons in Iraq, despite being recommended for a reprimand by one inquiry, was ultimately cleared of any responsibility for events by Admiral Church and later given a military award. In later trials where his testimony was requested, he took the military equivalent of the Fifth Amendment, protecting himself from self-incrimination. Lt.-General Ricardo Sanchez, the head of all military operations in Iraq, who under the doctrine of command responsibility should have known what was occurring by way of unauthorized brutality and humiliation, and who at one point had authorized harsh interrogation including the use of dogs to intimidate, was forced into retirement—not because he had fallen out of favor in the Department of Defense but because he might implicate higher authorities in prisoner abuse when required to testify in the Senate.[41]

Others who had been key in developing U.S. policy toward enemy detainees were advanced by President Bush. Gonzales was nominated to be Attorney General. Jay B. Bybee, a Justice Department lawyer who had written some of the early, permissive memos, was nominated to be a federal judge for the important Ninth Circuit Court of Appeals. William J. Haynes II, a Pentagon lawyer who had approved some of the early, permissive memos, was nominated to the Fourth Circuit Court of Appeals. It was apparently Haynes who had excluded critical lawyers from the policy-making process. Rumsfeld's two letters of resignation were not accepted.

## DOMESTIC REACTION

By and large, American society and the Republican majority in both houses of Congress did not want to delve deeply into the Bush policy toward enemy detainees during 2002–4. As Jean Paul Sartre had noted back in the 1950s in the context of the French-Algerian war, it is disturbing to face the question of what to do when co-nationals are in favor of pulling out fingernails, or something similar to it (Sartre's preface to Alleg 1958). It is painful to confront directly how much abuse of individuals might be justified when attempting to protect the nation.

No sizable grassroots public movement arose in protest, but this is not surprising. Even in the face of genocide, the American public has not roused itself to demand a proper response from its foreign policy officials (Power 2002). After all, the country, including civilians, had been attacked. Moreover, there is a dark side to a free society: the public is preoccupied with individual things—family, jobs, schools, health care, pensions, and so on.[42]

Congressional Republicans, caught up in the nationalistic reaction to 9/11, were especially reluctant to provide critical oversight of a Republican president. A few hearings were held, but military officials dissembled, the tough questions were not asked, and the issues were swept under the congressional rug.[43] Gonzales was confirmed as Attorney General despite his efforts to undermine much law. Because of the damage he had done to IHL, he was opposed by a number of high-ranking military officials. He said in his confirmation hearings that U.S. law against torture did not cover U.S. officials when interrogating foreign detainees outside the United States. Bybee was confirmed to sit on the Ninth Circuit appellate bench.

As time passed and American support for the war in Iraq waned, as American enthusiasm for the occupation there also declined, and as the President's approval ratings fell, some Members of Congress (MCs)—including Republicans—began to speak out about closing Guantanamo and about other prisoner issues. There was thus some unease about detention policies among Republicans as well as Democrats. Particularly in the Senate, led by Republican Senators John McCain, Lindsay Graham, and John Warner (all of whom were interested in notions of American and military honor, as well as international standards), there was finally open defiance of Bush policies on the question. In the context of increased publicity,[44] the Senate voted 90–9 to oppose any interrogation procedures that were not in keeping with those approved in U.S. military manuals.[45] The House followed suit, again with a comfortable majority.[46] The 2005 Detainee Treatment Act, containing these measures, passed the Congress easily.

Still, the Bush administration fought for an exemption from this provision that would allow nonmilitary officials, such as those of the CIA, to operate differently abroad.[47] The Bush administration formally caved in to congressional opinion by signing the legislation in question, since it was clear that a presidential veto could be overridden in each house. The

President, however, made comments that suggested he might not follow the law in certain situations.[48]

After the 2006 Hamdan judgment in the U.S. Supreme Court, President Bush and the Republican-controlled Congress agreed on new legislation that authorized presidential discretion to engage in exceptional detention and interrogation, and new military commissions that allowed for the possibility of coerced confessions and other violations of widely accepted notions of criminal due process. The statute also provided criminal immunity for U.S. officials that might have violated the law on prisoner treatment in the past. At the end of the day, President Bush got most of what he wanted regarding enemy prisoners, while his congressional critics secured only minor adjustments to presidential policies.[49]

The one element of the national media that did the most to try to keep a critical focus on the issue was the *New York Times*, which ran several prominent stories, not to mention editorializing against the relevant Bush policies. It was also important that the *Wall Street Journal* and the *Financial Times*, two conservative papers, published leaked prison reports and/or ran stories on the International Committee of the Red Cross (ICRC) and prisoner issues. But much of this was supportive of the Bush policies, and critical of those interested in the human dignity and rights of enemy detainees.[50] *Newsweek* also gave periodic coverage to prisoner stories.

Liberal groups, like the ACLU, Human Rights First, and the Center for Constitutional Rights, played important roles by using the Freedom of Information Act to get important documents into the public domain, such as the FBI memos expressing concern about harsh military interrogation at Guantanamo. Human Rights First, formerly the Lawyers Committee for Human Rights, pursued the subject of prisoner abuse with much determination. It also helped bring a lawsuit against Secretary of Defense Rumsfeld on behalf of certain former prisoners It was also important that certain Judge Advocate General's Corps (JAG) lawyers, concerned about disrespect for IHL—which, after all, is supposed to protect U.S. military personnel when detained by others—expressed their concerns to Scott Horton, head of the New York City Bar Association, Committee on International Human Rights, who then directed several trenchant studies (Greenberg and Dratel 2005: 558 and following), as well as engaging in public commentary in important media outlets such as the NewsHour with Jim Lehrer on PBS. Independent newspapers catering to military readers, such as the *Army Times*, editorialized in support of traditional notions of military honor and against many prisoner policies of the Bush administration.

The problem for critics, especially in the Democratic Party, was that they did not control the congressional oversight and budgetary process. Moreover, in elections, particularly the 2004 presidential campaign, they did not want to appear soft on national security issues, or to have to articulate an alternative policy to the one put in place by the Bush administration. So in that presidential race, the topic of treatment of enemy detainees was not raised by the Democrats in any central way, and certainly not by their presidential candidate, John Kerry.

Yet as public and congressional opinion shifted, congressional Democrats joined moderate Republicans in reemphasizing the legal ban against coercive interrogation. In the congressional debates leading to a reaffirmation of this ban in 2005, different arguments came into play: American exceptionalism (Americans do not torture), military honor (the proper soldier does not torture), reliance on law (various treaties prohibit torture), military self-interest (we need to protect our military personnel when captured in future wars), political self-interest (we cannot win the hearts and minds of the Arab-Muslim world when we torture). But the 2006 legislation undercut some of the intent of the 2005 statute by authorizing exceptional detention (and abuse) in nonmilitary sites, as well as not prohibiting coerced confessions in the post-Hamdan military commissions.

In this political context, U.S. courts slowly and gingerly stepped into the controversy, holding first that they did have jurisdiction over events at Guantanamo, then that habeas corpus did obtain.[31] This judicial position was apparently undermined when Congress voted in 2005 that Guantanamo detainees did not have the right of habeas corpus, but that when tried by U.S. military commissions, enemy detainees had the right to appeal to civilian courts.[52] The Bush team had resumed the use of military commissions to try "enemy combatants" in highly controversial procedures.[53] Vigorous defense of prisoners by their lawyers again caused the process to move slowly, in fits and starts.[54] When the American citizen Jose Padilla, who had been listed as an "enemy combatant" and thus stripped of his constitutional rights, was then placed by the administration under the jurisdiction of the civilian courts, and charged with traditional crimes, parts of the federal court system were not happy about the apparent arbitrariness of the use of legal categories.


INTERNATIONAL REACTIONS: NATO ALLIES

Bush policy toward enemy detainees contributed to a highly negative reaction among virtually all NATO publics, and in other circles already alarmed by the prospect of unchecked U.S. power.[55] After the *Washington Post* reported that the United States had interrogated certain detainees in "black sites" or secret interrogation centers in Europe, public reaction there was strongly and broadly negative. A number of legislative inquiries were launched, including by the Council of Europe and European Union.[56]

At the same time, the British, Swedish, Canadian, and certain other governments also engaged in rendition,[57] and some foreign governments probably cooperated in abusive interrogation at Guantanamo and other places like Afghanistan.[58] A former British diplomat went public with his view that the United Kingdom was cooperating with, and receiving information from, U.S. torture.[59] The British House of Lords, stimulated by U.S. policy, declared that information gained via torture was inadmissible in UK courts.[60] A British parliamentary committee urged the Blair government to speak out more strongly about Guantanamo.[61]

There was no doubt a certain governmental sympathy in NATO for U.S. policy, whatever parliaments and publics might think. It is highly unlikely that the CIA could have engaged in repeated flights in Europe transporting secret prisoners without European security managers being aware of what was happening, even though the British, Spanish, and other governments denied knowledge of relevant events. It is also doubtful that U.S. forced disappearances and concomitant interrogation could have occurred in certain European countries, whether Romania, Bulgaria, Poland, the Ukraine, or elsewhere, without knowledge by European security managers.[62] When the German government under Gerhard Schroeder learned that a German citizen had been seized by the United States in the Balkans and then transported to Afghanistan where he was abused, in a case of mistaken identity, the German government did not make a public controversy over the matter.[63] (Later, incoming Chancellor Angela Merkel did say publicly that eventually Guantanamo should be closed.)[64] It was finally established that while the Schroeder government was publicly protesting the U.S. invasion of Iraq, certain German intelligence agents were providing the United States with information, with the approval of high German officials.[65]

In Afghanistan, Canadian military forces turned captured suspects over to U.S. forces; given the high incidence of U.S. mistreatment of prisoners in that country, this action brought an expression of concern from the ICRC.[66] Later in Afghanistan, certain NATO governments, apparently led by the Dutch, insisted on a clear policy about the humane treatment of prisoners before they would agree to expand NATO's role in that country.

Many European governments wound up in a delicate position, cooperating to some degree with U.S. policies toward enemy detainees, but then having to confront an aroused public and deal with parliamentary inquiries.

A certain amount of hypocrisy was at work, as in the case of Germany noted above. The Italian government under Berlusconi may have publicly demanded the extradition and trial of the U.S. operatives who seized a suspect on Italian soil, but again it is highly unlikely that such a kidnapping could have occurred without some role for Italian security managers, especially given that the Berlusconi government was openly supportive of Bush policies in Afghanistan and Iraq.[67]

In early 2006 certain British officials called for the closing of the Guantanamo detention facility, but Prime Minister Blair hedged on the issue. All of this suggests that many NATO governments sought to distance themselves in public from U.S. policies toward enemy detainees, while maintaining a certain covert cooperation with, or tolerance of, those policies.

## INTERNATIONAL REACTIONS BEYOND NATO

The UN system reacted in various ways to this topic, especially through its secretariat, but without much impact on the Bush administration, predisposed as it was to dismiss most UN initiatives that interfered with desired policies.[68] As a general rule, UN criticism of Washington is taken less seriously than congressional criticism or U.S. court action.

The UN High Commissioner for Human Rights made a number of statements about U.S. treatment of enemy detainees, via Mary Robinson, Bertie Ramcharan, and Louise Arbour. None of these statements seemed to have had any impact on Washington. A group of UN human rights experts related either to monitoring bodies of particular treaties or to the UN Human Rights Commission (or to its subcommission) expressed concern about the reports of abuse at Guantanamo, Afghanistan, and Iraq. From 2004 they requested that certain UN human rights experts be allowed to visit Guantanamo. For a time Washington stalled in dealing with this request, then said a visit to Guantanamo would be allowed, although prisoners could not be interviewed. The UN officials in question then said they would not visit under this condition. In early 2006 they issued a closely argued report charging the United States with various violations of human rights and humanitarian law standards, and called for the closing of Guantanamo.[69]

International human rights groups played important roles in keeping the issue alive. Although it is impossible to track all NGO activity related to this subject, some examples can be given. Particularly important as a thorough record was a long and detailed report by Amnesty International (AI) in November 2004.[70] AI's release of its annual report in 2005 led to much controversy, stemming in part from its use of the word "gulag" to refer to Guantanamo. These semantics brought publicity to the issue, but also allowed the Bush administration and its friends to deflect the debate away from its policies and toward AI's judgment and reliability.

Human Rights Watch (HRW) also produced many reports on U.S. policy, including a major report about U.S. command responsibility for prisoner mistreatment.[71] HRW repeatedly called for an independent inquiry into the subject, given the limits and weaknesses of both DOD reports and congressional oversight. While congressional commentary picked up by 2005, at the time of writing no truly independent study had been allowed by the Bush team. Given the tenor of American nationalism, such an independent inquiry was unlikely.

The Center for Constitutional Rights teamed with some former detainees at Guantanamo to bring charges in a German court under the principle of universal jurisdiction. The defendants were Secretary of Defense Rumsfeld and others. German authorities did not pursue the suit.

All of this NGO activity, when linked to media reports and congressional actions, may have generated some pressure on the Bush administration to restrict the scope of coercive interrogation at U.S. military facilities.[72] At a certain point it was clear that the Bush team was prepared to clean up military interrogations but wanted to maintain abusive interrogation under the CIA. "Disappearances" and "renditions" continued, at least until halfway through 2006.

Publics and parliaments in Asia did not react as strongly against U.S. policies of renditions and forced disappearances as in Europe.[73] Many Asian governments seemed supportive of U.S. policies.

## THE ICRC

The one organization outside the U.S. government that knows in detail what is occurring at Guantanamo and in Afghanistan and Iraq, but not in the U.S. secret detention centers, is the ICRC.[74] This founding agency of the International Red Cross and Red Crescent Movement focuses exclusively on armed conflict and internal unrest. It has a mandate to engage in humanitarian protection, which includes protecting the human dignity of prisoners in war and unrest. Under GCs III and IV, it has a right to visit detainees in international armed conflict, in order to observe and comment on whether IHL is being properly implemented. It has a right to offer its services in civil wars and domestic unrest, in which case the visitation process can be almost the same as in international wars.

Exactly what it is doing, and how, and with what success, is difficult to say. In its humanitarian work since 1863, the ICRC prides itself on its independence, neutrality, and impartiality. These guiding standards do not preclude public comment, but discretion is its preferred mode of operation. Its basic approach to violations of human dignity is not covered in IHL but is spelled out in one of its doctrines, or general policy statements, No. 15—first articulated in 1981 and refined in 2005.[75] It normally does not make public comment about the details of what its delegates observe, since in its view this confidentiality promotes access, trust, and leads over time to positive developments. It may share detailed information confidentially with certain third parties in the quest for humanitarian improvements. It may make public statements and even public denunciations if discreet diplomacy does not yield significant progress over time, and if such publicity is judged to be in the interest of the victims themselves. Other doctrines, such as No. 58, allow the ICRC to make public comment for other reasons, such as to correct partial or inaccurate reports about its role.

The Bush administration, while resisting the application of IHL to Guantanamo, did nevertheless allow an essentially permanent presence there by the ICRC from early 2002. The ICRC did not agree that IHL was inapplicable to at least some of the Guantanamo detainees,[76] but consistent with its preferred policies it did not engage in protracted and acerbic legal debate in public, especially since it was active on the ground at Guantanamo on practical matters of humanitarian protection.

In May 2003, the ICRC went public about the deleterious effect of indefinite detention without prospect of charge or trial at Guantanamo. It did so it a fairly low-key way, which is typical of the organization, posting a statement on its Web site and allowing the head of its Washington office eventually to give an interview to the *New York Times,* saying the same thing as posted. More than thirty Guantanamo detainees had attempted suicide, given their despair. The fact that the United States was the largest donor to the ICRC budget, and had been for some time, providing about 28 percent of the wherewithal for ICRC operations around the world in 2004–5, did not affect the policy of the organization on this issue. (Nor had donor status affected ICRC support for the Ottawa Treaty banning antipersonnel land mines, which the United States opposed.)

We now know that during the period 2002–4, the ICRC lodged numerous discreet protests about certain U.S. policies at Guantanamo, involving such things as the treatment of detainees under the age of 18, the lack of prayer mats and Korans, the abuse of Korans by interrogators, the sexual humiliation of prisoners, the use of medical records by interrogation teams in violation of medical ethics, and other U.S. actions that in some cases were "tantamount to torture." At times the ICRC was prevented from seeing some detainees.[77] On some issues the ICRC representatives on the scene judged the policies serious enough to warrant a temporary suspension of visits, although no public statement was made.[78]

We also know that ICRC President Jacob Kellenberger went to Washington several times and met with high Bush officials, including the president in February 2005, to discuss Guantanamo (and Afghanistan and other subjects). Kellenberger also involved himself with Guantanamo and other IHL issues with the U.S. diplomatic mission in Geneva. So there was high-level ICRC diplomacy to try to effectuate change in keeping with international norms for human dignity.

What we do not know is the exact Guantanamo balance sheet of improvements and remaining problems. And we do not know the details of the ICRC cost-benefit analysis about staying or leaving with a public protest. We certainly do not know if the ICRC asked the Guantanamo detainees if it should stay or go with a protest. The organization sometimes poses this question to prisoners, and if they want the ICRC to continue with confidential visits, which give the prisoner a sole contact with the outside world, the ICRC can hardly do otherwise—even if humanitarian progress is slight to nonexistent.

Contrary to the assumptions of some observers, there has been some beneficial change at Guantanamo over time, stimulated by the ICRC's quiet diplomacy. We just do not know exactly how much. Kellenberger said in a press conference in 2005 that at Guantanamo the organization had achieved progress on some issues, although all of its requests had not been met by U.S. authorities.[79] This type of mixed record is usually enough for the ICRC to continue with its discreet diplomacy, at least where it can see some important progress.

In Iraq, where the United States accepted the application of IHL in general, the process of prison visits was not that different from Guantanamo. Interestingly, Geneva decided that the progress achieved by late fall 2003 was greater than in either Guantanamo or Afghanistan. This was partially because much of the abuse at Abu Ghraib was unauthorized by higher authorities, even if in reality they were negligent about proper planning and supervision. So the U.S. authorities in Iraq did not resist some of the changes demanded by the ICRC. But there were intentional policies of abuse also, such as the CIA "disappearing" persons, most of whom were abused in one way or the other, and at least one of whom died in captivity (Amnesty International 2004: 8). Also, there was slow U.S. action at times in response to ICRC reports, and on at least one occasion, a U.S. officer proposed that ICRC visits be announced in advance so as to not interfere with coercive interrogation (ibid.: 54).

This being so, some ICRC officials in both Iraq and Geneva wanted more than quiet suspension of ongoing visits. They wanted a strong public protest. But once again Geneva, after much debate, decided in favor of discretion. A leaked ICRC report about Iraq, published in the *Wall Street Journal*, did not come from ICRC sources but probably from dissidents within the U.S. executive. And even a certain faulty follow-up to ICRC reports by U.S. authorities in the fall of 2003 did not occasion a radical change of plan by Geneva.[80] By the time of Kellenberger's meetings with Bush, Rice, Rumsfeld, and others in February 2005, Iraq was not the top agenda item, but rather Guantanamo and Afghanistan. Many of the changes in Iraq were of course produced by the infamous pictures that circulated about Abu Ghraib, and not because of the ICRC confidential reports. Nevertheless, as at Guantanamo, there was a certain progressive change over time, perhaps more so in Iraq than at Guantanamo on these humanitarian questions. In both places, as the ICRC had reported privately, most of the detainees were nonpolitical. Thus eventually a number of releases occurred.

In Afghanistan, there were numerous and credible reports of detainees being abused while in U.S. captivity, whether at the Bagram or Khandahar military bases, or at regional bases, or at smaller "holding centers." Somewhere around twenty fatal cases of prisoner abuse were being investigated at the time of writing. From the beginning, it was clear that the ICRC did not have immediate access to all detainees in all detention facilities. U.S. prisoner policy in Afghanistan was a subject of high-level ICRC diplomacy with U.S. leaders on several occasions.

It is reasonable to conclude that much of the United States' abuse of enemy prisoners was unnecessary for the life of a democratic nation. One major problem with the necessity argument is that it tends to be applied very broadly. One engages in a war of choice in Iraq in 2003, not tightly linked to the security of the United States. But then abusive interrogation transpires, despite well-considered concerns that U.S. military forces should not have been sent there in the first place.[81] That invasion has probably harmed U.S. security, leading as it has to a laboratory in which anti-U.S. actors can perfect their deadly skills, with plenty of American targets.[82] Abuse was practiced widely at Guantanamo, even though many prisoners there had no actionable intelligence to give.[83]

By 2005, what one British scholar has called the "fight-back" against excessive executive claims found resonance in Congress, having been articulated earlier by some government lawyers, human rights NGOs, and media like the *New York Times* (Gearty 2006: 108). Led by a few senators with a strong sense of American exceptionalism and military honor, Congress did succeed in passing legislation that prohibited both torture and mistreatment wherever it might be considered in places under U.S. control. So once again it was Congress that insisted on serious attention to human rights, even if it had taken the better part of three years for that oversight and legislative reaction to materialize.[84] These 2005 gains, however, were greatly undercut by the subsequent 2006 legislation allowing exceptional detention and interrogation, as well as new military commissions that fell far short of international standards of due process.[85]

At the time of writing most courts in the United States were still often deferential to executive claims about the need for secrecy and broad executive power in national security affairs.[86] A divided U.S. Supreme Court, however, began to challenge executive legal claims in both the *Rasul* and *Hamdan* judgments. The latter case was potentially highly important, asserting a broad application of international legal protection to prisoners and defendants linked to armed conflict, given Common Article 3 from the Geneva Conventions of August 12, 1949.[87]

A clear casualty from Bush policies toward enemy detainees was a decline of U.S. reputation and soft power in the world. One can imagine that the next time the U.S. government engages in quiet diplomacy toward another state about torture, it will be similar to when a British diplomat talked to a Nazi official about the German concentration camps. The Nazi silenced the British diplomat when the former pulled off his shelf an account of the British concentration camps in the Boer War, in which almost 30,000 persons died, mainly women and children (Ferguson 2004: 232–33). Washington has made it more difficult to exercise influence for progressive causes around the world (Carothers 2006: 68). Certain insurgents in Iraq were carrying reproductions of the Abu Ghraib pictures of abuse when they were apprehended, which is clear evidence that widespread knowledge of prisoner mistreatment made the U.S. role in the world more difficult.[88] Abu Ghraib was no doubt a recruiting bonanza for al Qaeda. But Guantanamo and the rest of U.S. policy toward enemy prisoners made their own contributions to this problem.

It was highly ironic that in 2005 and 2006 the U.S. was pressing the Iraqi government to improve the treatment of prisoners in that country, in the interest of national reconciliation, when the U.S. itself had been so obtuse about the damage to U.S. goals and interests in Iraq and the world via its own policies of prisoner abuse.

Even if, from time to time, coercive interrogation may yield actionable intelligence of importance, there are many negatives involved in the process: the decline in reputation and hence soft power of the detaining authority, damage to its sense of proper identity and honor, undermining its effort to protect its own personnel when captured in the future, and above all the antagonism and hostility of foreign populations. The Bush administration seemed blind to all these considerations. It was rather Congress, led by moderate Republicans in the Senate, mostly with military backgrounds, that challenged administration abusive policies on these various grounds.[89] Even the centrist paper *USA Today* called in early 2006 for the closure of Guantanamo on grounds that it was not in the U.S. national interest to keep it open, given that it had become an impediment to better relations with the Arab-Islamic world. A British parliamentary committee said the same thing. But when President Bush transferred fourteen detainees from the "black sites" or secret detentions to Guantanamo, he thereby insured that the Cuban facility could not be closed in the near future.

The American polity, however, showed little inclination to do what HRW has called for: create a special prosecutor and/or special commission to examine the origins of prisoner abuse at highest levels, military and civilian, so as to correct the impunity now existing for such officials. Investigation of high policy makers, as Sartre noted long ago, is agonizing and requires great courage. As a perceptive journalist concluded (Lelyveld 2005: 39), the public and Congress agreed during 2002–4: "the less we know as a people about secret counterterrorism struggles and strategies, [and] the less we contemplate the possibly ugly consequences, the easier it will be for those in authority to get on with the job of protecting us."

# 4 Northern Ireland

*Violent Conflict and the Resilience of International Law*

Colm Campbell

A state that defines itself by an ideological commitment to the rule of law (usually, though not universally, coterminous with liberal democracy) tends to behave differently from more authoritarian states. Paradigmatically, the democratic state's agents operate within the framework of legal powers that we have come to understand as Weberian "formal rationality." In practice, no state fully conforms to this model, even in peaceful times. At best law has a "relative" rather than an absolute autonomy, and some degree of illegality characterizes the operation of all states (Abel 1995). A variety of substantive, procedural, and evidential factors operate to limit the reach of the law on state action, creating mutable legal "grey zones." Norms may be ambiguous or lacking; prosecutorial discretion may shield state operatives; the judiciary may display marked deference; and illegality may involve covert operations in which links with the state may be difficult to prove, particularly where official investigations are deficient.

When the liberal-democratic state faces severe violent challenge, there is likely to be pronounced pressure to depart from formal rationality (Balbus 1977). This departure may involve the imposition of a formal, or merely de facto, "state of emergency." During such periods of emergency new legal grey zones invariably manifest, and although a revised normative framework may not mandate prisoner abuse it may in practice facilitate it. There is likely to be a rise in covert operations entailing activities such as killings, in which links to the state may be difficult to identify (as Chapter 7 in this volume discusses). The *scale* of repression is nevertheless likely to be lower in democratic than in authoritarian states, suggesting a "damping" effect (Tilly 2003; Davenport 2004). Law contributes ambiguously to this effect—its limited effective reach enables the existence of grey zones, while its remaining presence helps to delimit them.

A similar ambiguity manifests at the level of international law. While international human rights law has greatly increased in scope since the founding of the UN, derogation clauses in the major conventions make explicit provision for the declaration of states of emergency, providing for restriction on all but a small core of "nonderogable" rights (Fitzpatrick 1994). These core rights nevertheless include those most under pressure during emergencies: the right to freedom from torture and a prohibition on arbitrary killings. Yet the "bite" of human rights law in emergencies is significantly reduced by doctrines such as that of the European Court of Human Rights, which allows states a wide "margin of appreciation" (Gross and Ní Aoláin 2001). There are also significant procedural and evidential obstacles. Domestic remedies must generally be exhausted unless it can be shown that the alleged abuses constitute state "administrative practice" (Harris, O'Boyle and Warbrick 2005), and covert activities generally leave few traces.

The protection of nonderogable rights is paralleled by restrictions in international humanitarian law ("the laws of war") on torture and arbitrary killings, but the reach of this area of law can be hampered by a separate issue: state sensitivity about acknowledging that "armed conflict" exists. Humanitarian law sanctions killing "combatants" (though the phrase is used only in relation to international armed conflicts) and might therefore be perceived to free the state's hands on the use of lethal force. But the law's application might also seem to convey status on violent challengers, either informally, or in the case of conflicts meeting particular technical requirements, by the formal award of "prisoner of war" status. From the state's point of view two alternative optimal results suggest themselves. The first is to recognize the existence of armed conflict (facilitating use of lethal force), while denying that challengers meet technical requirements for prisoner-of-war status. The second is to deny the existence of armed conflict while exploiting domestic law grey zones to employ the kind of lethal force against violent challengers that international humanitarian law permits against "combatants." If humanitarian law is ultimately judged applicable, the deaths may not have been in violation, particularly if when killed, challengers were taking "a direct part in hostilities," (though a violation of international human rights law may have occurred; see generally Kretzmer 2005).

Sensitivity around normative framing highlights that in many situations there exists not only violent conflict, but also "metaconflict"—that is, conflict about the conflict (McGarry and O'Leary 1995: 1). Claims about appropriate international legal norms are themselves claims about the conflict's nature. At one level, international law provides an external framework for evaluating conflict; at another, international law can be *within* conflict, helping to shape the identities and behavior of protagonists (Berman 1997). Conceptualization of international law as simply a set of objective norms offers limited potential to capture this dynamic. Much better possibilities are presented by viewing international law as a process "in which context is always important" (Higgins 1994: 8). Contextualization offers the possibility of taking account of the impact of conflict on the interpretation of international law; it also allows for the possibility that the nature and standing of particular states might impact on the law's bite. This is not to adopt a realist dismissal of international law as nothing more than power politics in disguise. Rather, it assumes a much more complex relationship between power and international law, in which the latter enjoys a significant degree of autonomy, while recognizing that international law can shift, and that powerful states can play particularly important roles in the change process.

Contemporary debates on terrorism, international law, and U.S. hegemony raise these questions in their sharpest form. While some have seen in the exercise of hegemonic power a rejection of the viability of international law (at least in its capacity to limit the hegemon; Bolton 2000), others have suggested that the optimal position for the hegemon may be neither to dismiss international law, nor to create a special regime for itself, but rather to shape international law in a way that furthers its own interests (Byers 2003). A project such as this is greatly assisted by the capacity of the hegemon not simply to shape the content of norms, but also to influence the identification of the appropriate normative framework.

This chapter uses the British experience in Northern Ireland to explore the international law dimension of protracted violent political conflict in a leading Western state with a formal commitment to the rule of law. While the Northern Ireland conflict differed in many respects from the current "war on terror," there are also points of correspondence (explored further below), making analysis of the example especially valuable for three reasons. The first has to do with shifting contextualization: the Northern Ireland conflict offers the advantage of having a beginning, a middle, and something like an end. Each of those phases can be considered to contribute to the context within which the behavior of the state can be judged and in which different degrees of leeway may be shown by the international community.

The second is that while the UK has not occupied the position of global hegemon since the nineteenth century, there are reasons for suggesting that its subsequent international standing has had hegemonic resonance. The effects of a period of hegemony may continue in complex ways, long after the power of the hegemon has waned (Keohane 1984). Britain remains a nuclear power with a permanent UN Security Council seat; it also played a key role in the creation of the European Convention on Human Rights (ECHR) (Simpson 2001).

Third, as Chapter 5 also emphasizes, current British antiterrorist legislation draws heavily on Northern Ireland experience, and the state has attempted to highlight the lessons of this experience in its "special" (if unequal) relationship with the United States. Particularly since the Suez crisis (1956), a key driver in British foreign policy seems to have been a perceived need to act in concert with the United States (Hourani 1989). Especially since 9/11, the UK has been facilitative of the exercise of American hegemony; in doing so it has been keen to project as capable of influencing the United States in a way that few countries can (albeit with little supporting evidence).

The first part of this chapter provides a backdrop for exploring the international law dimension of Northern Ireland's "Troubles," outlining domestic legal frameworks and security strategies adopted during the conflict's three main phases: outbreak and militarization (1968–1976), criminalization (1977–1994), and transition (1995 to the present). The international law analysis that follows is loosely structured around these phases, beginning with explorations of approaches employed by the UK in combating early Irish government attempts to raise Northern Ireland at the UN, and of British strategies in relation to international humanitarian law. This is followed by an analysis of the case law under the ECHR using the derogation cases as the main focus during the criminalization phase, and those in relation to the investigation of lethal force as the principal topic during the transition. The chapter then explores the extent to which the British experience in relation to the international law dimension of the Northern Ireland conflict may be applicable in relation to the U.S. experience in its "war on terror."

Overall, I address three salient issues. The first is the extent to which the standing of the British state may have impacted upon judgments of its behavior in Northern Ireland. The second is the extent to which changing contextualization over time may have impacted upon this adjudication, with particular reference to state activities in grey zones of domestic law. The third is the extent to which any of this analysis may be applicable to the United States, now or in the future, given its hegemonic position.


## DOMESTIC FRAMEWORKS

With over 3,500 deaths in a population of 1.5 million, Northern Ireland was easily Western Europe's most violent conflict in the post–World War II period. Though subject to an ambiguous claim by Ireland until 1998, Britain exercised sovereignty over the region, which in its constitutional law was part of the UK. Devolved government existed until 1972, with a separate legal system (still subsisting), and with emergency legislation (the "Special Powers Act") in force from the state's foundation (Campbell 1994).

The first phase of the conflict, (1968—1976) began with a civil rights campaign on behalf of a disadvantaged nationalist minority. A deteriorating public order situation saw the deployment of British troops in 1969 and the re-emergence of highly violent, and frequently quite structured paramilitary groups. The nationalist Irish Republican Army (IRA) sought re-unification with Ireland, while loyalist groups such as the Ulster Defence Association saw themselves as defending the union with Britain.

Internment without trial under the Special Powers Act was introduced in 1971. The legislation was replaced in its entirely by the Northern Ireland (Emergency Provisions) Act of 1973 (EPA), which provided for the continuation of indefinite detention and for the trial of terrorist-type offences in juryless, single-judge courts with special rules of evidence calculated to facilitate the use of interrogation-based confessions. In addition, a host of ancillary stop, search, arrest, and detention powers were given to the police and the army. From 1974 these were supplemented by a UK-wide Prevention of Terrorism (Temporary Provisions) Act (PTA), introduced following indiscriminate IRA pub-bombings in England. This provided for seven-day detention without charge and a system of executive-imposed "exclusion orders" (somewhat akin to internal exile).

Following the introduction of indefinite detention in Northern Ireland came a rash of claims of severe prisoner abuse (which I examine further below). There were also well-documented claims of abusive use of lethal force by the army. In addition to the statutory framework governing the latter issue, there existed an opaque range of nonstatutory (common-law) powers. At one point these had been invoked in a manner that came close to a form of martial law (Campbell and Connolly 2003). Furthermore, special rules on inquests hindered public scrutiny of the use of lethal force; prosecutions of security force personnel were rare, and convictions even rarer (Ní Aoláin 2000). The picture that emerged was of significant legal grey zones: many security force activities were characterized by ambiguous or absent legality, and infractions upon norms by these forces led to few criminal sanctions.

The second, "criminalization," phase (1977–94) saw a shift in which the military lost its lead role under a doctrine of "police primacy." Trial in Diplock courts assumed a central place in the government's security strategy, as internment had been abandoned in 1975. During the earlier phase, the security strategy had appeared to hover between war and criminal justice models. Criminalization marked the formal dominance of the latter, though attempts to treat prisoners as "ordinary criminals" were severely dented by the IRA's 1981 hunger strike, and elements of the war model appeared to survive in aspects of security apparatus behavior.

Under criminalization, the kind of highly *visible* egregious abuses that had characterized the earlier period were largely absent; if anything, though, covert activities appeared to increase in importance. What occurred was a succession of security initiatives, each of which raised concerns of abusive behavior. As pressure created by human rights NGOs forced the abandonment or alteration of particular strategies, further concerns arose; the overall pattern was one of displacement rather than elimination of abuse.

Some concerns involved questions about the fairness of Diplock trials; others involved continuing claims of prisoner abuse. In addition, there were two patterns of incidents in the 1980s and 1990s implicating the security apparatus in suspicious killings, raising a variety of concerns about "shadow state" activities. The first involved situations in which specialized units seemed to operate a "shoot-to-kill" policy of eliminating (generally armed) terrorist suspects in planned ambushes (Urban 1993). In effect, it appeared as though in these instances the security forces were operating according to laws-of-war rather than criminal justice standards. The second pattern involved some well-documented cases in which it appeared that elements in the security apparatus were colluding in assassinations with loyalist paramilitaries. The victims appear to have included a number of IRA suspects, some civilians, and two of Northern Ireland's leading human rights lawyers (J. O'Brien 2005).

The third phase is one of transition, beginning with the paramilitary ceasefires of 1994, and continuing with the 1998 Good Friday Agreement (Campbell, Ní Aoláin, and Harvey 2003) There has been a gradual reduction in the use of emergency and antiterrorist powers. Military deployment has greatly diminished; police reform (or possibly transformation) has proceeded (though some elements of the security apparatus have emerged unscathed or even strengthened); and the "past" has emerged as a major area of concern, with a particular focus on dealing with the legacy of disputed security force activities, particularly killings, that fell into legal grey zones (Bell 2003).

Legislatively this period has been one of consolidation. Security discourses and the structure of legislation in the earlier phases of the conflict tended to emphasize the exceptionality of Northern Ireland-related terrorism, and the temporariness of antiterrorist measures (the 1970s and 1980s saw a succession of EPAs and PTAs). This reflected London's generalized sense of Northern Ireland's "separateness," helping to explain why much harsher measures were tolerated locally than were employed in Britain itself. In succeeding decades, while the separateness persisted, the approach to legislation changed. "Emergency" powers gradually seeped into "ordinary" powers applicable throughout the UK, and violence in Northern Ireland became partly subsumed under the general (domestic and international) rubric of the "terrorist threat." Accordingly, the bulk of the powers previously found in the EPA are now located in the part of the Terrorism Act of 2000 that applies only in Northern Ireland. That act was subsequently amended with respect to Northern Ireland and has been supplemented by a raft of more general, post-9/11 legislation analyzed by Todd Landmann in Chapter 5 of this book.

## NORTHERN IRELAND: INTERNATIONAL LAW CONFLICTS

This domestic law framework sat alongside an extensive web of UK treaty commitments with respect to international law (including human rights law), reflecting Britain's significant status in the international law arena. From today's perspective, the international legal reference points framing the Northern Ireland conflict seem relatively well defined (principally by reference to the ECHR), but the position at the conflict's eruption was less clear. Most importantly, an assertive Irish government displayed a willingness to use UN mechanisms in an attempt to internationalize the issue. A further factor was that militarization in Northern Ireland overlapped with the opening of the Diplomatic Conference on the Reaffirmation and Development of International Humanitarian Law in Armed Conflicts, which continued from 1974 to 1977 (Moir 2002). The conference's concern with unconventional armed conflicts posed implicit questions about Northern Ireland's categorization. Given the UK's formal commitment to international law, and its questionable Northern Ireland record, the challenge it faced was to manifest engagement with the law while short-circuiting potential criticism; how to avoid rather than evade condemnation?

### Eruption: Northern Ireland at the United Nations

Interactions between the UK and Ireland at the UN at the start of the conflict are best seen as a metaconflict in which both states sought to use international legal reference points to bolster competing narratives about the conflict. In a situation of deteriorating public order, the Irish government in 1969 requested an urgent meeting of the Security Council, calling for the dispatch of a UN peacekeeping force to Northern Ireland (Ireland 1969). This request was repeated in the address by the Irish minister to the Security Council when the procedural question arose of the possible inclusion of the Irish letter on the Council's provisional agenda. His address emphasized the government's policy in relation to Northern Ireland, which was that the state did "not in any way concede to . . . [the UK] the right to exercise jurisdiction there," implying that the domestic affairs exception in Article 2(7) of the Charter was inapplicable. Alternatively, he suggested, drawing parallels with UN approaches to apartheid, that British objections be overridden. The UK response was to insist that Article 2 operated to preclude UN involvement. Despite Soviet support for the Irish position, the meeting was adjourned without taking a decision on whether to adopt the suggested provisional agenda, and the matter was dropped.

Ireland then sought to have its concerns included on the agenda of the forthcoming UN General Assembly session. Its request referred to the UN Decolonization Declaration (resolution 1541, adopted in 1960), and asked that Northern Ireland be examined with a view to ending discrimination and establishing human rights, citing various articles of the Charter. The item made it on to the provisional agenda, but following a British objection that debate was precluded under Article 2(7), further discussion was deferred, and the issue died. Thus in both instances, the UK used procedural devices to foreclose discussion of substantive issues. In effect, the British narrative of the conflict ("an internal matter") won out at the Security Council and General Assembly.

### International Humanitarian Law: Closing the Door

Given the sustained and organized nature of the violence in Northern Ireland, humanitarian law might seem an obvious reference point for assessing the behavior of participants. This was particularly the case in the early 1970s, given the intensity of the fighting and the control of "no go" areas by nonstate entities. In fact, for much of the conflict there was little attempt to view violence through the lens of humanitarian law, apart from an occasional airing in the context of the status of IRA prisoners (Walker 1986), and some later attempts by human rights NGOs to monitor paramilitary activity by referring to humanitarian principles (Human Rights Watch 1991). There was therefore limited examination of the potential applicability of humanitarian law provisions governing guerrilla or noninternational armed conflicts (principally Common Article 3 of the 1949

Geneva Conventions, and the conventions' two 1977 protocols). In general, the Northern Ireland conflict tends to be viewed as having hovered between some form of noninternational armed conflict (governed by Common Article 3 and meeting at least some of the requirements of Protocol II of 1977), and the lower intensity category of "situations of internal disturbances and tensions."

The important point is that while the applicability of the law during the conflict is an open question, the UK nevertheless took considerable pains to avoid the possibility of creating fresh obligations. This wariness appears to have been based on a combination of diffuse and quite specific status concerns. If "armed conflict" existed, the state was a *participant* in it, as indeed were armed opposition groups. At a more specific level, there appear to have been concerns about 1977 Protocol I, which granted prisoner-of-war status to combatants captured in conflicts where "peoples are fighting against colonial domination and alien occupation . . . in the exercise of their right of self-determination . . ."[1]

In retrospect, although self-determination claims were important elements in the Northern Ireland conflict (and its resolution), it is difficult to see how Protocol I's conditions of applicability could be said to have been met. As regards procedural issues surrounding international exploration of a possible "colonial" dimension to the conflict (with obvious implications for the applicability of Protocol I), Britain's influential position at the UN again came into play. When between 1988 and 1990 the U.S.-based Brehon Law Society sought to have the UN Decolonization Committee interest itself in Northern Ireland, the Committee insisted that its mandate meant that it would require a resolution of the General Assembly or a referral by the Secretary General before it could hold hearings on the region (M. O'Brien 1996; Harvey 1990) No such resolution or referral was forthcoming.

Protocol II did not grant prisoner-of-war status but did provide for prisoner release at the conflict's end. These provisions, though, were binding only in noninternational armed conflicts which met the protocol's high thresholds for applicability. Although the UK was an early signatory of both protocols, it declined to ratify them for many years, and at the time of signing it made a declaration with respect to Protocol I (Roberts and Guelff 1989), aspects of which appear designed to negate its possibility of applicability to Northern Ireland.

Eventually, the Geneva Conventions (Amendment) Act of 1995, enacted a year after the Northern Ireland cease-fires, provided for ratification of the protocols (Rowe and Meyer 1996). The legislation was not immediately brought into force. Ratification was eventually accomplished only in

January 1998, the IRA cease-fire having been ended and restored in the meantime, suggesting that the imperative to avoid arguments over the applicability of the protocols to violence in Northern Ireland played a part in British calculations. Furthermore, ratification was accompanied by a number of reservations in respect of Protocol I, which although textually different from the earlier declaration, also seemed designed to exclude any applicability to Northern Ireland. As regards Protocol II (the applicability of which was a more likely bet), while the UK has never indicated that it viewed the conflict as coming within the instrument's terms, it could, if it felt mindful to do so, make a claim that the early release of prisoners under the Good Friday Agreement met the amnesty requirements of the protocol.

At one level, the strategies pursed in relation to Northern Ireland at the higher reaches of the UN and with respect to international humanitarian law functioned as straightforward shielding devices for the UK. At another, they can be considered effective contributions to the metaconflict. As such, they confirm that particularly at conflict's outbreak, leading Western states are well placed to define international legal frameworks and contexts in ways favorable to their interests.

## Derogation and the Entrenchment of the Conflict

The international humanitarian law concept of "armed conflict" overlaps but is not coterminous with that of "public emergency threatening the life of the nation" in derogation articles of human rights treaties. While the occurrence of armed conflict in a particular area would amount to such a threat to the nation's life, violence at a level not technically amounting to armed conflict might yet constitute an emergency. It was this distinction that allowed Britain to claim that although there was no armed conflict in Northern Ireland, there was a "public emergency" under Article 15 of the ECHR and Article 4 of the International Covenant on Civil and Political Rights (ICCPR). The distinction was an important one on several levels. While humanitarian law's possible applicability raised awkward question of status, few such issues arose with derogation; rather, the mechanisms were essentially facilitative for the state.

Conceptually, the term "emergency" is locked in a dichotomous relationship with the norm against which it is defined. Implicit in this relationship is the temporariness of emergency. Were emergency not temporary, there could be no norm. This relationship has been variously described in terms of a governing paradigm of "normalcy-rule, emergency-exception" (Gross 1998: 440), or of the "implicit counterpoint between emergency and normality," producing the "emergency/normality" antimony (Marks 1995: 85).

Northern Ireland fits uneasily within this conceptual framework, since from its foundation the state has been in a permanent emergency. Having ratified the ECHR in 1951, the UK derogated in 1957, and continuous derogations were in force until 1984. The 1984 derogation withdrawal was not marked by an abandonment of emergency legislation, and when in 1988 the legislation's detention provisions were found to be in breach of the convention, further derogations were entered which were kept in place until 2001. Although fresh derogations were entered later that year (subsequently withdrawn), these were focused not on Northern Ireland, but on international terrorism.

The most important issues aired under Council of Europe mechanisms in the early period involved allegations of the abuse of prisoners who were detained without trial in 1971–72. These cases prefigured in many respects the debate on "torture lite" and "torture heavy" in the recent "war on terror." The interstate case *Ireland v. UK* (involving "torture lite") focused mainly on the use of the "five techniques" of "interrogation in depth": hooding, wall-standing, food deprivation, sleep deprivation, and the use of "white noise" (though allegations of more traditional brutality also figured).[2] The European Court of Human Rights found that the "five techniques" had been approved at a "high level" and therefore constituted administrative practice. While conceding that a public emergency existed at the time, Ireland claimed inter alia that the scale of detention was not strictly required, and that the techniques to which some of the detainees had been subjected amounted to torture, and therefore to a violation of a nonderogable right .

The court's decision has been analyzed extensively elsewhere; rather than reproduce this criticism here, two aspects of the judgment will be highlighted. The first is the degree of deference shown to the state's estimation of the situation. While the court accepted its duty to decide whether an emergency justifying resort to derogation existed, it accompanied this with a strong validation of the doctrine allowing states a "margin of appreciation." This paved the way for the finding not only that an emergency existed, but that detention without trial on the scale involved was not in violation of the convention, and that there was no discrimination in its operation.

The second notable feature was the finding by the majority in relation to the "five techniques" that the state had inflicted inhuman and degrading treatment upon the detainees (and therefore had violated a nonderogable right under Article 3 of the ECHR), but—in contrast to the earlier finding of the European Commission on Human Rights—that this did not amount to torture. This was despite a finding by the court that the techniques' application caused "at least intense physical and mental suffering to the persons subjected thereto and also led to acute psychiatric disturbances during interrogation."[3] Nevertheless, their use "did not occasion suffering of the particular intensity and cruelty implied by the word torture." Three judges dissented on this point, arguing in separate opinions that use of the "five techniques" constituted torture.

Another set of allegations (with "torture heavy" resonance) was aired in the *Donnelly* case,[4] involving seven applicants, several of whom had received substantial compensation payments. The aspects of ill treatment in *Donnelly* have been discussed primarily in relation to allegations of physical brutality (several applicants were hospitalized), and secondarily in relation to allegations by three applicants that interrogators secretly administered mood-altering drugs (Boyle and Hannum 1972, 1976, 1977). A third category of claims has heretofore attracted little attention, though events in Abu Ghraib now put it in a different light: one of the detainees described being made to "bark like a dog" and squat on all fours, and being subject to a serious sexual assault (a brush shaft forced into his rectum).

In a somewhat technical decision, the European Commission ultimately ruled the case inadmissible. There was no administrative practice because toleration of the alleged activities had not been shown to exist at a sufficiently high level of the state apparatus: toleration "at the middle or lower levels of the chain of command . . . does not . . . necessarily mean that the state concerned has failed to take the required steps to comply with its substantive obligations" (p. 85). That police investigations of complaints had taken place was seen by the commission as crucial, despite accepting that no successful prosecutions were mounted, that the investigations were "open to criticism," and that at least some were "incomplete" (p. 83). This approach seemed much more indulgent to state claims than is evident in the *Greek* case, which involved prisoner abuse at the time of the Greek military junta of 1967–74,[5] suggesting that the democratic character of the British state may have been implicitly factored into the commission's assessment.

In *Ireland v. UK* the structure of adjudication had been predicated upon the viability of the emergency-normality dichotomy. This was perhaps understandable given that the case arose from the early stages of the Troubles, but by the 1980s increasing entrenchment of the emergency raised the question of its continuing appropriateness. The issue was revisited in *Brannigan and McBride v. UK*,[6] which saw a challenge to the PTA provisions allowing detention of terrorist suspects for up to seven days, a power relying upon a derogation from Article 5(3) of the ECHR.

Given that the Northern Ireland emergency was in at least its twentieth year when the detentions complained of took place, an obvious question mark arose over the viability of the kind of analytical and evaluative approaches evident in *Ireland v. UK*. Although permitting a wide margin of appreciation may be understandable in the turbulence of a sudden onset of emergency, and for a limited period, such a rationale largely disappears in an entrenched and relatively predictable (though violent) situation. Accordingly it was argued before the court that if a state is to be allowed a margin of appreciation, that margin should become narrower the longer the "emergency" continues.

Rather than engage meaningfully with this argument, the court fell back on stock phrases, validating the claim that a "wide margin of appreciation" should be granted to the state in assessing both the existence of the emergency and the measures taken on foot of it. This paved the way for the validation of the regime in the interrogation centers.

Although the finding that the level of violence in Northern Ireland threatened the life of the nation might be considered unremarkable, the validation of the safeguards in the interrogation centers is quite another matter, and was out of step with the approach taken in other international forums. In its consideration of the first periodic report of the UK under the Torture Convention in 1991,[7] members of the UN Committee against Torture subjected the safeguards in the interrogation centers to scathing criticism. Criticisms continued in later periodic reports. In 1993 the Council of Europe's European Committee for the Prevention of Torture was sufficiently concerned at the situation in the "holding centers" that it judged a visit to Northern Ireland "to be required in the circumstances," after which it issued a highly critical report. Following a further intervention in 1999, it issued a (successful) call for the closure of the main center.

In *Brannigan and McBride*, therefore, the European Court afforded a degree of deference to the UK that other international human rights bodies were unwilling to display. The general deference to state claims displayed by the court was also much greater than that afforded to Turkey in *Aksoy*,[8] in which the safeguards applicable to the extended detention of terrorist suspects were found to be inadequate. This again suggests that the liberal-democratic character of the British state (in contrast to Turkey's flawed democratic record) may have been implicitly factored in to the court's assessment. Although occasionally a more stringent approach to the use of emergency powers has been evident from ECHR organs,[9] subsequent case law has tended to dampen expectations that such cases opened a route to innovative challenge to state action (at least while violence continued).[10]

## Transition and the International Law Context

Although ECHR jurisprudence on Northern Ireland up to 1994 showed considerable deference to state claims, it has been markedly different since. Of the fourteen conclusive rulings available at the time of writing, thirteen found state breaches.[11] For illustrative purposes this essay focuses on one subset, those relating to deaths caused either by direct security force action or where it was alleged that security forces had acted in collusion with loyalist paramilitaries.

Given the extent of the sea change in European adjudication, any worthwhile explanation is likely to be multifactorial, but one factor, timing, cannot be ignored. All judgments were handed down after the start of the transition in Northern Ireland that began with the 1994 paramilitary cease-fires and has continued to the present by way of the 1998 Agreement. Although the language of "transition" has not been invoked explicitly by the European Court, it is difficult to avoid the conclusion that the changed Northern Ireland context has been factored in to some degree.

In at least four respects this jurisprudence marks a departure from previous European case law on Northern Ireland. The first relates to context. The *Gibraltar* case involved the shooting dead by SAS troops, in a preplanned operation, of three IRA members who were believed to be involved in an overseas bombing mission but who were subsequently found to have been unarmed. In assessing the killing, the court explicitly mentioned the context of terrorism, but in effect viewed this context as being trumped by the primacy afforded to the "right to life" (Article 2 ECHR). This approach was markedly different from that taken by ECHR organs in earlier lethal-force cases from Northern Ireland, in which considerable leeway had been afforded to the state.[12] This suggests that the primacy attached to Article 2 itself reflected a changed broader context.

The second departure is a shift in focus away from the instant of killing toward structural and procedural issues, either preceding the killing or in subsequent investigations. For instance, in *Gibraltar* a substantive breach of Article 2 was found in which the authorities were judged to have committed errors in planning, control, and organization before the killings. In others, breaches of the procedural requirements of Article 2 were found on the basis of inadequate investigations of deaths. A critical effect was that the focus of responsibility was shifted from the direct perpetrators toward those higher up the chain of command, inviting the question of ultimate responsibility for "shadow state" activities.

The third departure is an extension of concern with killings caused directly by security force personnel to killings alleged to have resulted from collusion between security force members and loyalist paramilitaries. The political sensitivity of such killings cannot be underestimated, given their "dirty war" resonance. Breaches of the procedural requirements of Article 2 of the ECHR were found on the basis of the lack of a prompt or effective investigation into allegations of collusion, the lack of independence of the police officers investigating the incident from the security force personnel allegedly implicated in collusion, and the exclusion of the collusion issue from the scope of the inquest. Among the investigations impugned in these rulings was the one concerning the assassination of the human rights lawyer Pat Finucane.

A final point of departure from past approaches is the "fit" between the Northern Ireland, Turkish, and Chechen cases. The divergence between *Brannigan and McBride* and *Aksoy* has already been noted; by contrast, the jurisprudence evident in cases such as *Shanaghan* and *Kelly* meshes virtually seamlessly with *Kaya* and similar rulings from Turkey, [13] and with judgments in the Chechen cases brought against the Russian Federation.[14] This suggests an erosion of the perception that the Northern Ireland experience is exceptional.

The picture that emerges is one in which international law increasingly reaches into former grey-zone state activity. Similar approaches have been evident in recent case law covering the relationship between the fair trial and the interrogation regime, and relating to the protection of intelligence sources. This suggests that the "pull" of the state on the law is affected by context. While conflict continues, human rights law may display a variable tendency to accommodate itself to the requirements of powerful democratic states, but absent violent challenge, the situation may be partly reversed, with human rights law displaying an increasing pull *on* the state, even in relation to retrospective judgment on acts committed during the former conflict.

## WHAT LESSONS FOR THE "WAR ON TERROR"?

There can be no simple transposition of the Northern Ireland experience to the global conflict. Assessment of whether any lessons are applicable must take account of both similarities and differences. Some elements suggest the viability of comparison: both the United States and UK are liberal democratic states; both conflicts have involved structured political violence with complex ethnic and religious dimensions; the long-standing alliance between the two states has resulted in significant ongoing exchanges of security experience; and both states have similar (common law) legal systems, with relatively robust judiciaries.

Yet there are also important differences. Most obviously the "war on terror" raises questions about the use of force in international law, absent in Northern Ireland, and the United States occupies the position of a global hegemon, much different from the standing and interests of the UK during the Northern Ireland conflict. Other important differences relate to the nature of the threat, to conflict categorization, and to domestic and international legal frameworks.

The nature (and possible novelty) of the contemporary threat have important implications for the leeway likely to be initially allowed to the state (the "margin of appreciation" in ECHR jurisprudence). In that regard, five differences between the conflicts can be noted. Al Qaeda's structures and goals appear much more diffuse than those of groups such as the IRA, affecting a much larger number of states. While Northern Ireland saw some appalling atrocities by nonstate entities, the overall percentage of civilian casualties tended to be significantly lower than in many al Qaeda attacks. Al Qaeda has made extensive use of suicide bombers, posing interdiction problems that were not present in Northern Ireland, and there have been persistent claims that al Qaeda is intent on employing weapons of mass destruction (though its actual attacks have been technologically low level).

Turning to conflict categorization, the UK, after some initial ambiguity, was careful to construct a narrative of its behavior in terms of a criminal-justice-based response to "terrorist criminality" (despite significant militarization). This entailed rejection of a "war" formulation, even if elements in the security forces seem to have exploited legal grey zones to engage in some activities, such as killings and coercive interrogations, typical (though not all legitimate) in wartime. By contrast, the United States has been prolix in the depiction of its activities variously as the *"war* on/against terror(ism)," or more recently the "long war," formulations sufficiently broad to cover the 9/11 attacks, the conflicts in Afghanistan and Iraq, and antiterrorist initiatives at home and abroad, neatly eliding war-as-metaphor with war-as-armed-conflict.

As regards international humanitarian law, both the United States in the current conflict and the UK in Northern Ireland sought to avoid conferring prisoners with actual or perceived status, but there are important differences in approach, corresponding to the alternative optimal strategies (from the state's perspective) outlined earlier. The British approach, consistent with its criminalization strategy, was to deny the applicability of humanitarian law while seemingly making some use of lethal force with varying degrees of (unacknowledged) accordance with "laws of war' standards. The U.S. approach, following from its "war" rhetoric, has entailed assertions that the "laws of war" entitle it to use lethal force against suspected terrorists, while resisting claims that detainees such as those from the Taliban met the technical requirements for prisoner-of-war *status.*

With respect to other areas of international law, the two states differ in their scale of human rights treaty ratification. The UK has ratified a wide range of treaties including the ECHR, which provides for individual complaints. The United States is subject to the individual complaint mechanism of the Inter-American Commission on Human Rights through the OAS charter and the American Declaration of the Rights and Duties of Man. By contrast, the United States has declined to ratify (though it has signed) the American Convention on Human Rights. It has, however, ratified the ICCPR and the UN Convention against Torture (and is therefore subject to these conventions' reporting requirements); it is also a party to the UN Charter and subject to UN thematic human rights procedures. The United States has declined to invoke the derogation mechanisms under the ICCPR. Its formal position is that activities necessitated by the "war on terror" fall outside international human rights law. This view has been rejected by UN human rights bodies, which have been heavily critical of U.S. treatment of terrorist suspects.

The overall result has been the creation of deliberate ambiguity and confusion about the reach and interrelationship of legal norms in the current conflict. Whereas some have seen in this the attempted creation of legal "black holes" (Steyn 2004), others have pointed to continuing reliance by the United States on legal classification and representation, even in regimes such as that at Guantanamo (Johns 2005). Rather than representing a completely new phenomenon, the U.S. approach in the "war on terror" may be considered a particular example of attempted exploitation of legal "grey zones," bearing some similarities to (and differences from) the British experience in Northern Ireland (Campbell and Connolly 2006).

Inevitably, this comparison raises the question of the relationship of the hegemon to international law. It is unnecessary for the purposes of this essay to go into the voluminous current material on "hegemony"; suffice to say that the literature tends to identify at least two major uses of the term at the international level, with divergent views on the relationship of the hegemon to international law (Byers & Nolte 2003; Byers 2003; Vagts 2001; Krisch 2005). One tends to emphasize hegemony as "dominance," with connotations of unilateralism in international affairs, and a dismissive "realist" approach to the question of the capacity of international law to bind the hegemon. The second focuses on more subtle exercise of power, emphasizing the long-term desirability for the hegemon of employing multilateral-ist strategies. On this view, as discussed above, the optimal position from the hegemon's perspective may be to employ, and attempt to shape, international law in a way calculated to advance its interests.

If, ultimately, the exercise of hegemonic power by the United States approximates the former model, the British experience in Northern Ireland offers few pointers. If, however, the latter model prevails, the hegemonic resonance of the UK's status may offer some valuable clues. Powerful states may be well placed to influence the metaconflict in a way that furthers their interests, and adjudication of applicable legal norms displays a tendency to accommodate itself to the state's interests. Varying contexts, however, can lead to international law's displaying significant resilience. This may create challenges for attempts to invoke international law to buttress hegemony; the possibility of law-based challenge will be continually present, with shifting contextualization potentially increasing its changes of success.

The example of Northern Ireland suggests that the UK's liberal-democratic character, coupled with its strong international standing, resulted in its being granted greater leeway during violent conflict by international human rights mechanisms than were countries with lesser democratic credentials. This leeway, while not unlimited, operated to shield state activities in domestic legal grey zones. In the postconflict environment, the context of terrorism was still taken into account when adjudicating actions from the past; that context, however, seems to have been partly trumped by the implicit context of transition since 1994.

These assessments suggest three tentative propositions about the bite of international law in relation to the "war on terror." First, particularly in the early stages of conflict the United States could be expected to be afforded considerable leeway in assessing the extent of the threat and of the necessary response. This is particularly the case in view of the relative novelty of al Qaeda's structures and tactics. Second, as the conflict persists the state is likely to attract increasing criticism, both through treaty-based reporting requirements and from thematic human rights mechanisms focusing on patterns of abuse, particularly in relation to such nonderogable rights as the prohibition on torture.

These two propositions help to explain why, immediately after 9/11, international mechanisms were so facilitative of U.S. approaches, and why human rights criticism of the "war on terror" was initially so muted. But it also helps to explain why, as the "war" has continued, increasing friction in international mechanisms has become apparent.[15]

The third proposition is based upon the assumption that, like the "Hundred Years' War," the "long war" (or parts of it) will eventually come to an end of sorts. Such a transition from violent conflict may produce critical ex post facto judgments on how the "war" was pursued. It may be, therefore, that the bite of international human rights and humanitarian law will increase significantly, if in part retrospectively.

# 5  The United Kingdom

## The Continuity of Terror and Counterterror

Todd Landman

[T]he world has changed and there needs to be a debate on whether some erosion of what we all value may be necessary to improve the chances of our citizens not being blown apart as they go about their daily lives.

DAME ELIZA MANNINGHAM-BULLER, Head of MI5, September 1, 2005

If people start to believe that decisions at the European Court, in operating the European Convention, are not broadly in accordance with a consensus about how rights should be defended, then there will be some very difficult questions about the convention itself in Britain.

CHARLES CLARKE, Home Secretary of the United Kingdom,<br>September 8, 2005

[W]e may have to modify some of our freedoms in the short-run in order to prevent their abuse by those who oppose our fundamental values and would destroy our freedoms and values in the long-term.

JOHN REID, Home Secretary of the United Kingdom, August 9, 2006

We, of course, wanted far tougher laws against terrorism. We were prevented by opposition and then by the courts in ensuring that was done.

TONY BLAIR, Prime Minister of the United Kingdom, October 1, 2006

These statements from the head of MI5, two home secretaries, and the prime minister provide a strong indication of the general mood in the government of the United Kingdom concerning the relative protection of human rights while combating terrorism. Since the September 11, 2001, attacks and with renewed vigor since the London bombings in July 2005, the Labour government has been attempting to fortify its response to terrorism through legislation (e.g., the Anti-Terrorism, Crime, and Security Act 2001, the Terrorism Act 2006, and the Immigration, Nationality, and Asylum Act 2006) to expand the powers of the Home Office, the police, and security services across a wide range of issues relating to the establishment and main-

75

tenance of terrorist organizations, the incitement of terrorist acts on British soil, the involvement in international terrorism, and the support more generally of terrorist organizations and acts, as well as the glorification of terrorism itself. These legislative developments suggest that long-held attachments to the protection of certain rights are being increasingly brought into question; as in many of the countries considered in this volume, the curbing of liberties is seen as an essential and necessary requirement to combat terrorism. These new attempts to expand the depth and breadth of government authority over the rights of citizens (and noncitizens) in the UK met stiff opposition and delivered Prime Minister Tony Blair's first Commons defeat since taking power in 1997. But beyond the recent unfolding of events, the current counterterror response must be seen as the culmination of a long history of battling domestic and international terrorism, which has been given new impetus in the post-9/11 era (see also Gearty 2005; Gearty 2006).

Within the context of the countries considered in this volume, Britain has a number of unique and in many ways paradoxical features that make its consideration particularly warranted for an analysis of the democratic response to terrorism. First, it has a long history of enshrining civil liberties that dates from the Magna Carta in 1215; it has been a key arena for the popular struggle for the civil, political, and social rights of citizenship (Marshall 1950; Barbalet 1988; Foweraker and Landman 1997; Robertson 2005); and it has in many ways been the home for the normative debate for the Hobbesian and Lockean solutions to the tension between and among order, security, rights, and liberty (Ingram 1994; Jones 1994; Ishay 2005; Tesón 2005). Second, despite this historical and theoretical commitment to rights, Britain does not have a written constitution that delineates these rights or outlines explicitly the powers of the different governmental institutions that may protect them. Rather, the power and authority of government has evolved. Since the brief hiatus of the Cromwell years in the seventeenth century, power has shifted increasingly from the Crown to Parliament and has given rise to the principle of parliamentary sovereignty, the House of Commons has become the primary chamber following the 1911 Parliament Act, and the executive (i.e., the government) has dominated the Commons, effectively leaving less room for the kind of horizontal accountability typical of modern liberal democracies. Third, Britain has been a key architect in the development of the European human rights "regime" (Donnelly 1986, 2003) as one of the authors of the 1950 European Convention for Human Rights (Moravcsik 2000; Simpson 2001), whose articles were finally brought into the domestic legal system through the enactment of the 1998 Human Rights Act. Participation in the European regime has meant that Britain has been subjected to the judgments of the European Court of Human Rights, particularly in relation to its policies in Northern Ireland, and open to scrutiny by other institutions within the Council of Europe (e.g., the Human Rights Commissioner). Finally, Britain has had a "special" relationship with the United States that has resulted in joint military participation in two world wars, two Gulf wars, and the 1999 Kosovo bombing campaign, and assistance in the overthrow of unsavory regimes, most notably the Taliban in Afghanistan in 2001 and Saddam Hussein in Iraq in 2003. In the "war on terror" Tony Blair has been a staunch ally of George W. Bush, an unlikely partnership that draws on a similar sense of the politics of conviction (Dionne 2005).

Unlike the United States, Britain shares with the other countries considered in this volume a long history of battling domestic forms of terrorism. Indeed, it has had to deal with domestic terrorism since the days of Guy Fawkes in the early 1600s and the Puritans, who were prosecuted as "terrorist fanatics" during the restoration of Charles II (Robertson 2005: 171). The troubles in Northern Ireland posed either an international or national threat depending on how the crisis is viewed, while Britain has been the victim of international terrorism relating to Palestine, Kenya, Malaysia, Cyprus, Aden, and Libya (Taylor 2002; Walker 2003; Parker 2005). With the July bombings in London in 2005, the UK has become the victim of international terrorism committed by British-born militants that have adopted radical versions of Islam, which seek to transcend the governmental systems of nation-states through the implementation of Islamic law.[1]

The current attempt to fortify and make permanent counterterror measures thus sits within these features, paradoxes, and commonalities of the British case. On the one hand, Britain has been a beacon of liberty to the world, has been a key player in the development of one of the strongest regional systems for the protection of human rights, and has recently and formally domesticated its rights commitments through the 1998 Human Rights Act. On the other hand, in dealing with domestic and international terrorism it has established the strongest and most draconian set of restrictions on its citizens in Europe (Haubrich 2003), requiring it to derogate from some of its legal obligations under the European Convention for Human Rights, and has stood shoulder to shoulder with the United States in prosecuting the current "war on terror," even when such behavior put the Labour government at great political risk and has made it the subject of sustained domestic criticism. Tony Blair's support for the war on terror, and in particular the war in Iraq, has been identified as one of the key reasons why he has been forced to step down as leader.

This chapter locates Britain's response to terrorism in these larger domestic and international dynamics and addresses the main questions posed by this volume. First, it argues that the post-9/11 response to terrorism must be seen in light of a legacy of counterterror measures and policies, particularly in relation to the Troubles in Northern Ireland since 1969. Counterterrorist legislation passed just before 9/11 and since 9/11 has made the temporary counterterror measures adopted in the context of Northern Ireland permanent, deeper, and broader in scope. There is thus continuity between the pre- and post-9/11 legislation, although the sense of urgency, perception of domestic and international threat, and the level of support in government for such measures have only become stronger since the London bombings and have been reinforced by the foiled attack on trans-Atlantic flights in August 2006. Second, it argues that the response to terrorism coincides with and in many ways stands in contrast to the electoral victory and sustained dominance of the Labour Party for three parliaments, during which time the government has pursued a larger agenda of constitutional reform, devolution, freedom of information legislation, and the enactment of the Human Rights Act. Third, it argues that terrorism in the UK has been cast as a problem of *criminality* and *criminal justice* and that the response has shifted to one of "proactive policing and the management of risk" (Walker 2003: 16), where counterterror laws are "normalized" to be more in line with existing legislation while at the same time criminalizing increasingly larger sets of citizen (and noncitizen) activity. Finally, the chapter argues that there are at present limited forms of vertical and horizontal accountability with respect to decision making and the centralization of authority over the response to terrorism. This means that only through considerable political will and a significant change in rights culture within the UK will the intrusion on liberties be checked.

## TERROR AND COUNTERTERROR CONTINUITY

The United Kingdom has long been subjected to domestic and international forms of terrorism, including domestic groups carrying out acts against UK targets, domestic groups carrying out attacks against foreign targets, foreign groups carrying out attacks against UK targets, and foreign groups carrying out attacks against foreign targets on UK soil (Taylor 2002: 198–207). The largest numbers of terrorist acts carried out against British targets have been associated with the conflict in Northern Ireland, and the main acts have included outright deaths and injuries from political violence. Between 1969 (the start of the Troubles) and 2003, political violence associated with the con-

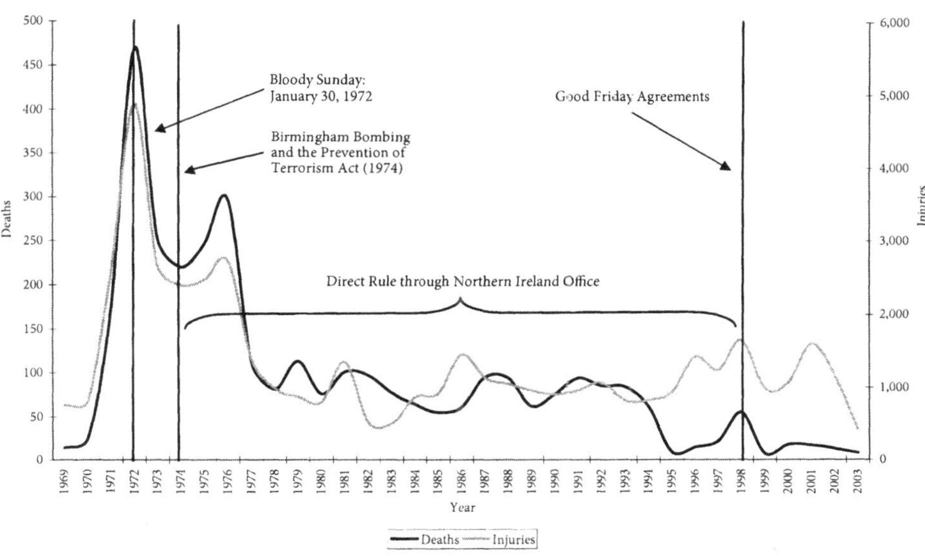



Figure 5.1. Total Deaths and Injuries in Northern Ireland as a Result of the
Troubles (1969–2003)

flict in Northern Ireland led to 3,297 deaths overall and well over 10,000
injuries (see Figure 5.1). In addition, the conflict has led to 35,798 shootings,
15,351 bombs, 21,049 armed robberies, as well as the discovery of 11,605
firearms and 115,517 kilograms of explosives (Taylor 2002: 202–3). These
totals do not include the terrorist campaign on mainland Britain, which
included multiple assassinations and bombings throughout the period, the
last of which were the 1996 bombings in Canary Wharf and Manchester city
center. Clearly, the violence was most pronounced in the early years of the
conflict, especially during the years surrounding Bloody Sunday (1972) and
the Guildford and Birmingham bombings (1974), and then declined dramatically during the period of direct rule (1974–98), which ended with the Good
Friday Agreement of 1998. While deaths and injuries followed roughly the
same patterns, they diverged in the 1990s, with outright deaths peaking in
1998 (especially with the Omagh bombing) and then declining to near zero
in the first few years of this century. Ironically, or fortuitously, as part of the
Northern Ireland peace process, the Irish Republican Army (IRA) declared an
end to its armed campaign shortly after the July 2005 terrorist attacks in
London, a declaration that coincided with confirmation from the de
Chastelain commission that the IRA had put its weapons "beyond use."

Beyond the terrorism associated with Northern Ireland, mainland Britain experienced a large number of additional terrorist attacks and events throughout the 1970s, 1980s, and 1990s. For example, Palestinian militants exploded a bomb in a Marks and Spencer department store in London (1969), Black September militants killed an Israeli counselor with a letter bomb (1972), Palestinian militants assassinated the prime minister of Yemen in London (1977), the former premier of Iraq was assassinated outside the Intercontinental Hotel in London (1978), the aircrew from El Al airlines was attacked outside the Europa Hotel in London (1978), militants killed two hostages in a siege of the Iranian embassy (1980), a policewoman was killed in front of the Libyan embassy (1984), 259 passengers and 11 people on the ground were killed when Pan Am flight 103 was blown up en route from Frankfurt to New York over Lockerbie in Scotland (1988) (Cook and Stevenson 1996: 200–204), a car bomb was set off outside Balfour House in London, which housed a Jewish charity (1994), and an airliner from Afghanistan was hijacked in Pakistan and diverted to Stansted Airport outside London (2000) (Taylor 2002: 206–7).

Against this backdrop of political violence, death, injuries, assassinations, hostage events, and bombings, it is obvious that the threat of terrorism has been real, immediate, and harrowing for generations of Britons. In response to such threats, Britain has had a considerable record of counterterror legislation on its statute books, most of which has been directed toward the problems in Ireland, and since 1921, Northern Ireland. Indeed, between 1761 and 1972, there have been twenty-six legislative acts with provisions for combating Irish nationalism, including special courts, detention without trial, and the suspension of habeas corpus (Wilson 2005: 32; see also Gearty 2006: 99–101). Since the 1970s, a range of legislative measures have been introduced to combat domestic and international terrorism, including laws concerning hostage-taking, transport and use of nuclear materials, aviation and maritime security, and terrorist acts committed in Northern Ireland and on mainland Britain as part of the struggle for Irish nationalism (see Campbell's chapter in this volume).

In general, the legislation introduced included measures for proscribing and banning certain terrorist organizations; powers to stop, question, and search suspects throughout the United Kingdom; powers to attack terrorist finances and material assistance to terrorists; powers to arrest and detain suspects without charge; and the use of special tribunals and internment in Northern Ireland (Bonner 2000: 40–47). Interrogation tactics used on detainees have included such practices as hooding; the deprivation of sleep, food, and water; as well as exposure to loud noise. In *Ireland v. UK* (1978)

TABLE 5.1  Counterterror Legislation in the United Kingdom

1. Tokyo Convention Act 1967
2. Suppression of Terrorism Act 1978
3. International Protected Persons Act 1978
4. Taking of Hostages Act 1982
5. Aviation Security Act 1982
6. Nuclear Material (Offences) Act 1983
7. Prevention of Terrorism (Temporary Provisions) Act 1984
8. Prevention of Terrorism (Temporary Provisions) Act 1989
9. Aviation and Maritime Security Act 1990
10. Northern Ireland (Emergency Provisions) Act 1991
11. Criminal Justice and Public Order Act 1994
12. Northern Ireland (Emergency Provisions) Act 1996
13. Criminal Justice (Terrorism and Conspiracy Act) 1998
14. Terrorism Act 2000
15. Anti-Terrorism, Crime and Security Act 2001
16. Crime (International Cooperation) Act 2003
17. Civil Contingencies Act 2004
18. Prevention of Terrorism Act 2005
19. Terrorism Act 2006
20. Immigration, Nationality and Asylum Act 2006

the European Court of Human Rights found that such practices were in breach of Britain's international legal obligations under the European Convention on Human Rights since they constituted cruel, inhuman and degrading treatment, though the court found that such practices did not constitute torture (Boner 2000; Parker 2005: 123).[2] It was not until 2000 that these counterterror measures were made more comprehensive, coherent and *permanent* through the passage of the Terrorism Act (Haubrich 2003: 23), which came into force well *before* 9/11 (see Table 5.1). But before considering these and other developments in Britain's fight against terrorism it is first necessary to reflect on the rise of the Labour government and its program for constitutional reform.

## LABOUR DOMINANCE AND CONSTITUTIONAL REFORM

The introduction of permanent counterterror legislation presents an interesting paradox in the context of the three successive electoral victories for a

Labour government that sought to bring about significant constitutional reform and to "bring rights home" through the enactment of the 1998 Human Rights Act (Blom-Cooper 2005). In 1997, New Labour was elected with a parliamentary majority of 179 MPs and had a constitutional reform agenda that included removing life peers from the House of Lords; devolving power to national assemblies in Wales, Scotland, and Northern Ireland; establishing separate governmental institutions for London; introducing freedom of information legislation (FOI); introducing proportional representation for the devolved assemblies; and enacting significant human rights legislation. Of these initiatives, Lords reform, devolution, FOI, and human rights were successfully enacted, although many commentators have argued that these reforms had not gone as far as were promised in the election manifesto and/or had not gone far enough in bringing about progressive political reform.[3] Most relevant to this chapter is the enactment of the 1998 Human Rights Act, which came into force in 2000 amid much fanfare that the Labour government had indeed brought rights home. The act is meant to domesticate into British law or "to give further effect" to the articles found in the European Convention of Human Rights (ECHR). Domestication of convention rights in practical terms has meant that all public bodies (national and local) are required to act in ways that are compatible with the convention, and individuals (not groups) can bring cases through the judiciary to seek remedies should they feel their rights have been infringed in some way by any public authority.[4] The judiciary can declare acts of Parliament "incompatible" with the convention rights, and, in certain instances (forty to date), can change elements of existing legislation to make it more compatible with convention rights without consulting Parliament.[5]

These new judicial powers are in no way akin to the powers of judicial review in the United States that have evolved since *Marbury v. Madison*, but they have in some way led to a quiet revolution in those areas where the judiciary has been able to challenge parliamentary sovereignty. For the government, the introduction of the Human Rights Act avoided the need for a full written constitution, the enactment of a full bill of rights, and a constitutional court, all of which would have significantly undermined parliamentary sovereignty (Blom-Cooper 2005: 238). In practice, the government could ignore the fact that its acts are incompatible with convention rights; however, it either introduces amendments to existing legislation or new legislation that addresses the issues of incompatibility. Alongside the Human Rights Act, a Joint Committee on Human Rights comprising members from both Houses of Parliament has been established, which hears testimony and evidence from human rights scholars and practitioners, considers the human rights implications of all legislation proposed by the government, and files regular reports on its findings. It has filed numerous reports and findings since the 2000–2001 session of Parliament, and has provided comprehensive and in many cases robust comments and criticisms on counterterror legislation.[6]

New Labour won again in both the 2001 and 2005 general elections, although its majority dropped to 167 and then 66, respectively (Crewe 2005: 200). This narrowing majority was accompanied by a series of backbench rebellions and a variety of close votes on public bills introduced to Parliament, and has created a mood that the government must take greater care and consideration when introducing new legislation (Allen 2005). Coupled with the enhanced power of the judiciary as a result of the Human Rights Act, the Labour government has found itself repeatedly challenged on its attempts to introduce counterterror legislation that undermines the protection of long-cherished civil liberties. And it is within this context of heightened concern in the judiciary and on the backbenches that we can now consider the current period of the fight against terror in Britain.

## FROM 9/11 TO 7/7

In the immediate aftermath of the 9/11 attacks and still enjoying a majority of 167, the Labour government was fast to act in introducing new counterterror legislation that enhanced the powers found in the 2000 Terrorism Act. In less than a month in late 2001,[7] the government enacted the Anti-Terrorism, Crime, and Security Act 2001, which has often been compared to the 2001 Patriot Act in the United States, the Sicherheitspaket II in Germany, and the Loi de la Sécurité Quotidienne in France (Haubrich 2003: 9–10). The most controversial measure within the 2001 Act is found in part IV, sections 21–23, which allows for the indefinite detention of foreign nationals where deportation may lead to their torture or execution within the recipient country (Parker 2005: 129) . This measure required a further provision (found in section 33) that renounces Britain's legal obligations under Article 5 of the ECHR protecting the "right to life and liberty," which is made possible under Article 15 of the ECHR "at time of war and other public emergency threatening the life of the nation." Out of the forty-one member states of the Council of Europe at the time, Britain was the only state to declare a state of emergency in order to derogate from its Article 5 obligations under the ECHR (Haubrich 2003: 19).

Shortly after the act came into force, Home Secretary David Blunkett used his newfound powers to detain fourteen terror suspects indefinitely in Belmarsh Prison in Southeast London. The derogation from Article 5 of the ECHR, the detention provision, and its use by the Home Secretary for the "Belmarsh 14" as they became known, caused much reaction within the legal profession, among many MPs, and among human rights groups such as Liberty, Justice and Amnesty International. In December 2004 the Law Lords ruled 8–1 that the power to detain foreign nationals without charge for an indefinite period was indeed incompatible with the ECHR on grounds that it was a *disproportionate* response to the threat posed at the time of its introduction and *discriminatory* since it applied to foreign nationals only.[8] In heeding the Law Lords' declaration of incompatibility, Home Secretary Charles Clarke responded by proposing a series of measures that would allow him (or any future home secretary) to impose "control orders," such as house arrest, curfews, electronic tagging, and other restrictions on any individuals (foreign or British) suspected of involvement in terrorism. In this way, the government argued that it was addressing both the concerns of proportionality and discrimination through the introduction of such measures.

But the government was under significant pressure to turn these proposals into proper legislation, so it introduced the Prevention of Terrorism Bill in January 2005. The existing powers to detain the Belmarsh suspects were due to expire on 14 March, thus creating ever more urgency to get the bill through Parliament. In the event, the debate and arguments surrounding the passage of the bill into law featured as one of the most prolonged and contested pieces of legislation, requiring the third longest sitting of the House of Lords (Quinn 2005: 21). The government found it necessary to make an increasing set of concessions to get the bill through Parliament, including transferring the power of house arrest from the home secretary to the judiciary,[9] pledging that the powers would be reviewed in a year's time, and raising the standards of proof needed to detain any suspects. After bouncing between both houses four times, the bill received the Royal Assent on March 11, just three days before the powers to detain the Belmarsh suspects expired. The release of the detainees on bail and subsequent imposition of the control orders was not particularly well handled by the government, effectively leaving the newly freed men (they were all male suspects) unsure of how much freedom of movement, association, and communication they actually enjoyed.[10]

Just as the nation and Parliament was catching its breath from the debates over the Prevention of Terrorism Act 2005 and the fiasco over the implementation of the control orders, London was bombed on July 7, fol-

TABLE 5.2  The Labour Government's Twelve-Point
Counterterror Plan

1.  New grounds for deportation and exclusion
2.  New counterterrorism legislation
3.  Refusal of asylum for anyone who has had anything to do with terrorism
4.  Enhanced powers to strip British citizenship from dual citizens and naturalized citizens
5.  Time limits on all extradition cases
6.  Significant extension of pretrial detention
7.  Extension of control orders against those who cannot be deported
8.  Enhancement of court capacity to hear deportation and control order cases
9.  Proscription of extremist organizations
10.  Raise the threshold for British citizenship
11.  Powers to close places of worship that espouse extremist views
12.  Speed up border control plans to include biometric data

lowed by a further attempted bombing on July 21. The July 7 suicide bombings in three separate locations on London's tube and on a bus during the morning rush hour killed 56 people and injured a further 700, making it the worst terrorist attack in Britain since the 1988 Pan Am disaster. The attacks prompted a cross-party consensus on the need for counterterror action, in which Tony Blair pledged to introduce new laws that would include bans on the preparation of, incitement to, and/or training for terrorism. In August, he issued a twelve-point plan to combat terror (see Table 5.2), which would be realized through a combination of the new Terrorism Bill, the new Immigration, Nationality and Asylum Bill (to deprive nationality and to redefine refugees), new administrative measures (such as memoranda of understanding with recipient countries to guarantee deportees would not be tortured), and some executive intervention in court cases.

Of these measures, the Terrorism Bill received the widest attention. Under its provisions for encouraging terrorism and disseminating materials on terrorism, it created a new offence of *glorifying* terrorism (part I, section 1), which many human rights groups saw as an infringement on freedom of speech. While the control orders enacted under the Prevention of Terrorism Act 2005 were still in force, the new Terrorism Bill sought to create new powers of pre-charge detention for terror suspects that could last up to a maximum of ninety days. Existing statutes have provisions for pre-charge detention of up to fourteen days, but the government made the argument that more time was needed on the grounds that investigating international terrorist activity carried out by foreigners or British nationals would incur time delays owing to international evidence gathering, mapping and investigating mobile phone networks, and examining multitudes of personal computers with large amounts of encrypted data.

In an October 6 letter to Home Secretary Charles Clarke, the assistant commissioner of the Metropolitan police, Andy Hayman, outlined the case for the "operational requirements for an extension to the maximum period of detention without charge to three months." The accompanying briefing note accepted that judicial oversight was crucial, but that the nature of the police investigations into terrorist activity that now use sophisticated technology requires extensive forensic expertise that may in certain circumstances require a full ninety days' detention of certain suspects. His argument was based on a combination of actual case studies and a theoretical case study constructed with the assistance of the Crown Prosecution Service involving statistics from real cases and a scenario of the most likely set of events.

The Bill passed its second reading with a majority of 379 votes, but it faced fierce opposition during the committee stage, which considers proposed legislation on a line-by-line basis. It was in this process that government suddenly became quite vulnerable over the issue of ninety-day precharge detention. The Liberal Democrats argued for fourteen days in line with existing legislation, the Conservatives argued for twenty-eight days, while the government stuck to its claim that it needed the full ninety days. The ensuing debate saw many Labour backbenchers arguing for a shorter period, while the substantive arguments focused on the degree to which it would be possible to strike a balance among traditional liberties, the rule of law, and the need to protect the country. Ultimately, the ninety-day detention provision did not carry the vote (twenty-eight days did), with MPs saying "no" by a majority of 31 votes, where 49 of 322 "no" votes came from the Labour benches. In early 2006, Parliament returned to debate section 1 of the Terrorism Bill on the glorification of terrorism, which passed the Commons with a majority of 38 votes on February 15, while an additional Bill on the introduction of identity cards passed with a majority of 31 votes just two days previously.

Two additional developments in this long chain of events have been the Law Lords ruling on December 8, 2005, that secret evidence obtained through torture is not admissible against terror suspects in UK courts, and the June 2006 ruling from the High Court that the use of control orders violated the ECHR. In 2002, the Special Immigration Appeals Committee

(SIAC), a body set up in 1997 to decide on deportation cases made on security grounds, decided that in its deliberations it was entitled to consider evidence obtained under torture. The December Lords ruling nullified that decision. Home Secretary Charles Clarke responded by saying, "I welcome the decision, which gives clarity about the extremely important and very difficult issue that requires more than ill-informed reaction," and continued by affirming that "The exclusion of evidence obtained by torture from SIAC hearings will not change, weaken or detract from our ability to fight terrorism."[11] As for the High Court ruling in 2006, it was clear that the use of control orders deprives individuals of their liberty without a trial. In his October press conference discussing the fact that two suspects subjected to these control orders had actually disappeared, the prime minister responded by saying, "I wanted to make sure that the original counterterrorist legislation was maintained in full. Control orders were never going to be as effective as detention."[12]

Thus, in the year since issuing the twelve-point plan, the government has used various instruments to try to achieve its main aims and objectives for countering terrorism. The government's own review of these measures in July 2006 claims that nine of the twelve points have been "actioned," two have completed their process of consultation, and one is still under review. In a more critical appraisal, the *Financial Times* claimed that of the twelve points, three have now been implemented, six remain incomplete, and three have not been enacted. The points in the plan that are still the subject of controversy include the deportation and exclusion of terror suspects, time limits on extradition cases involving terrorism, the extension of detention without charge, the use of control orders, the expansion of court capacity to deal with terror suspects, the power to close "places of worship" that foment extremism and the banning of foreign imams who are "not suitable to preach," and the tightening of border controls.[13]


HORIZONTAL AND VERTICAL ACCOUNTABILITY

What are the larger lessons to be learned from this set of developments in Britain's experience in fighting terrorism? There has been a legacy within the UK that comes from the long fight against terrorism—primarily but not exclusively against those terrorist acts associated with the troubles in Northern Ireland, which in many ways set the stage for the current period of counterterror. The perception of international threat after 9/11 and the raised sense of urgency after 7/7, combined with the already permanent counterterror legislation may have created the impression in government that the argument of necessity would override any concern for human rights, since it was in the national interest to defend Britain against this new evil. The Labour government used its democratic mandate over three successive elections to introduce a series of measures that broadened and deepened its authority and sought to win the argument by appealing to the increased sense of threat. But as this chapter has shown, that democratic mandate and dominant political position could only push the argument of necessity so far, where the concerns over human rights as well as the mechanisms for their protection put limits on the government's attempts to fight terrorism.

In an abstract sense, it is easier for nondemocracies to fight terrorism on the domestic front since they are less accountable to their citizens and can introduce a range of measures that curb any rights protections that may have existed or that citizens may have been able to exercise in the absence of formal legal protection. In contrast, it is much harder for democracies to fight terrorism since they are accountable to their citizens and in liberal democracies rights are enshrined in national constitutions or find expression through other legal mechanisms. Of the many options open to democracies in responding to terrorism—a criminal justice model, a war model, or "the causes of terrorism" model (Large 2005)—Britain has by and large followed a criminal justice model for dealing with its threat of terror, although there remains a significant temptation for the criminal justice model to be superseded by a "security model based on fear and suspicion" (Gearty 2006: 137). In the past, when its democratic institutions were not yet fully developed, it defined terrorists as criminals and developed its legal response accordingly. For a brief period in Northern Ireland, terror suspects were treated as prisoners of war, but since then they have been treated as criminals. It is no surprise, then, that the 2001 antiterrorism act refers to terrorism *and* crime and that the new Terrorism Bill seeks to criminalize a wider range of activities than have been criminalized in the past.

This combination of a criminal justice model in a liberal democracy trying to fight terrorism creates many of the same tensions among security, liberty, rule of law, and rights found in the other countries in this volume. It also raises significant questions about the degree to which mechanisms for vertical and horizontal accountability are working. On the issue of fighting terrorism, mass public opinion has waxed and waned over the years, and support for the war in Iraq has seen a general decline since the March 2003 invasion. But the public has been generally in favor of greater powers for the government to tackle terrorism at home. MORI polls have shown that between Blair's first and second term in office public identification of terrorism and foreign affairs as significant issues facing the country has risen dramatically from an average of 6 percent (1997–2001) to 31 percent (2001–5) (Quinn 2005: 8). During the run-up to the war in Iraq, public opinion was sharply opposed to the war; in February 2003 between 750,000 and 1 million people participated in a protest march in London (Allen 2005: 67). Yet, for fighting terrorism at home, a BBC poll conducted in April 2004 showed that 62 percent of respondents supported indefinite detention of foreign terror suspects, while 63 percent would be willing to extend such detention to British suspects, and a further 58 percent supported detaining individuals *associated* with terror suspects (Parker 2005: 129). An ICM poll for *The Guardian* conducted in August 2005 after the announcement of Tony Blair's twelve-point counterterror plan showed that 73 percent of the public claimed that it was right to lose some civil liberties to improve security against terror attacks. On specific measures such as banning organizations, deportations, and detentions, support ranged from 24 percent to 48 percent, while 52 percent supported the notion of parliamentary sovereignty in counterterror matters and were opposed to judicial review that could over-turn parliamentary decisions.

Finally, during the debate in Parliament on the ninety-day pre-charge detention provision in the Terrorism Bill, the public was largely persuaded by the case made by the police and the home secretary for the maximum detention period, and when the provision failed and the detention period was reduced to twenty-eight days, the tabloid headlines screamed that the British public had been "betrayed" and that "democracy had been under-mined" by MPs.[14] During the fallout after the vote, MPs from both the left and right were quick to defend the gap between public opinion and the result of the vote, and made appeals to the Burkean notion of the "enlight-ened" representative of the people passing judgment and making decisions that are in the best interests of the public good and not as elected "dele-gates" for their particular constituencies. Such a mismatch between public opinion and the outcome of parliamentary votes is common in all democra-cies on such emotive issues as the death penalty, abortion, and terrorism, and it seems unlikely that public opinion will shift drastically in favor of a rights-protective regime while Britain is under the threat of terror.

Human rights NGOs such as Liberty, Justice, and Amnesty International made a set of rights-based arguments that contrasted starkly with the pub-lic mood and the organizations have suffered a certain degree of hate mail and ostracism as a result.[15] These organizations have issued press releases and briefing papers on counterterror legislation for years and offered sig-nificant advice on the Terrorism Bill as it worked its way through

Parliament. For example, Liberty's main claim is that rights and security do not have to be in conflict and that counterterror legislation can be rights-compatible with the proper forms of oversight and judicial review in place. The organization argues further that some rights such as the protections against detention without charge and the use of torture are absolute, while other rights such as speech, assembly, and privacy may not be absolute, but that the government should only take measures that are necessary and proportionate—a position similar to that taken by the Law Lords in their decisions on the indefinite detention of foreign terror suspects and the use of evidence obtained through torture. Finally, they argue, in line with much analysis carried out on the conflict in Northern Ireland, that counterterror measures that restrict liberties and undermine long held rights commitments can in the long run be counterproductive: since the potential for making mistakes and mistreating innocent people is so great, many individuals who become marginalized, alienated, and disillusioned with the state may be recruited into extremist organizations.[16]

There are thus mixed forms of vertical accountability in terms of public opinion and civil society organizations, which may not lead to the greater call for the protection of human rights in the fight against terror. But like the Spanish and German cases in this volume (discussed in Chapters 7 and 9, respectively), the UK is subject to an additional form of vertical accountability represented by the regional regime for the promotion and protection of human rights within the Council of Europe, which has the ability to determine whether national level legislation violates international human rights legal obligations. In the context of the fight against terrorism in Northern Ireland, the European Court of Human Rights made a decision in favor of the complaints lodged by the Irish government with respect to the ways in which terror suspects were being treated. Despite this judgment in 1978, the post-9/11 and post-7/7 attempts by the government to introduce new measures to combat terror are again pushing the limits of human rights law. Though not as powerful in legal terms, the views of the European Human Rights Commissioner about the protection of human rights in the current fight against terror have carried some weight with domestic groups struggling to maintain Britain's long-held commitments to protecting human rights.

Like vertical accountability, horizontal accountability has manifested itself in mixed fashion in relation to the reaction to the government's attempts to combat terrorism. The Terrorism Bill had built-in review procedures to detain suspects up to a maximum of ninety days, when police would have needed court approval to detain suspects every seven days. The defeat of the measure in the Commons demonstrates that such guarantees did not satisfy a majority of MPs and represents a certain degree of democratic control of the legislature over the executive, which tends to be much more pronounced in presidential than in parliamentary democracies. But for human rights advocates, the result of a twenty-eight-day detention still means that suspects can be detained without charge for almost a month, a measure that far exceeds the powers enacted in similar liberal democracies across Europe. The outcome thus represents classic features of British democracy: political compromise and elite accommodation.

The two major decisions coming from the Law Lords, however, have shown that some measures proposed and enacted by the government to combat terrorism have simply gone too far. The indefinite detention of foreign terror suspects was found incompatible with the ECHR rights protected under the Human Rights Act, as was the use of evidence gained from interrogation techniques that include torture. In the words of Blom-Cooper, these decisions have evoked "discombobulation" (Blom-Cooper 2005: 236) in governmental circles and certainly find resonance with the 2004 *Hamdi v. Rumsfeld* decision by the U.S. Supreme Court, and the U.S. Congress's December 22, 2005, refusal to extend the USA Patriot Act beyond a month without revisiting some of its provisions. In both cases, the extension of governmental authority that violated long-held commitments to human rights simply could not be upheld in the long run. Liberal democracies are founded on the combination of majority rule and minority rights protection, which are institutionalized through various mechanisms that are meant to have checks in place to curb the worst forms of centralized power and authority. While these checks are more institutionalized and more obvious in the American system of government, the recent unfolding of events in the UK surrounding the government's attempt to combat terrorism demonstrates that the writ of rights runs long and deep. With time, rights arguments can take hold, with unintended consequences for governments. This may just yet provide the kind of complementarity between rights and security that the war on terror needs.

# 6 Torturing Democracies

## *The Curious Debate over the "Israeli Model"*

Gershon Shafir

In 1949, the Israeli writer S. Yizhar (the pen name of Yizhar Smilansky) published a series of short stories about the Israeli War of Independence. In "The Prisoner," a unit of the home guard takes an Arab shepherd and his sheep captive; during the interrogation of the frightened and confused man, the soldiers mechanically, yet systematically, kick and beat him to pry out information. Though the shepherd cannot tell his own age and seems innumerate, he is tortured to reveal the exact number of the Egyptian soldiers in his village and their armaments. In this macabre scene the shepherd is eager to be helpful, but his tormentors do not believe a word he says. Yizhar gives voice to the soldiers' approach:

> Because if you want the truth, beat him! If he lies, beat him! If he tells
> the truth . . . beat him so he won't lie later on! Beat him in case there is
> more to come. Beat him because you've got him at your feet! . . . And if
> someone doesn't agree, let him not argue. He's a defeatist, and you can't
> make wars with that kind. Have no mercy. Beat him! They have no
> mercy on you. (Yizhar 1962: 165)

Though Yizhar, the acclaimed writer of the generation of 1948, portrays the Palestinian victim vividly, the main character emerges from the group of three soldiers ordered to drive the shepherd to an interrogation center. Yizhar's unnamed protagonist's earnest Sartreian struggle of conscience between choice and fate is also an adventure gone wrong, a battle against a youthful prank, and against the power of nationalist slogans that lead to conventional cruelty and unthinking obedience. Should he free the shepherd and send him back to his village and wife and accept the "honor" of being held accountable and punished, or keep mum and take the shepherd where he might be kept for years or even, as repeatedly suggested by his fellow soldiers, be "finished off"? The story delves deeper and deeper into the soldier's growing despair but ends without ever resolving his dilemma.

Yizhar, who expressed some of his generation's scruples—later to be named the "shooting and crying" syndrome—was from Israel's mainstream and paid no public price for his outspokenness. He received the coveted Israel Prize for literature in 1959 at age 43, and served as a Member of Knesset from the ruling Mapai Party and later Rafi. The openness he brought to the topic of torture, however, disappeared after the Israeli conquest of the heavily populated Palestinian West Bank in 1967.

When the *Sunday Times* of London broke the topic wide open in 1977 (in stories on June 19 and July 3 and 10) by concluding after a five-month investigation that "Israeli interrogators routinely ill-treat and often torture Arab prisoners" and had done so "throughout the ten years of Israeli occupation," the Israeli government's denials were feeble and unconvincing. The official inquiry a decade later by the Landau Commission concluded that the "the Israeli General Security Service lied for 16 years" (*Jerusalem Post*, November 1, 1987).[1] By the time of the Landau Commission's report, almost forty years after Yizhar's story, torture was no longer practiced by citizen-soldiers but by an official, though secretive, state organ. Nor was it part and parcel of a war, but part of a protracted struggle over occupation and colonization in the territories occupied by Israel in the June 1967 war.

The Landau Commission decided to lift the veil on this taboo subject as did Yizhar in his day. All the same, the members of the commission—who, like Yizhar, also wrestled with the conflicting values of individual and national security versus human dignity—resolved to sanction as a matter of policy the application of (the euphemistically phrased) "moderate physical pressure" when "necessity" seemed to dictate.

Israel these days is rarely held up as a model, let alone a positive one. But since 9/11, the nexus of Israeli torture of Palestinian suspects has acquired added significance in the United States, and a debate has ensued over the application of the "Israeli model" to suspected al Qaeda terrorists. Assistant Attorney General Jay Bybee's memo dated August 1, 2002, to then White House Counsel Alberto Gonzales held that the president's constitutional power as commander-in-chief includes the right to authorize torture, and should an American be charged for using torture he could rely for his or her defense on the Israeli model, under which national security necessitates physical and psychological coercion of unlawful combatants.[2] But Bybee's justification was offered in bad faith: the model he invoked had already been rejected in Israel itself.

On September 9, 1999, the Israeli Supreme Court (sitting as the High

Court of Justice), in an opinion written by Chief Justice Aharon Barak, forbade the GSS from using several methods of physical pressure against terror suspects, though it did not close all loopholes (Israel, Supreme Court, 1999, hereafter SC). In short, Israel stands out not only for having legalized certain forms of physical pressure falling under "torture and other cruel, inhuman, and degrading treatment" as described in the UN Convention against Torture, but also in having reversed that decision in a meaningful way (if not fully).

In contrast to Bybee, in November 2005 Senator John McCain, on NBC's "Today" and on Fox "News Sunday," cited Israel as a country that is successful in combating terrorism without resorting to torture. In substantiating his Senate antitorture amendment, McCain stated that "the Israeli Supreme Court outlawed torture, outlawed cruel and inhuman treatment. And I have talked to Israeli officials, and they say that they do very fine without it."[3] McCain's information, however, was far from accurate: physical pressure of Palestinian terror suspects has not ceased, even after the Supreme Court decision.

Alan Dershowitz, who was also inspired by Israeli practice and had advocated his ideas to the Israeli government before offering them to the United States (Shank 2001: 21), constructed a third (albeit considerably muddled) model. Whereas the Landau Commission sought to bring the practice of physical pressure under legal control by authorizing it as a matter of policy, Dershowitz, seemingly more humane, advocates the issuing of prior "torture warrants" only in specific cases. But in justifying the torture of terror suspects, Dershowitz invokes the Israeli Supreme Court's 1999 decision, which upheld the necessity defense even as it outlawed physical pressure. In fact, whereas the Court will consider necessity only as an ex post facto defense, Dershowitz is willing to authorize it in advance (Dershowitz 2002: 139–41).[4]

It is valuable to study the "Israeli model" not because it shows that torture is necessary, nor because it demonstrates that it is not, but for two other reasons. First, civilian and military leaders, lawyers, and scholars in the United States rehash many of the arguments, in particular the necessity defense, already tried out in the Israeli debate (which itself is built on prior French and British models). An examination of the reasoning and practices of these "torturing democracies" demonstrates not only the uses but also the abuses of the model. Second, and more important, if there is an Israeli model, its use is in illuminating the social and political conditions under which democracies are likely to engage in torture openly or surreptitiously, by themselves or through third parties. While upholding the constraints on torture is a key component of the fight against it, only changing the very conditions that give license to torturing terror suspects is likely to do away with it.

Accordingly, I examine the central contours of the Landau Commission's report and the Supreme Court's decision. I then present the social and political context in which license is given to torture in democratic states, and the constraints imposed on the use of torture, cruel, inhuman, and degrading treatment by domestic and international law. I further analyze the justification, limits, and practice of the "necessity" defense. In conclusion I ask the following question: If, in our study of democracies' approach to the terror-torture nexus, Israel is to be interrogated as a model, what is it a model of?

## THE LANDAU COMMISSION AND "MODERATE PHYSICAL PRESSURE"

The Israeli government officially appointed the "Commission of Inquiry into the Methods of Investigation of the General Security Service Regarding Hostile Terrorist Activity"[5]—known by its Chair, retired Supreme Court Justice Moshe Landau—in the wake of the Nafsu affair. In 1987, the Supreme Court overturned the 1980 conviction of a former IDF lieutenant, Izat Nafsu, for espionage on behalf of Syria. The Court ruled that Nafsu's conviction was based on a confession extracted under duress by GSS interrogators who falsely testified in court to cover up their illegal actions. Being an Israeli citizen of the Circassian minority, Nafsu's mistreatment generated the kind of legal alarm that another famed case of abuse of Palestinian Arab terrorists by the GSS three years earlier did not. In April 1984, Israeli troops stormed a number 300 bus hijacked by four Palestinian terrorists, killed two of the terrorists, and freed their Jewish hostages. Though two of the terrorists survived, they were later pronounced dead. It was later revealed that they were beaten to death, apparently under the orders of Avraham Shalom, GSS's head. When the attorney general (who in Israel roughly combines the tasks of the solicitor general and the government's legal counsel) refused to halt his investigation into the beating deaths, he was fired; Shalom and his underlings, who lied to cover up the beating but cooperated with the investigation, were pardoned by the Israeli president.[6]

The Landau Commission determined that GSS personnel had been using physical pressure on terrorist suspects and lying to cover it up in court during the preceding sixteen years (Israel, Landau Commission, 1987 [henceforth LC]: 2.27–2.28, p. 23; Kremnitzer 1989: 218] At the same time, having accepted prima facie the GSS's view that physical pressure was necessary to conduct effective interrogation of terror suspects, the commission members expressed fear of moral corruption resulting from infringement on the rule of law. In struggling with this dilemma they compared and contrasted the options of lawlessness, hypocrisy, and justification. They were unwilling either to place the GSS outside or above the law or to countenance the hypocrisy of ignoring torture carried out in the name of national security (LC 4.1–4.8, pp. 77–81). In adopting this approach they, in fact, retraced the footsteps of the Wuillaume Commission, which investigated torture in French Algeria in 1955 and also wished to do away with the hypocrisy and secrecy surrounding it (See Vidal-Naquet 1963: 33–36; the text of the report is in the appendix, pp. 169–79).

The commission's preferred option was to confront the dilemma openly and, by justifying the exceptional use of force under the "necessity" defense, to make permissible the use of "moderate physical pressure" (LC 4.7, p. 80; Gross 2004: 372; Kremnitzer 1989: 217). Such pressure, the commission, asserted, should "never reach the level of physical torture or maltreatment or grievous harm to his honor which deprives [the suspect] of his human dignity" (LC 3.16, p. 61). Though the commission established a regulatory mechanism to oversee its use, the part of its report that specified what constituted allowable physical pressure—in defiance of international conventions and norms—remains secret to this day.

The Landau Commission's report was approved by the Israeli government. A special ministerial committee monitored and routinely renewed its guidelines. During 1988, the second year of the mostly nonviolent intifada, when the GSS expressed its need for better information, the monitoring committee authorized the GSS to use "enhanced physical pressure" (B'Tselem 1991: 34; Pacheco 1999: 6). Physicians were to examine the suspect and fill out a "form of medical fitness," which, according to Ruchama Marton of the Association of Israeli-Palestinian Physicians for Human Rights, served to certify their fitness to be interrogated in a fashion which "leads to torture" (see form in Marton 1995: 37). In fact, the main five methods of physical pressure used by the GSS—widely documented by the Palestinian al Haq and about half a dozen Israeli human rights organizations and admitted to by the GSS in court cases—have become well-known. The following descriptions are taken from the 1999 Supreme Court decision that made them illegal:

1. Shaking: "the forceful shaking of the suspect's upper torso, back and forth, in a manner which causes the neck and head to dangle and vacillate rapidly." Affidavits submitted to the Court assert that "the shaking method is likely to cause serious brain damage, harm the spinal cord, cause the sus-

pect to lose consciousness, vomit and urinate uncontrollably and suffer serious headaches." This is considered the harshest of the five methods (SC 3; B'Tselem 1997: 11).

2. The "Shabach" position, in which the suspect is seated on a small, low chair, whose seat is tilted forward, toward the ground. One hand is tied behind the suspect and placed inside the gap between the chair's seat and back support. His second hand is tied behind the chair, against its back support. The suspect's head is covered by an opaque sack, falling down to his shoulders. Powerfully loud music is played in the room. According to the affidavits submitted, suspects are detained in this position for a prolonged period of time, awaiting interrogation at consecutive intervals.

Affidavits further claim that "prolonged sitting in this position causes serious muscle pain in the arms, the neck and headaches" (SC 3; Bowden 2003: 64).

3. The "Frog Crouch": "refers to consecutive, periodical crouches on the tips of one's toes, each lasting for five minute intervals" (SC 4).

4. Excessive tightening of hand or leg cuffs, which, as affidavits assert results in "serious injuries to the suspect's hands, arms and feet, due to the length of the interrogations." In some cases the applicants complained of the use of "particularly small cuffs, ill fitted in relation to the suspect's arm or leg size" (SC 4).

5. Sleep deprivation that results from "being tied in the 'Shabach' position, being subjected to the playing of powerfully loud music, or intense non-stop interrogations without sufficient rest breaks" (SC 4; Bowden 2003: 64). (For a detailed description of these and additional methods, see B'Tselem 1998.)

This is not an exhaustive list of physical pressure methods used by GSS interrogators. For example, on January 31, 2006, the GSS agreed to pay compensation, without admitting wrongdoing, to twenty-eight Palestinians who complained of having been tortured in more extreme fashion, including having been severely beaten, after their arrests in 1996 and 1997.[7]

According to an 1998 estimate by B'Tselem, the Israeli Information Center for Human Rights in the Occupied Territories, the GSS annually interrogated 1,000–1,5000 Palestinian suspects and "some 85 percent of them—at least 850 prisoners a year—are tortured during investigation" (B'Tselem 1998: 8). On the higher end, the Israeli attorney Allegra Pacheco, who defended many Palestinian terror suspects, puts the number of Palestinians tortured by Israel at 50,000 (Pacheco 2001). These coercive interrogations took place in detention centers and prisons in Tul-Karem, Jenin, Nablus, Farah, and Hebron that were maintained by the GSS (Langer

1995: 77). In the 1980s, GSS interrogators also collaborated with interrogators of Israel's surrogate Southern Lebanese Army in the Khiam prison in southern Lebanon, where the use of similar methods was reported (Sherry 1999).

During the first intifada, about "sixteen Palestinians are reported to have died after punitive beatings at the time or shortly after arrest by Israeli forces. At least eight others died in detention centers" (Amnesty International 1994: 21). One of them, Abdel Samad Harizat, died as a consequence of having been administered violent shaking, a fact not denied by the GSS (Pacheco 1999: 7). Two GSS interrogators were sentenced to six months in jail for causing Khaled Shaik Ali's death by negligence (Amnesty International 1994: 21). The Public Committee against Torture in Israel (PCATI), founded during the first intifada, and additional human rights organizations repeatedly petitioned the Supreme Court to review the Landau Commission guidelines and revoke them, and to have its secret annex made public. Though the Court issued *order nisis* (interim injunctions) to the GSS to show cause for further use of physical pressure against individual suspects, it left these cases pending for several years (Pacheco 1999 reproduces these petitions).

## LICENSE TO TORTURE

Torture happens when it is licensed by political and social sanctions. In authoritarian regimes and dictatorships the very act of engaging in acts of political opposition earns one the label of "enemy." As such, the regime's "enemy" is exposed to the hostility of, and sometimes torture by, the regime. In democracies, however, such divisions are not ideological or political alone.

From a sociological viewpoint, the more clearly it is possible to divide terrorist suspects and their victims into distinct categories, whether ethnic, national or religious, the lower the ethical standards are likely to be during their confrontation. "Torture and racism may mutually reinforce each other" (Ruthven 1978: 285–86) since torture is a process of dehumanization and, consequently, is most easily applied to those already dehumanized through social exclusion and racism. Terrorists drink from the same well. In general, the depiction of the enemy as illegitimate, or as one not following the rules, plays a crucial role in justifying torture as much as it does in justifying terror, binding the two phenomena into a single nexus.

Deep social and political divisions rank hierarchically the opposing parties by stratifying their respective human dignity and apportioning them into separate legal frameworks. The origins of the legalization of such division are ancient indeed: Roman law established that "barbarians could be tortured but not Roman citizens" (Millett 1994: 98; Ross 2005: 4–7). Pope Innocent IV in 1252 adapted this division to the religious purposes of the Inquisition by proclaiming that "heretics deserve torture" (Millett 1994: 99; Levinson 2003a: 2031; Ross 2005: 10). One accomplishment of the Enlightenment is that torture no longer has a legal foundation, but it continues to occur, based (even in some democracies) on the effective segregation of suspects underwritten by a body of peripheral legislation, such as the suspension of constitutional rights and various forms of special powers, which create "circumstances whereby torture can be practiced in secret" (Millett 1994: 99).

## Social License

The discourse of national security commonly reinforces the construction of national boundaries and the divisions among citizens, individuals, and groups of various levels of standing within the state. The Landau Commission's licensing of moderate physical pressure in interrogations, as Mordechai Kremnitzer observed, was based on the painting of the terrorist organizations and the GSS in contrasting hues of black and white (Kremnitzer 1989: 223). In 1987 the PLO was an illegal organization in Israel, and the Landau Commission shared the Israeli political consensus that Palestinian terrorism threatened not only the lives of innocent civilians but that the PLO's objective of "the destruction of the State of Israel" also posed a threat to Israel's national life (LC 2.9, p. 11; Gross 2004: 372–74). In this spirit the Landau Commission also accepted Israel's broad definition of terrorism, which included not only acts or threats of violence but also "political subversion which is prohibited by law in Israel or the [occupied] territories," namely the whole range of activities expressing Palestinian nationalism (LC 4.8, pp. 80–81; Hajjar 2004; Kremnitzer 1989: 225 n. 14). Consequently, PLO terrorists in the commission's view fell in a special category of suspects who "have no moral right to demand that the State for its part maintain towards them the usual civil rights" (LC 4.5, p. 79). Conversely, the GSS's interrogators were held by the commission to be trusted professionals with solid and reliable judgment (Kremnitzer 1989: 223).

This legal dualism removes the concern that the use of torture might be used against Israeli Jews. "Israelis don't fear their own security services because [its] victims are all Palestinians," a clearly delineated and hostile outgroup that resides beyond the territorial boundaries of the affected nation. As Michael Gross points out, there are no reports of torture against Israeli Jews, but Arab citizens of Israel arrested during the September–October 2000 riots were subjected to inhuman and degrading treatment by the Israeli police (Gross 2004: 380). Democracy is identified with Israel's Jewish citizens and, consequently, is viewed not as threatened but defended through the use of torture.[8]

Under Israel's 1950 Families of Soldiers Who Fell in Battle Law, victims and their families are entitled to compensation and rehabilitation for terrorist attacks if these were carried out by an organization defined as "hostile" to the state of Israel. Thus, the four Israeli Arab citizens killed and twelve wounded by Eden Natan Zada on August 4, 2005, in a shooting spree on a bus in the city of Shfaram, were not compensated. Natan Zeda was a uniformed Israeli soldier and thus not considered a member of a group hostile to the state of Israel, even though he deserted from the military and was a supporter of the late Rabbi Meir Kahane's Kach party, which had been outlawed for seeking the expulsion of Israel's Arab citizens. Such an attack is considered ordinary crime, as Jews cannot be legally treated as terrorists. Though the Shfaram victims were never defined as victims of terror, after Prime Minister Sharon condemned the perpetrator (who sought to thwart his planned unilateral Israeli withdrawal from Gaza) unusually bluntly as "a bloodthirsty terrorist who sought to harm innocent Israeli civilians," they were offered compensation as an exceptional measure.[9]

The danger of Jewish terrorism in Israel is not imaginary: religious extremist groups and individuals have in the past carried out terrorist attacks on a range of targets with the intention of avenging Palestinian terrorism or, conversely, derailing the Israeli-Palestinian peace process. In May 1980 a synchronized attempt was made to kill several Palestinian mayors, in March 1994 Baruch Goldstein perpetrated a massacre at the Machpela Cave, and in November 1995 Prime Minister Itzhak Rabin was gunned down as he was leaving a peace rally. Among terrorist plots discovered and prevented by the Israeli security forces, there were at least four to set fire to or bomb the al Aqsa Mosque.[10] Yuval Diskin, the current head of the GSS, admitted as recently as 2006 that his service shows "more leniency toward Jewish terror suspects than toward Israeli Arab or Palestinian suspects."[11] The dual standards of the Israeli security forces in fighting terrorism—letting the armed Goldstein, wearing an Israeli army uniform, into the Machpela cave during Muslim prayer; not protecting Rabin from Jewish extremists—had severe consequences. Hamas unleashed its first suicide bombing campaign in response to Goldstein's terrorism, and Rabin's murder severely impacted the peace process.

## Political License

Ethnic, national, and religious divisions are usually polarized under particular political circumstances. Systematic Palestinian terror acts aimed at civilians created a national security doctrine assessment of grave threat to the state and its Jewish population (Barzilai 1998) and placed the country "on a permanent war-footing against terrorism" (Waxman 2000: 16). In addition, Israel had all four of the main conditions that increase the likelihood that terror suspects (even in democratic societies) will be tortured: military conflict or war, military occupation, colonialism, and colonization.

Years of colonial rule, in which a dominant group controls another, reinforces the dominant group's sense of superiority. When this dominance is challenged by a rising nationalist movement, such as in British India, "torture, previously seen as a manifestation of native barbarism, come[s] into the white man's service" (Ruthven 1978: 286). In Kenya, after the Second World War, the British imprisoned up to 1.5 million Kikuyu, nearly the entire population of the country's largest ethnic group, in detention camps and fortified villages. Many of the detainees were tortured with the intention of putting down the Mau Mau rebellion. Whereas the British accused the Kikuyu of acts of barbarity against British settlers, the colonial administration mistreated the Kenyans in order to restore its authority, under the guise of a civilizing mission (Elkins 2005: xi–xvi). Other forms of ill-treatment and torture by British authorities abound. Cyprus and Aden had no British settlers, but the attempted suppression of their nationalist movements included harsh torture at British hands (Sellars 2002). Where occupation was practiced in Europe, by the 1960s the British pioneered the use of "torture lite" in Northern Ireland. The most extensive documentation involves the abuse by the British of detained IRA suspects. The European Court, in its judgment on a suit brought by Ireland against the UK, recognized multiple techniques of coercive interrogation as ill-treatment. Less known is the Donnelly case, in which the UK was accused of brutal treatment of seven detainees, but which was dismissed by the court on the technical ground that domestic remedies were not exhausted (see Chapter 4 in this volume; Boyle and Hannum 1977: 316).

Torture "has always been part of the arsenal of colonial police practices," but it was transformed into its "principal weapon" as part of the French theory of "counterinsurgency warfare" (Robin 2005: 46). During the war in Indochina, French intelligence gathering on the Viet Minh was entrusted to small *Bandes Noires* (rogue units), later renamed *Détachments Opérationels de Protection*, composed of Viet Minh deserters, local thugs, and criminals.

Under the command of French NCOs, these units engaged in the dirty work of brutalizing and torturing suspects and captured Viet Minh guerrillas, executing them and disposing of their bodies (Porch 1995: 381–83).

In Indochina, David Rieff observed, torture by French forces did not become a systematic aspect of the war in spite of its ferocity. The reason, in his view, was that the Viet Minh fought a conventional war of liberation and, "unlike the FLN," was "not tempted by terrorist tactics" (Rieff 2002: 107). But I will argue that the significant circumstance that distinguished Vietnam from Algeria is that Vietnam experienced a war of liberation against French colonial authorities and later U.S. occupation; Algeria, by contrast, was also the site of French colonization, with 1 million European settlers to 9 million Arab Algerians. In Algeria, "the FLN was not just fighting a war against the French army but a terrorist war aimed at driving out the European settlers" (Rieff 2002: 107).

The intensity of the French repression of the resistance and terrorism of the FLN and the extensive use of torture and summary executions provides the most compelling example of the terror-torture nexus that evolves when all four aggravating conditions coexist. The French argued for the indissolubility of France and Algeria but treated the majority of the Algerians as colonial subjects. The strategy of the Algerian nationalists included a systematic campaign of terror against civilian targets, both French and Muslims friendly to France. The French response was unashamedly described in 2001 in the shocking memoir of Paul Aussaresses, the intelligence officer in charge of implementing the French policy. Aussaresses's memoir definitively put the lie to the official version that torture was an exception resorted to by a few caught up in a brutal war; he demonstrates that it was, as was known at the time in France and faithfully reproduced by Gillo Pontecorvo in *The Battle of Algiers*, an officially sanctioned policy from the seat of the French government in Paris, one supported by both left and right (Aussaresses 2001: 128; Rieff 2002: 106, Macmaster 2002: 450). The response to terrorism by the French military and the French police of Algeria, which worked hand in hand, was torture and summary execution.

The ability of the French military to create a regime of torture in putting down the FLN's uprising in Algiers was due entirely to the colonial nature of its control. The decision of the French government to dispatch General Massu's Tenth Parachute Division to repress the uprising was part and parcel of its attempt to elide the distinction between police work and war. Torture, as Neil MacMaster points out, "cannot be understood in isolation, but only as one key component in a wider, integrated system of repression" that allowed arbitrary arrests and long-term imprisonment, since it was predicated on the suspension of "the normal protection of due process, habeas corpus, access to lawyers and the courts, proper indictment and fair trial" (MacMaster 2004: 6). In the colonial context, the French state could refuse to recognize that it was at war in Algeria and classify the FLN members and recruits as common-law criminals, outside the protections of international humanitarian law and the Geneva Conventions. It was also able to authorize the executive, under the French Parliament's Special Powers Act of March 16, 1956, to introduce by administrative order any form of repressive measure it saw fit (MacMaster 2004: 6). Enabled by the exceptional circumstances of the Algiers casbah's enclosed and dense traditional urban layout, Massu did not seek to arrest the FLN bombers selectively but detained 30 to 40 percent of all males, namely anyone who plausibly could be thought to be associated with the FLN (Rejali 2004b). "The French won the Battle of Algiers," Darius Rejali concluded, "primarily through force, not by superior intelligence gathered though torture" (Rejali 2004b).

But it was also due to the colonial nature of the confrontation that even though General Massu's paratroopers were able to suppress the FLN and bring its terrorism to an end, the population of Algeria became increasingly estranged and the world outraged until international pressure isolated France at the UN and brought French rule in Algeria to its end by 1962 (Danner 2004b: 74). The internal damage done to French institutions was just as great: only the willed ignorance, dishonesty, and corruption of the judiciary, military, and the administration made the grim horrors of torture possible. Having been ignored, they were not corrected for a long time. "The consensus that emerged in France, one accepted by the mainstream Left and center-Right political parties, as well as by many ex-soldiers who had served in Algeria," including recently General Massu, "was that the use of torture had constituted an unspeakable catastrophe" (MacMaster 2004: 9). France won the battle but lost the war. And yet, the "French school" of counterterror, as Marie-Monique Robin's interviews demonstrate, had been exported through instruction provided in the École Supérior de Guerre, by dispatching military attachés, instructors, and liaisons, via the publication of reference books and the elaboration of a global theory of "counterinsurgency warfare" to Latin America, especially Argentina, "leading to an epidemic of torture" (Robin 2005: 44, 49–53; Macmaster 2004: 8).

The United States, which also learned from French experts, including Aussaresses (Macmaster 2004: 8), adopted a more systematic policy of torture and assassinations in Vietnam than the French did, though even here it was carried out in cooperation with and later transferred into the hands of a local allied regime. In late 1960s, during the Vietnam War, "Operation Phoenix" was launched by the CIA in collaboration with the South Vietnamese intelligence to uncover and destroy the network of noncombatant Viet Cong operatives engaged in recruiting and training insurgents within South Vietnamese villages and assassinating local leaders loyal to the South Vietnamese government. Many of the captured suspects were tortured and subsequently executed, sometimes by being thrown out of helicopters; in fact "Operation Phoenix" is most commonly recognized as an assassination campaign. About 20,000 suspected Viet Cong cadres were "neutralized" in 1969 alone. By 1969 the operation became public knowledge, the CIA began distancing itself, and the day-to-day operations were transferred to South Vietnamese units accompanied by U.S. advisers.[12]

## CONSTRAINTS ON TORTURE

Though the legal domain of civil liberties and international human rights is sometimes described as nebulous, there exist multiple layers of legal constraints on the torture and cruel, inhuman, and degrading treatment of all and any suspects, making this one of the strongest extant legal proscriptions, indeed, construing it as taboo. I will survey three domestic and three international layers of prohibitions.

### Domestic Protections

Three types and levels of constrains in Israeli law serve to protect suspects from torture: interrogation law, penal law, and constitutional law, most specifically the 1992 Basic Law: Human Dignity and Freedom. Later in this chapter I examine how effective these constraints are.

In 1965 Justice Landau himself stated in another context that "the interrogation practices of the police in a given regime are indicative of a regime's very character."[13] Since torture almost invariably takes place during the interrogation stage, the regulation of interrogation is a major form of protection for suspects. As Kate Millett points out, "detention without trial or charge is responsible for torture to a greater extent than any other modern factor" (Millett 1994: 113). Access to lawyers and the writ of habeas corpus play a major role in affording suspects the legal protection that precludes the preconditions under which coercive interrogation may flourish. Detained residents of the West Bank and Gaza, under article 78 of the military occupation's Security Regulations Order, may be deprived by the official in charge of the interrogation from the right to meet with their attorney for a period up to fifteen days. Higher ranking and military court authorities may extend this order up to six months (PCATI 2001: 19). Thus, unless the Supreme Court, sitting as a High Court of Justice, accepts an appeal and permits a meeting, the detainee is in fact isolated from the outside world for a considerable amount of time.

The Penal Law is explicit in making physical pressure illegal. It states in section 277, "Oppression by a Public Servant," that an official who "uses or directs the use of force or violence against a person for the purpose of extorting from him or from anyone in which he is interested a confession of an offence or information relating to an offence," or even "threatens any person, or directs any person to be threatened, with injury to his person or property" to extort such a confession "is liable to imprisonment for three years" (quoted in Kremnitzer 1989: 242). Though in the West Bank, and Gaza until 2005, Israeli retained the respective Jordanian and Egyptian legal codes, Israeli citizens are subject to Israeli criminal and administrative law. Consequently, GSS interrogators, who all are Israeli citizens and as such public servants, are subject to Israeli law, including penal law (B'Tselem 1991: 16). At the same time, Israeli penal law also exempts from criminal responsibility the authors of acts committed under conditions of "necessity" (Uildriks 2000: 87). (This topic is discussed in detail below.)

Though Israel lacks a formal constitution or "bill of rights," human rights had been protected in Israel by a "judicial bill of rights," a body of judicial decisions that gradually and cumulatively established the basic freedoms as norms governing the conduct of the state authorities. In addition, in 1992 the Knesset adopted two constitutional laws related to certain fundamental human rights, and the Supreme Court used the occasion to claim the right of judicial review in areas that fall under these two laws. At the same time, the applicability of even these basic laws is limited. Of the two, only Basic Law: Freedom of Occupation was entrenched, rather weakly, with a stipulation that it could be amended only by another basic law enacted by a majority of Knesset members. Basic Law: Human Dignity and Freedom, which protects the rights to life, liberty, dignity, the integrity of the body, private property, privacy, and movement in and out of the country, was not entrenched in this way, because of its possible implications for the validity of religious legislation. Furthermore, the rights guaranteed by the two laws can be infringed upon by subsequent primary legislation, provided that such legislation is consistent with the values of Israel as a Jewish and democratic state, is enacted for a worthy purpose, and the infringement does not exceed what is necessary for that purpose. In addition, all legislation that had been on the books prior to the enactment of the two basic laws is immune forever against scrutiny for its accordance with Basic Law: Human Dignity and

Freedom (Kretzmer 1992: 240–42; Gavison 1997: 93–100; Shafir and Peled 2002: 267). Even so, the petitions submitted by PCATI, the Association for Citizens' Rights in Israel (ACRI), and several Palestinian individuals which led to the Supreme Court's 1999 decision to ban extant forms of "moderate physical pressure" were in part framed by reference to this new law (Pacheco 1999: 12–13).

## International Protections

Three layers of international law prohibit torture: international humanitarian law, the 1987 Convention against Torture, which singles out torture for absolute proscription, and customary international human rights law (Imseis 2001: 331). These protections have been domesticated into national law by both Israel and the United States.

International humanitarian law regulates the conditions of armed conflict and the relationship between states and the citizens of their adversary, such as in the governing of occupied territory. Though the term itself is of recent origin it is understood to include the 1907 Hague Conventions, the 1949 Geneva Conventions, and related documents. The obligations undertaken under these treaties are binding only between signatory states to them, though the International Committee of the Red Cross (ICRC) holds that they should be viewed as a series of unilateral commitments entered into solemnly in front of the world (Fleck 1995: 9–10). These conventions, especially as amended after their frequent violation during the Second World War, require the humane treatment of prisoners of war since they pose no further threat to their captors. Nor can POWs, even those held to be war criminals or those involved prior to their capture in war crimes, lose these protections (Fleck 1995: 321, 336). As the Third Geneva Convention specifies, POWs are required to provide only personal military information and "no physical or mental torture, nor any other form of coercion, may be inflicted on prisoners of war to secure from them information of any kind whatsoever" (GC III, Article 17.4; Fleck 1995: 345–46). More broadly, the Fourth Geneva Convention of 1949 states in Article 31 that "no physical or moral coercion shall be exercised against protected persons, in particular to obtain information from them or from third parties." Though Israel argues that in absence of a recognized sovereign power in the territories it occupied in 1967 it is not obligated to observe the Geneva Conventions' provision, it committed itself to follow its humanitarian principles, which include Article 31, voluntarily. The U.S. Uniform Code of Military Justice explicitly incorporates the Geneva Conventions.

Already the original Universal Declaration of Human Rights that was adopted by the UN's General Assembly on December 10, 1948, stated in its Article 5 that "no one shall be subject to torture or to cruel, inhuman or degrading treatment or punishment." The very same language reappears in Article 7 of the International Covenant on Civil and Political Rights. Though it allows states during "time of public emergency which threatens the life of the nation" to take measures derogating from their obligations under the covenant, it does not extend this to the permission of torture. There is no derogation from Article 7; the prohibition on torture is unconditional and absolute.

In 1984 the UN adopted the "Convention against Torture and Other Cruel, Inhuman and Degrading Treatment or Punishment" that went into effect in June 1987. As of 2002 it has been ratified by 127 states, including Israel in 1991, and is one of the handful of human rights treaties signed by the United States (Levinson 2003a: 2014–16; 2003b). Though the U.S. Senate opted for a more restrictive definition of torture—under which torture means the infliction of severe rather than "normal" pain and suffering, and "prolonged" mental harm —it accepted Article 2.2, which provides that "no exceptional circumstances whatsoever, whether a state of war or a threat of war, internal political instability, or any other public emergency, may be invoked as a justification for torture" (Levinson 2003a: 2015–16; 2004: 1). Furthermore, the U.S. Congress in special legislation criminalized torture committed by foreign nationals inside, and U.S. nationals outside, the United States (Levinson 2003a: 2016).

Even if a country were not a signatory to the Geneva Conventions and the Convention against Torture, it would still be obligated under customary international law to respect the prohibition on the use of torture. This prohibition has assumed over time the status of customary international law. Falling under universal jurisdiction, which overrides sovereignty itself, it is one of the few genuine norms of *jus cogens* (Levinson 2003a: 2013; Imseis 2001: 331). The protection of life and bodily integrity were a crucial demand of the Enlightenment's struggle for penal reform as well as the foundation of human rights; the history of the three is inextricably intertwined, and major human rights organizations such as Amnesty International have made their early mark and built consensus around this very set of concerns. More recently, opposition to torture is couched in the language of the protection of human dignity, which has become a cornerstone of human rights legislation. The right to dignity is understood to be the right to being human, to act freely and self-consciously in shaping oneself and one's world. The torture of a suspect by an interrogator, whose goal is the destruction of his or her self-respect in order to attain a self-incriminating confession, transforms the suspect from a subject into an object, thus landing a blow to his or her human dignity (Kremnitzer 1989: 250). In Lisa Hajjar's cogent characterization, the universalization of this norm makes the body itself sovereign (Hajjar 2000). The right not to be tortured, in fact, is recognized as stronger than the right to life, since it is unconditional: there are no circumstances under a which person can legally be tortured (Hajjar 2004).

## THE "NECESSITY" DEFENSE

The main legal significance of the Landau Commission's recommendation to permit the use of "moderate physical pressure" on the basis of an a priori "necessity" defense lies in the legitimation of this defense, in making it the source of legal governmental authority to inflict such pressure. Hence an examination of the uses and abuses of "necessity" and, in particular, the continued reliance on it by the very Supreme Court decision from 1999 which struck down "moderate physical pressure" will demonstrate that the legal basis for such "physical pressure" persists in Israel.

The necessity defense is based upon the "unique, isolated and extraordinary character of the situation which makes it an exception to the rule" (Kremnitzer 1989: 238), in this case the rule of law. Under such circumstances an individual is not expected to act in accordance with the law but, under the pressures of the moment, in an ad hoc fashion (Kremnitzer 1989: 238). Section 22 of the Israeli Penal Law of 1977 recognizes the "necessity" defense in a "particularly elastic and open ended" fashion (Dershowitz 1989: 196):

> A person may be exempted from criminal responsibility for any act or omission if he can show that it was done or made in order to avoid consequences which could not otherwise be avoided and which would have inflicted grievous harm or injury on his person, dignity or property or on the person or dignity of others whom he was bound to protect or on property placed in his charge. (quoted in ibid.)

At the same time, the law requires that the defendant who invokes it to demonstrate that "the harm caused by him was not disproportionate to the harm avoided." The test is exacting; in balancing the two evils the judicial review must be comprehensive of the situation and the proximate, distant, direct, and indirect ramifications, including legal and moral consequences. It is not enough to argue that human life was endangered; one also must demonstrate the degree of certainty and proximity of the danger (Kremnitzer 1989: 247). For example, the criteria for invoking the necessity defense in the defining case of torturing a suspect involved with a "ticking bomb" would require the following confluence of conditions: "a firm assurance that the suspect is telling the truth, that his information is complete, that he will talk in time to diffuse the bomb and that there is no chance that the device will be reprogrammed or moved" (Gross 2004: 374).

A summary of the Israeli experience conclusively establishes that any authorization of physical pressure under the necessity defense inevitably and invariably leads to an inflation of its use and purported effectiveness—extensively if it is authorized a priori, but often even when it is allowed to be invoked ex post facto. An emergency measure, such as the "necessity" defense, Dershowitz argued, "is not suited to situations which recur over long periods of time" (Dershowitz 1989: 197). Ironically, Dershowitz justifies his "torture warrant" by the inflation of the necessity defense in Israel. During a visit to Israel in the late 1980s, he wrote, "I realized that the extraordinary rare situation of the hypothetical ticking bomb terrorist was serving as a moral, intellectual, and legal justification for a pervasive *system* of coercive interrogation, which, though not the paradigm of torture, certainly bordered on it" (ibid.) It is the systemic nature of this practice under the necessity justification that Dershowitz sought to limit, though not eliminate, by putting it under public accountability (Dershowitz 2002: 140–41).

But this inflationary process is not a circumvention of the Landau Commission's opinion; rather, it is enabled by it. The commission allowed room for this inflationary process in at least three ways: using a sliding scale of torture, ignoring the question of the effectiveness of torture, and putting its trust, as one would expect in a deeply divided society, unreservedly in the Jewish interrogators.

By replacing the absolute prohibition on torture with one based on distinction between degrees of physical pressure, the commission, in effect, contributed to the erosion of the law's restraining influence. Though the Convention against Torture, as its full name indicates, equally proscribes "cruel, inhuman, and degrading treatment," the Landau Commission, through a notional comparison of measures of pain, legalized the infliction of "moderate physical pressure," namely pressure on a level that purportedly would not deprive the suspect of his human dignity (LC 3.16, p. 61). Although such pressure might be more moderate than other methods of torture, it is not necessarily moderate in itself. The UN Committee against Torture, as well as studies by Human Rights Watch and on occasion on the basis of interrogators' own admissions, repeatedly reached the conclusion that a range of Israeli interrogation methods "constitute torture" as defined by the Convention against Torture (Human Rights Watch 1992, 1994, 1998). A case in point is Michael Koubi, the former chief interrogator for the GSS, a self-proclaimed master of the dark art of interrogation. Koubi claims that "only in rare instances did he use force to extract information from his subjects; in most cases it was not necessary" (Bowden 2003: 62). In fact, Koubi's own description of his methods demonstrates just the opposite. His success depended on preparing, that is softening, the subject properly through bringing him into interrogation "roughly handled, bound, hooded (a coarse, dirty smelly sack serves the purpose perfectly) and kept waiting in discomfort, perhaps naked in a cold, wet room, forced to stand or to sit in an uncomfortable position." All of this after having kept him "awake for days prior to questioning, isolated, and ill-fed" (ibid.: 63–64). During interrogation, Koubi would "slap [the suspect], knock him off the chair, set guards on him," as well as "have associates loudly stage a torture or beating session in the next room" (ibid.: 65). The binding directive of the commission which enumerated and regulated allowable forms of "moderate physical pressure" does not seem to have been overly effective.

The commission also inflated the incidence of permissible torture by not addressing the vexing question of the reliability of information obtained through physical pressure. Nor did its report, in spite of the requirement of Israeli penal law to examine necessity through the prism of proportionality, draw distinctions between different levels of dangers on the basis of their imminence and the concreteness of their threat (Feller 1989: 207). Consequently, any information that may be of service in the fight against terrorism could have fallen under the designation of necessity (Kremnitzer 1989: 231–34, 244). Nor did the commission draw the obvious conclusion as to the ineffectiveness of torture from the fact that nearly 50 percent of interrogations resulted in dismissal of charges or in no legal steps taken against suspects (Kremnitzer 1989: 257), although around 85 percent of suspects were tortured (B'Tselem 1998: 8).

Similarly, the forgiveness shown by the commission toward past actions of the GSS and the trust extended to its interrogators, in spite of the very reason for the committee's appointment—the false confession extracted from Nafsu, and commission's admission that it caught the GSS in sixteen years of lying—further eroded the latter's commitment to the rule of law (Kremnitzer 1989: 223, 252, 254). "Few things predict future torture," Darius Rejali concludes trenchantly, "as much as past impunity" (Rejali 2004b). The 1995 annual report of Miryam Ben-Porat, the state comptroller, based on an inspection of interrogation facilities between September 1991 and December 1992, concluded that the rules and restrictions the commission laid down were systematically ignored and that "even after the release of the Landau Commission Report, the habit of telling lies did not cease among GSS investigators."[14] Justice Landau himself admitted to feeling betrayed by the GSS's practice of regularly exceeding the constraints his commission sought to impose (Felner 2005: 39).

The Israeli experience is not unique. In his memoir, General Aussaresses, the unabashed apologist for French torture in Algeria, also went on to offer the classic scenario of the "ticking bomb" that has been used by so many others, including the Landau Commission and Dershowitz, to justify the torture of terror suspects. Notwithstanding the ritual invocation of this justification, no democratic political regime that authorized a policy of torture under the "necessity" provision has ever restricted its application to such cases.

As the analysis of the colonial examples demonstrates, torture is not a way of interrogating individual suspects but the paradigmatic act of waging war against both terrorism and resistance. Torture is the military strategy of counterterror and conveys the warring, occupying, colonizing power's thinking about the illegality of its enemy. The systematic execution in Algeria of terror suspects who "had directly participated in deadly attacks," but also those who were only "dangerous or thought to be so," and even those who had confessed, clearly indicates that the aim of French counterterror was not just the gathering of information (Aussaresses 2001: 119–23, 127). In Aussaresses' words, "summary executions were . . . an inseparable part of the tasks associated with keeping law and order. That was the reason why the army had been called in" (Aussaresses 2001: 127). Aussaresses rationalized that it was preferable to "neutralize" the prisoners once they were interrogated since charging them would have clogged the court system and allowed many to avoid any punishment (ibid.: 126). Nor did Aussaresses wish to stop his campaign after suppressing the FLN in Algiers: he intended to carry the battle into France and "neutralize" French intellectuals who were supportive of the FLN (ibid.: 152–156). Tragically, the license Aussaresses gave himself to stop at nothing in fighting terrorists, the ultimate illegitimate combatants, mirrors the ultimate rationalization of terrorists themselves who choose not to distinguish between combatants and civilians or distinguish between methods of war and, consequently, abandons the painfully accumulated legacy of warfare regulation.

Overall, then, the "ticking bomb" rationale, which lies at the heart of the "necessity" defense, does not act as a constraint on coercive interrogation but serves as a license that enables its widespread practice. It does so, above all, by violating liberal principles and liberal democracy; David Luban argues that in a "world of uncertainty and imperfect knowledge, the ticking bomb scenario should not form the point of reference" (Luban 2006: 46). To recap, the justification for torturing a terror suspect under this scenario requires the following confluence of conditions: "a firm assurance that the suspect is telling the truth, that his information is complete, that he will talk in time to diffuse the bomb and that there is no chance that the device will be reprogrammed or moved" (Gross 2004: 374). In fact, the more the interrogator knows in advance the less likely he will need to resort to physical pressure, and in the case of a true "ticking bomb" scenario he or she will have to have such an abundance of information, covering all the points mentioned above, that the resort to torture will not be necessary, let alone justified. When such justification is nevertheless invoked it amounts to an intellectual fraud, as its aim is the detachment of the practice of torture from its illiberal roots (Luban 2006: 36). In the United States in fact, in contrast to Israel, the necessity defense is not recognized by federal statutory law and has emerged only as a judicially created defense. Where it has been argued in court, it was never in case of pending violence nor was it ever successful (Luban 2006: 65–67).

In a renowned article from a quarter-century ago, Henry Shue asked whether, even in situations in which torture seems justified, its prohibition should be relaxed (Shue 1978: 143). His answer was an unequivocal "no." Shue held that great distance remains "between the situations which must be concocted in order to have a plausible case of morally permissible torture and the situations which actually occur" and that it should not be closed. If indeed, he added, anyone believes that he was justified in using torture, he "should be in roughly the same position as someone who commits civil disobedience." The torturer then has to defend himself in court, precisely because torture remains illegal (Shue 1978: 143). But there also exists a great distance between "morally justified" torture and civil disobedience. As Rejali explains, civil rights protesters break the law in full view of the public and are willing to have their day in court. Torturers, in contrast, operate in darkness and specialize in techniques that manipulate the body but leave no visible marks (Rejali 2004b: 4). If there were Israeli court cases of GSS investigators invoking the necessity defense, I am not aware of any.[15]

Finally, the "necessity" defense, especially where it is relied on extensively, is available to a host of claimants, not only to those engaged in civil rights disobedience or their purported equivalents. Dershowitz, for example, pointed out in the late 1980s when he was critical of the "necessity" defense and before he found his new zealotry, that had it existed in the United States, government officials such as Oliver North could have relied on it in justifying lying to Congress and President Nixon to excuse the Watergate break-in and its cover-up. More pertinently to our topic, Dershowitz also asked, "what if Palestinian rock-throwers raised the defense of necessity in defense of their 'honor and property?' Would the courts be forced to chose—on an entirely political basis—between conflicting claims?" (Dershowitz 1989: 198). Other political justifications, such as the controversial doctrine of preemptive war, also fall squarely under this defense. And, of course, in addition to their ideological and religious rationalizations, terrorists frequently invoke their relative weakness and the nature of asymmetric warfare as the "necessity" which drives them to disregard the Geneva Conventions. Moral and legal distinctions over the necessity defense are easy to blur. Indeed, Dershowitz's main criticism of the Landau Report in 1989 was that its justification of "physical pressure" was based on "a legal doctrine that is essentially lawless and undemocratic" (Dershowitz 1989: 200).

## CONCLUSION: THE ISRAELI MODEL

The Landau Commission's report issued on the eve of the first intifada (December 1987– November 1993) has "inadvertently" given license to interrogators to use "a list of humiliating and brutal coercive techniques" against thousands of suspected Palestinian terror suspects (Lelyveld 2005: 60). Some six years after the signing of the Oslo Declaration of Principles and Israeli withdrawal from Gaza and the West Bank towns, the threat posed by the PLO and Palestinian terror could no longer be defined as one against the "survival of Israel" (Gross 2001: 31), and the Supreme Court moved to make the Landau list illegal.[16] The Supreme Court in its decision boldly asserted that "although a democracy must fight with one hand tied behind its back, it nonetheless has the upper hand. Preserving the rule of law and recognition of an individual's liberty constitutes an important component in its understanding of security. At the end of the day, they strengthen its spirit and its strength and allow it to overcome its difficulties" (SC 15). Pursuant to this decision, Attorney General Elyakim Rubinstein carefully circumscribed the GSS's interrogation practices in an internal memo in which he explained that in the future "means of interrogation immediately necessary to yield vital information" cannot be used as a routine matter or be part of ongoing investigation to gather information about terrorist organizations. When such means were used, he stated his intention to weigh the threat's immediacy, concreteness, and gravity, alternatives available and the interrogator's state of mind, and the involvement and deliberations of upper echelons in each case separately. And the methods to be used are never to amount to "torture" as defined in the Convention against Torture (Israel, AGD, 1999: paragraph 7)

About a year after the Supreme Court's decision a second intifada broke out and has seen the extensive use of horrific suicide bombings in restaurants, discos, bus stations, shopping malls, festivities, and other locations by Hamas, Islamic Jihad, Fatah's al Aqsa Martyrs' Brigades and the Popular Front for the Liberation of Palestine. Whereas the first intifada was by and large nonviolent, Human Rights Watch's report on the second intifada concluded that "the scale and systematic nature of these attacks . . . meet the definition of a crime against humanity. When these suicide bombings take place in the context of violence that amounts to armed conflict, they are also war crimes" even when perpetrated on civilian settlers.[17] Even against the backdrop of such purposeful and indiscriminate attacks on Israeli civilians, the Supreme Court's decision and the Attorney General's legal opinion had a clear restraining impact. The GSS trained new interrogators, disciplines and monitors them, requires them to work in pairs, and videotapes interrogations. The low, tilted chairs used in the "Sabach" position were replaced with regular chairs; suffocating hoods with blackened goggles, the violent shaking methods with repeated shoving. No detained terror suspects died in custody. All the same, while legal constraints always matter a great deal, physical pressure had only been reduced by the Court decision, not eliminated.

Lisa Hajjar, one of the most astute participants in the torture debates in Israel and the United States, aptly captures the meaning of the Supreme Court decision: "A qualified victory in this struggle was achieved in September 1999, when the Israeli High Court finally rendered a decision against the commonplace use of state-sanctioned 'pressure' tactics, although this decision does not go so far as to close the widow of opportunity for continuing torture" (Hajjar 2000: 105). The decision in fact covers neither illtreatment during the predetention period when the suspects are in the hands of the military or the police, nor forms of "moderate physical pressure" not on the Landau Commission's list. The court also acceded to the infliction of "sleep deprivation" when it was not an end in itself but a side effect of the interrogation (SC 12). The Supreme Court, significantly, retained the ex post facto necessity defense for the use of physical pressure in the case of "ticking bombs" and, as the Landau Commission before it, allowed for its expansive use by defining the "imminence" of the threat to mean that "the danger is certain to materialize," "even if the bomb is set to explode in a few days or even in a few weeks" (SC 13). The Attorney

General's guidelines, following this ruling, also allowed for the "necessity" defense (Israel, AGD, 1999: paragraph 7).

In general, Itzhak Zamir, a former Israeli attorney general, laments that "it is particularly difficult in Israel to reach a suitable balance between the interest of national security and that of human rights. The special conditions which prevail here foster an extreme approach, which tends to assign absolute priority to national security above all other interests, and to disregard the need to strike a balance between them" (Zamir 1989: 377). Zamir reached this conclusion in 1989; but as Gad Barzilai noted, notwithstanding the economic, social, and legal liberalization of Israel in the 1980s and the 1993 Israel-PLO agreement, the Supreme Court continued to emphasize security considerations in its decisions in the 1990s as well (Barzilai 1998: 263).

The Court also chose a narrow legal basis for concluding that the prior authorization of specific practices was unlawful. It held that the executive branch alone could not adopt such a policy and that it had to be done, if it was to be done, by the legislature. At the same time, though the Court did not invoke the Basic Law: Human Dignity and Liberty as the grounds for its decision, it pointed out that legislation will have to, thus raising a high barrier to the passing of such a law (SC 15).[18] Parliamentary and governmental attempts to adopt such a law, significantly, came to naught (B'Tselem 2000).

Even in the wake of the Supreme Court decision, as documented in PCATI's April 2003 report, there exists ongoing ill-treatment of terror suspects and in some cases torture. Many of these took place during arrest and on the way to the GSS detention facility, such as tight shackling for many hours with hard-plastic disposable shackles that can be tightened but not loosened, detention in open air without food and provisions, beatings with riffle butts and slapping, and threats against relatives (PCATI 2003: 9). Though the number of terror suspects subjected to "special methods" declined from hundreds during the first intifada to dozens a year during the second, the use of such methods persists (Lelyveld 2005: 66). A major adverse outcome in the aftermath of the court's decision has been its unwillingness to hear subsequent petitions of terror suspects concerning incidents of torture. PCATI had submitted 124 petitions requesting permission for detainees to meet with their lawyers during the course of their interrogation, but the court accepted none (PCATI 2003: 8). In 2002, the GSS acknowledged that since the Supreme Court ruling 90 Palestinian terror suspects were defined as "ticking bombs" and subjected to physical pressure, though PCATI believes that the actual number might be higher.[19] The state prosecutor referred complaints to the GSS itself for investigation, and the latter had found none in which physical pressure was deemed unnecessary. Finally, though the attorney general, as we have seen, defined the applicability of the necessity defense very narrowly in his guidelines (Israel, AGD, 1999: paragraph 7) he granted his approval ex post facto for every single case in which physical pressure was used (PCATI 2003: 12).

On December 22, 2005, the U.S. Congress passed Senator John McCain's antitorture amendment, which requires that all U.S. personnel, whether military, CIA, or members of any other branch, not engage in cruel, inhuman, or degrading treatment of detainees. This was a significant victory, as was the Israeli Supreme Court decision which Senator McCain invoked, for those wishing to affirm the values guiding interrogation, rule of law, as well as international humanitarian law, the Convention against Torture, and customary international human rights legislation. But when President George W. Bush signed the bill on December 30, 2005, the White House issued a statement that asserted that "the executive branch shall construe [the law] in a manner consistent with the constitutional authority of the President to supervise the unitary executive branch as a Commander in Chief" and reiterated the same during the signing ceremony of the reauthorized Patriot Act on March 9, 2006.[20] This is the very same rationale and language used by the Justice Department's Office of Legal Council in 2001 and 2002 to reduce U.S. obligations under the Geneva Convention to those defined as "unlawful combatants." Since that legal limbo served as the license for Abu Ghraib and related cases of torture by U.S. personnel in the "war on terror," this presidential interpretation leaves one with deep doubts as to the implementation of the new law.

Particularly telling are the provisions of the October 17, 2006, Military Commissions Act, which authorized the president to establish military commissions to try unlawful enemy combatants. Suspects being tried by such commissions cannot invoke the Geneva Conventions as a source of rights during proceedings, or file habeas corpus petitions in federal court. The courts may allow hearsay evidence to be admitted during proceedings and makes U.S. interrogators subject to only a limited range of "grave breaches" of Common Article 3 of the Geneva Conventions.[21] These provisions are the very warning signs in democracies that have weakened their legal barriers to allow the use of physical pressure and stepped onto the path of torturing terror suspects. It seems obvious that neither the United States nor Israel has done away yet with torture in their battle against terrorism.

Israel cannot serve as a model for the successful but sparing use of "physical pressure" when "necessity" demands, as Bybee argued, since even in the wake of the Landau Commission's report it was used systematically and expansively. Nor can it serve as a model proving that judicial action, such as the Supreme Court's striking down in 1999 the practices permitted by the Landau Commission, will abolish torture, as Senator McCain hopes. Nor can other democracies engaged in antiterror campaigns in the context of war, military occupation, colonialism, and colonization in deeply divided societies provide such a model. Legislative and judicial remedies for prohibiting torture, cruel, inhumane, and degrading treatment have served as an important barrier to torture in Israel, the United States, the UK, and elsewhere where they were accompanied by vigilant enforcement. But as the case of Israel has shown, and the debate and the assertion of presidential authority foreshadows, under certain conditions their effect will remain limited. "There have been limited victories on limited terrain," as Stanley Cohen eloquently put it, since "law can be a shield if not a sword" (Cohen 1991: 28).

Alan Dershowitz's observation that torture is very likely to be used against terror suspects, and certainly in the "ticking bomb" case, rings true on the basis of the analysis above, but his suggestion that it be regulated by prior "torture warrants" to reduce its incidence is mistaken and misguided. Dershowitz, after all, never inquires as to the conditions under which terrorism flourishes. These are, as I have argued, the cumulative result of war, occupation, colonialism, and colonization; Israel is a model for the licensing of torture when these conditions persist. The French "special procedures," British "depth interrogations," American "stress and duress" techniques, and Israeli "moderate physical pressure" (Cohen 2005: 24–25; Massimino 2004: 74) were the offspring of some or all of these circumstances. Neither legislation, nor a priori "torture warrants" are likely to do away with torture since, as the record of the Landau Commissions' implementation demonstrates, "physical pressure" was used against 85 percent of Palestinian terror suspects, and even after the Supreme Court's restrictive ruling it continues to be employed. Though Dershowitz promised to reconsider his proposal on the basis of "empirical claims," he has not done so (Dershowitz 2004: 281). To render torture exceptional rather than systematic, let alone bring about its elimination and the upholding of international human rights law, requires facing the pernicious effects of war and occupation and, even more, colonialism and colonization.

# 7  Democracy, Civil Liberties, and Counterterrorist Measures in Spain

Salvador Martí, Pilar Domingo, and Pedro Ibarra

The chapter examines the evolution of counterterrorism legislation in Spain following its transition to democracy from two perspectives. We look at both the *formal legal framework* for and the *practice and discourse* of counterterrorism in terms of their compatibility with human rights and due process, and their impact on broader democratic values. We examine the development of formal aspects of antiterrorist legislation beginning in 1978, when Spain began its transition to democracy, and assess the extent to which they contradicted democratic commitments to civil liberties and due process. We also consider the practice of government and public authorities, which in some cases exceeded the formal legal framework, and the evolution of counterterrorist discourse in a young democracy.

In the course of the chapter we develop five main points. First, the Spanish democratic state inherited a terrorism problem from the Franco dictatorship in the form of ETA, the Basque nationalist movement. Spanish democracy from its inception thus had to develop counterterrorism legislation. However, because democracy was new to Spain and there was little history of liberal values and traditional liberal rights, in the early transition years the inevitable tension between civil liberties and the exigencies of counterterrorism did not feature prominently in public debate—and in fact has not done so until very recently.

Second, Spain's authoritarian legacy has never been fully addressed through a meaningful public reconstruction of Franco-era repression. This lack of public historical memory to some extent may account for later unlawful practices in the treatment of terrorist suspects that have been the object of domestic and international denunciation.[1] The most flagrant violation of state commitments to human rights and the principle of due process took the form of paramilitary action, with the Anti-Terrorist

Liberation Groups (Grupos Anti-Terroristas de Liberación; GAL) under the first government of the Spanish Socialist Workers' Party (Partido Socialista Obrero Español; PSOE) from 1982 to 1996.

Third, once the GAL scandal was brought to public attention and properly investigated, subsequent governments have been more careful to act within the law. Under the subsequent Partido Popular (PP) government (1996–2004) the strategy has been twofold: to toughen the laws on terrorist (and associated) activity, and to develop a rhetoric of radical political polarization by which all dissenting voices are discursively "criminalized." Nonetheless, it is important that government efforts were now directed toward acting *within* the law, albeit a tougher law.

Fourth, the new dramatic rhetorical tone attached to the PP's counterterrorist strategies, while not illegal as such, served to undermine democratic values of tolerance and freedom of association and expression. This has created a polarized political climate that has heightened tension around regional politics. More dramatically, the PP government effectively and deliberately politicized, for party and electoral purposes, the language and practice of counterterrorism. This strategy ultimately—and ironically—cost them the election of March 2004.

Finally, overall, and despite Spain's different democratic trajectory, a comparative glance at Spanish antiterrorist measures does not set Spain apart from the general trend among contemporary democracies described in this book. Nonetheless, public debate on the issue did not address the concerns of human rights incompatibilities in any significant way until recently, with the new PSOE government following the Madrid train bombings of March 11, 2004.

## RULE OF LAW, CIVIL LIBERTIES, AND COUNTERTERRORIST LEGISLATION UNDER A DEMOCRATIC REGIME

Rule of law refers to the structure of normative principles and institutional mechanisms that act to maximize the protection of civil rights. At one level, rule of law refers to the principle of limited political and public power according to a preestablished and broadly accepted constitutional contract; at another level, and as part of this limiting constitutional contract, it refers to the set of rights and obligations that defines the relationship between state and society (and between members of that society). Rule of law, then, is predominantly about limited government, but specifically with a view to protecting individual rights.

The modern liberal democratic state, however, is also called upon to protect its citizens and their rights from other individuals engaging in any activity that limits or constrains these rights and liberties. The criminal justice system, with its punitive measures which effectively act to restrict the freedoms of those found guilty of criminal acts, has traditionally been justified on these grounds. However, under democratic rule some minimum guarantees of due process and respect for the basic human rights of the accused form part of the normative texture that regulates criminal justice procedures. These can be judged in part according to internationally set standards, and overall there is a sense of some minimum normative consensus regarding what is considered appropriate state action. Of course, notions of good practice in terms of due process have changed over time.

In liberal democracies, terrorism has come to be considered a "special" type of crime that affects a state's national security concerns. As such, it is often the justification for hardening criminal justice procedures. Indeed, it reasonably can be argued that democratic states legitimately can develop special laws to deal with terrorism. The question is whether terrorism warrants such severity of state action that due process and minimum guarantees toward suspects can be legitimately compromised.

Not only are democratic regimes entitled to engage in effective counterterrorist measures, they are compelled to do so under their obligation to ensure minimum levels of law and order to protect their citizens. However, to relinquish the primacy of democratic values around civil liberties is to concede victory to terrorist activity. Contemporary notions of liberal democracy are morally premised on abiding by minimum standards of due process and respect for the rights of *all* individuals—including suspected and convicted terrorists. In this sense, the second half of the twentieth century saw the normative consolidation of a universal human rights regime as a moral standard by which to judge state action. This standard has acquired an unprecedented level of global acceptance, at least on paper if not in practice, and the legitimacy of democratic regimes is now measured to a large extent on its terms. However, in recent times we are also witnessing what could constitute a shift in the boundaries between this moral standard and a widening parallel discourse of counterterrorist practices that are justified in the language of national and public security—even to the point of putting at risk historical gains in civil liberties.

The Spanish case presents a young democracy at pains to overcome a recent authoritarian past which has manifested itself in state response to terrorism. The laws have changed over time, and so have the practices and rhetoric of counterterrorism—not always in tandem, and not always abiding by democratic values or principles of due process and human rights.

These changes have been neither unidirectional nor necessarily progressive in terms of democratic consolidation. Thus, the Spanish example illustrates the complexity of the relationship between counterterrorism and the democratic process.

In considering the Spanish case it is useful to distinguish among three types of counterterrorist strategies. First, there are outright violations of principles of human rights and due process. Second, there are measures that can be considered "hard-line" in terms of cracking down on terrorist activity—such as lengthening prison sentences for certain types of crimes, isolating terrorist suspects and convicts from other members of the targeted organization, and cracking down on financial operations—but which strictly speaking do not breach core principles of due process. These have the strategic objective of weakening the organizational capacity of terrorist groups. And third, there are measures aimed at weakening the political presence or capacity of the terrorist group through banning the activities of groups or political parties found to be supportive of the use of illegitimate violence. This has a long-standing tradition in the form of political party laws that ban political organizations that support violent or undemocratic practice (such as Nazi parties). It is not the object of this chapter to discuss in depth the merits or effectiveness of these measures in reducing terrorist activity. But these categories are useful for understanding the different legal measures that have evolved in Spain since the transition to democracy.

We also distinguish between the *legal* dimension and those aspects that have to do with the *rhetoric* and the *practice* of counterterrorism. All three dimensions may have varying levels of compatibility with democratic values and human rights. Moreover, they may be in contradiction with one another:

- The law itself either may violate principles of due process and human rights, or may provide sufficient loopholes for public authorities to resort to discretionary practices not in keeping with democratic values and civil liberties.

- The law may fall generally within the remit of accepted human rights principles and notions of due process, but the practice of counterterrorism measures (e.g., in the treatment of prisoners) may violate aspects of due process, or take advantage of lacunae in the law that allow for discretionary practices, or may involve outright violations of due process.

- State actors may demonstrate outright disregard for the law, as was witnessed in Spain with the state's recourse to GAL paramilitary activity during the 1980s.

- In some cases, the state response may exceed its original mandate and become politicized (e.g., in the use of counterterrorist rhetoric), in some cases very evidently for electoral purposes. A clear example of this, as we shall see, was the PP government's manipulation of the fight against ETA.

- In a related development, counterterrorist discourse can reach proportions that exceed not only the mandate but also the objective of fighting the targeted terrorist group. Thus, this slippery slope, unless checked, can result in the discursive "criminalization" of other social groups by association—an association stressed and even invented in popular counterterrorist discourse. Again, in the case of ETA the PP government promoted a political language in which all expressions of regional nationalism (as well as antiglobalization and other "undesirable" activities) were implicated with terrorist activity in a monstrous distortion of reality. The complicity invented by this discourse contributes to undermining, if not civil liberties directly, then certainly more broadly democratic values of tolerance, freedom of expression, and association.

## TERRORIST ACTIVITY IN SPAIN

Spain has experienced three forms of terrorism. First, there is the Basque separatist group ETA, which was born during the Franco dictatorship and has been responsible for most terrorist activity since the 1970s. The second type of terrorist activity has come from extreme right-wing groups. The third type of terrorism left its mark on March 11, 2004, when a series of bombs exploded at the Atocha train station in Madrid, an act for which an al Qaeda affiliate claimed responsibility.

### ETA and the Basque Question

ETA (Euskadi ta Askatasuna) represents the most radical expression of Basque separatism and justifies the use of armed violence to achieve its ends. The Basque question is over a century old. It revolves around the claim by a sector of the Basque population that the Basque country is a nation and should be granted autonomy (here there is no consensus within the Basque population on the degree of autonomy or, indeed, complete separation from the Spanish state).[2] From 1959 the nationalist claim took on a violent expression through ETA's activities, which were inspired somewhat by urban guerrilla movements in Latin America. ETA initially acted against members of the Spanish state. Over the years it has become increasingly indiscriminate with regard to its victims. In the last four decades, according to official statistics, ETA has killed 831 people, kidnapped 70, and injured 2,392 (Human Rights Watch [henceforth HRW] 2005b: 14).

With the return to democracy in 1978, the conflict in the Basque country took on a new dimension. First, the Estatuto de Autonomía of 1979 (the decentralization law LO 3/1979) gave the region a considerable degree of self-government. Second, from 1980 on, the Basque country has been governed by different coalitions of Basque nationalist parties (PNV, Partido Nacionalista Vasco, and EA, Eusko Alkartasuna). For its part, ETA has rejected the form of regional self-government that came about with democratization, and has continued in the use of violence, even increasing the number of casualties per year.

At the same time, in 1980 Batasuna (Unity) emerged as a radical nationalist political party which justified ETA's use of violence, and which has achieved regional electoral support of 9–14 percent. By contrast, approximately 60 percent of the Basque electorate supports Basque nationalist parties (including Batasuna). The other 40 percent vote for the main Spanish political parties (mainly PSOE and PP).

The Spanish government response to terrorism has varied over time. Under Franco, authoritarian methods with total disregard for due process and rights were the norm. Following the transition to democracy a series of laws has been passed, mostly within the body of criminal justice legislation, which amount to an accumulative process of antiterrorist legal measures (outlined in the next section). In parallel form, the informal practice and discourse of counterterrorism has changed over time—not necessarily in the direction of strengthening due process and democratic values. Finally, the international context has also changed; in particular, slowly growing collaborative police efforts with France to suppress ETA across the border. The continued presence of ETA, and its capacity to carry out attacks, attests to the relatively ineffective nature of the state response. At the same time, the intensity and deadliness of ETA's attacks have also varied over time due to a complex combination of internal, state, and international factors.

## Extreme Right-Wing Terrorist Activity

Activity by extreme right-wing terrorist groups was concentrated mostly in the transition period, although incidents occurred as late as 1989. This form of terrorism was rooted in the latter years of the Franco dictatorship and manifested itself in groups linked to some political actors associated with the regime (such as erstwhile police officers) and even members of the public administration, some of whom engaged in paramilitary activity.[3] These groups began to operate in the 1970s and early 1980s, operating under various names, such as the Anti-Communist Apostolic Alliance (Alianza Apostólica Anticomunista; AAA or "Triple A"), Antiterrorismo ETA (ATE), the Armed Spanish Groups (Grupos Armados Españoles; GAE), the Warriors of Christ the King (Guerrilleros de Cristo Rey), the Spanish Basque Batallion (Batallón Vasco Español; BVE), and an assortment of smaller groups. The actions of these groups, which have not been the object of much public discussion, included approximately forty murders, notably the massacre of trade union lawyers in 1977 (the "Atocha killings"), and the deaths of various active and ex-ETA militants, as well as a number of civilians with no political links.

As democracy began to become consolidated, and after a failed coup attempt on February 23, 1981, these groups began to dwindle. It is believed that some of their members would participate in the paramilitary activities of the GAL.

Recently the Spanish high court (the Audiencia Nacional) ordered reparations to be paid to family members of a victim of the group Guerrilleros de Cristo Rey under antiterrorist legislation (*El País*, January 24, 2006). This and other recent judicial decisions marks a new trend in terms of a more overt public acknowledgement of the terrorist nature of acts committed by an assortment of extreme right-wing groups since the transition to democracy.

## March 11, 2004, and the Atocha Bombs

The al Qaeda–linked bombings in Madrid on March 11, 2004, took place three days before a general election. The Partido Popular under the leadership of Prime Minister José María Aznar had brought Spain into the war on Iraq as an ally of the United States (although with limited military involvement) against majority public opinion. Nonetheless, at the time of the election the polls showed the PP to be in the lead, following eight years of government since 1996. On March 11 bombs exploded in Madrid's Atocha train station, killing almost 200 people. By the second day of investigations, it became evident that the bomb attacks were the work of Islamic fundamentalists, and not ETA as the government had insisted. This had an immediate impact on the election. The PP's aggressive discourse against regional nationalism—including all forms of Basque nationalism—had become an important point in the electoral campaign, contributing to a polarization of the Spanish political scene along regional cleavages. More significantly, during the three days following the Madrid bombings the government deliberately attempted to mislead the public (and also the international community) by insisting upon ETA's responsibility. Time ran out for the government amid accumulating police evidence implicating an Islamic group, evidence that could not be kept from public knowledge. The perceived intention to mislead the electorate led to public indignation, causing electoral defeat for the PP, which ironically had presented itself as the hard-line antiterrorist champion, both domestically and internationally (Woodworth 2004; Sampedro 2005). Aznar's government was also chastized from abroad.

## THE EVOLUTION OF COUNTERTERRORISM MEASURES

Given Spain's authoritarian legacy and its long-standing threat, the construction of the rule of law was inevitably compromised from its inception. The Franco regime did not develop the kind of special emergency legislation that emerged in other European countries as a response to the social unrest and terrorist activity of the 1960s and 1970s. Germany and Italy faced a relatively short-lived experience of terrorist activity and applied a variety of punitive and emergency measures (Silveira 1998: 90). The UK, facing its own long-standing threat from the IRA, developed its own state response. These are all cases of democratic systems looking for ways to combat terrorism through measures of exception (Chapters 4, 5, and 9 in this volume discuss these cases in detail).

By contrast, the Franco dictatorship (itself born of a coup d'etat against a democratic government and following three years of civil war) was an authoritarian regime founded on the arbitrary and systematic elimination of all political opposition, and with no concern for civil liberties.[4] With the emergence of ETA in the late 1950s, authoritarian methods of counterterrorism with total disregard for civil liberties were the norm. The transition to democracy occurred without a concomitant process of transitional justice, of truth-telling regarding the human rights abuses of the past. This has perhaps indirectly perpetuated patterns of security-force impunity that would continue into the 1990s.

This history, combined with a weak presence of liberal values regarding civil rights, explains the absence of any substantive public debate on the degree of compatibility of some aspects of antiterrorist legislation with civil liberties and democratic commitments. The political left showed little interest in promoting public discussion on the issue until the eruption of the GAL scandal in the 1990s. A more forceful political discussion has only really emerged in the wake of the Atocha bombings, in the context of a wider international debate on counterterrorism practices in the post-9/11 environment, especially in the United States. By observing events elsewhere, Spain has only recently begun to examine its own history of counterterrorism (of which more below).[5]

## From the Transition to Democracy to the End of the First PSOE Government: 1978–1996

Indeed, Spain did not develop specific antiterrorist laws; rather, such measures were incorporated into the criminal justice procedures that were reformed during the late 1970s and 1980s under the governments of the Unión de Centro Democrático (UCD; 1978–82), and the first PSOE government (1982–96). Nor did the transitional government draft emergency measures. Rather, its measures were incorporated into various laws and decrees after 1978, mostly within the body of law dealing with criminal justice (Serrano-Piedecasas 1988). As mentioned earlier, under Franco no laws had been drafted for this purpose[6].

The starting point the development of counterterrorist measures was the reform of the criminal code (Código Penal), and the code of criminal procedures (Ley de Enjuiciamiento Criminal). Thus began an accumulation of legislative acts that would constitute a growing body of counterterrorism law. The Spanish constitution also established the framework for the development of antiterrorist legislation in its article 55.2, by which

> [a]n organic law may determine the manner and the circumstances in
> which, on an individual basis and with the necessary participation of the
> Courts and proper Parliamentary control, the rights recognized in
> Articles 17, clause 2 [preventive detention], and 18, clauses 2 [inviolabil-
> ity of the home] and 3 [secrecy of communication], may be suspended
> as regards specific persons in connection with investigations of the
> activities of armed bands or terrorist groups.

Table 7.1 gives a chronological list of the relevant pieces of antiterrorist legislation introduced between 1977 and 1996. As a consequence of this legislation and its implementation with regard to ETA terrorism, Spain has been the object of some scrutiny by international human rights organizations (notably Human Rights Watch and Amnesty International), as well as some public international human rights bodies, for reported instances of human rights violations and for loopholes that allow for discretionary practices and the (informal) disregard for principles of due process.

This body of legislation involves several problematic issues. First, the question of incommunicado detention: its duration, insufficient levels of judicial supervision, limitations on the right to counsel, shortcomings

TABLE 7.1 Development of Counterterrorist Legislation in Spain, 1977–1996

| Name | Date | Description |
| --- | --- | --- |
| *Foundations of antiterrorist measures in the criminal justice system* | | |
| Real Decreto Ley 1/77, 3/77 | January 4, 1977 | Creates high court (Audiencia Nacional), which has jurisdiction on terrorist activity, displacing the Franco tribunal of public order (Tribunal de Orden Público). |
| Ley orgánica (LO) 11/80 | December 1, 1980 | Limits the principle of presumption of innocence and the right to *juicio ordinario* recognized in Constitution art. 24.4. |
| *Conditions of detention* | | |
| LO 14/83 | December 12, 1983 | Art. 527 establishes that terrorist suspects held incommunicado have the right to legal counsel, but not to a lawyer of their choice, and cannot notify relatives or a third person of their arrest. |
| LO 6/84 | May 24, 1984 | Limits habeas corpus. A judge may authorize incommunicado detention in cases of suspected terrorist activity. |
| LO 4/88 | May 25, 1988 | Art. 520 bis allows for incommunicado detention to be extended to five days. |
| *New types of criminal acts* | | |
| LO 10/95 | November 23, 1995 | Introduces "individual terrorist"; suspect need not belong to an armed group. Introduces prison sentence for "collaboration," including "any suspected form of cooperation" Introduces criminal act of expressing support for terrorist activity. |

regarding the right to medical examination, and the serious implications of secret legal proceedings for due process (HRW 2005b). These concerns deal directly with the leeway provided for disregarding due process.[7] The mere fact of incommunicado detention provides the opportunity for human rights abuses. There are also concerns about a lack of will to carry out investigations on reported abuses and incidents of torture.

The UN Committee against Torture, in its report *Conclusions and Recommendations of the Committee against Torture* of December 2002, invited the Spanish government to consider preventive measures in cases where terrorist suspects are held incommunicado (such as video recordings during police interrogation, or examinations by the forensic doctor and a doctor known by the suspect). The UN Special Rapporteur's 2003 report held that incidents of torture were probably sporadic and incidental, but it was nonetheless a risk given the nature of the conditions of incommunicado detention, and recommended that the government draw up a plan to eliminate all risks of torture. The last report by the Council of Europe's Committee on the Prevention of Torture, from a visit carried out in July 2001, expressed concern regarding the lack of interest on the part of Spanish authorities to carry out its recommendations concerning due process guarantees for suspects held incommunicado, and reported abuses denounced by Basque prisoners (OVDH, 2003: 7). In the same tone, reports by Amnesty International in 2003 and 2004 denounced the reluctance to carry out proper investigations in suspected cases of torture (Ubasart, 2005).

Additional concerns involve measures that are less problematic in terms of human rights violations but are objects of some protest. One example is the dispersal of ETA prisoners, by which they are removed from their place of origin and kept separate from members of the same organization who are also imprisoned.[8] The arguments for this practice are that resocialization is hampered by concentrating members of the same organization, and that ETA's organizational capacity can be undermined by weakening communication among convicted members (HRW 2005b). The practice does impose an additional penalty on the detainees and adds to the visiting costs of family and friends. Those burdens are relatively benign, however, insofar as they do not obstruct due process and are arguably justifiable from a strategic perspective.

While the legislation provides some loopholes that allow for the disregard of due process, the most alarming aspect of Spain's response to terrorism during this period was the existence of a "dirty war" in which the state engaged in paramilitary action (or state terrorism) against ETA through the GAL. This only served ETA's cause of appearing as the victim of a repressive state, and was contrary to basic notions of the rule of law, due process, and human rights.

GAL was a paramilitary organization financed by the state, protected by the ministry of the interior, and created by public functionaries. It was not the first example of "dirty war" tactics against ETA by Spain. The last years of the Franco dictatorship and early years of the transition saw similar paramilitary activity and a permissive attitude toward some extreme right-wing terrorist groups (such as Triple A, BVE, ATE, and the Comandos Anti-Marxistas). As mentioned earlier, much of this activity petered out after 1981 (Cerdán and Rubio 1997; Woodworth 2004).

GAL concentrated its activities in Spain's Basque country (and in the French Basque region), which took the form of kidnappings and disappearances, torture, and financial crimes. The first crime that came to light was the killing of Joxe Antonio Lasa and Jose Ignacio Zabala in 1983 (they had been kidnapped, tortured, and subsequently murdered and buried in Alicante). GAL was active until 1987. Twenty-three people were murdered at their hands, in addition to many more victims of threats and intimidation. As became evident in the subsequent trials, GAL's activities were carried out by French mercenaries contracted by members of the Spanish police, and received financial support from special funds of the ministry of the interior. Much of this was coordinated by public functionaries involved in counterterrorism.

Throughout the early 1990s, the GAL question became the object of judicial investigation and political scandal. High public officials were convicted, including Minister of the Interior Jose Barrionuevo, Director of Public Security Rafael Vera,[9] Ricardo Garcia Damborenea (the PSOE general secretary in Vizcaya), Franciso Alavarez (the head of the counterterrorism unit), Miguel Planchuelo (the head of the information brigade in Bilbao), Jose Amedo (a police officer), and Julian Sancristóbal (a police officer). It seems that Spanish justice fell somewhat short of pressing further the links between the GAL and other echelons of the PSOE government. Indeed, the PSOE initially denied all knowledge of, or connection with, the GAL case, and publicly condemned their crimes. PSOE President Felipe Gonzalez, however, never allowed a full investigation to take place regarding the use of special funds. The PP government under Aznar subsequently pardoned most of the high public officials who had been found guilty.

The scale of disregard for human rights principles and the rule of law evidenced by the state's complicity with GAL was a damning indictment of Spanish democracy. That it was possible reflects, first, a legacy of impunity, in which all means are justified in terms of state action in the war against "enemies" of the state. The GAL episode was a grisly reminder of the fragility of democratic values within the establishment, and certainly within the security forces. Second, it might also have been a consequence of the leeway conceded to the security forces by the newly inaugurated and possibly uncertain PSOE government in 1982—especially in the wake of the 1981 coup attempt, in which Congress was occupied by security forces—and at a time when democratic consolidation was still an aspiration and not a certainty (Woodworth 2002, 2004).

In any event, GAL's activities went well beyond what the law and constitution permitted in terms of state response to terrorism. The first lesson learned from the GAL experience by the entire political class was that that acting outside of the law is politically very costly (the scandal surrounding the GAL contributed in no small measure to the electoral defeat of the PSOE in 1996). The scandal was also a profound lesson in democracy in terms of making evident that the illegal and illegitimate practice of state-sponsored paramilitary activity and terror tactics are neither compatible with nor acceptable under democratic rule. Moreover, they are punishable crimes. It is significant that investigations took place and convictions were carried out. There is no doubt that the GAL scandal had an impact on the *practice* of state responses to terrorist activity, and also on the *discourse* of counterterrorism. The PP learned the lesson, and subsequently chose the path of acting "within the law, but with the full force of the law," including toughening up antiterrorist legislation.

## The Partido Popular and the Escalation of Discourse

The government of the Partido Popular can be divided into two periods. During the first legislature (1996–2000), the PP appeared to act with some caution and restraint. Laws were passed to toughen up antiterrorist measures. At first, though, the *discourse* of counterterrorism was one that emphasized political alliances outside the PP, mostly (if ironically) with moderate nationalist groups in Catalonia and the Basque country. The PP initially needed the support of the regional nationalist parties, but by the end of the first legislature, the relation between the central government and the regional nationalists (not only in the Basque country) was beginning to shift toward a polarization that would escalate dramatically in the second legislature (2000–2004), when the PP governed with an absolute majority of parliamentary seats and was thus no longer dependent on the restraining presence of the regional parties.

The PP also adopted a different style of counterterrorism strategy from the first PSOE administration. On the one hand, the PP toughened the law on acts of terrorism—and overall acted within the law. But it also took on an entire new *rhetoric* by which suspected subversive or associated activities or opinions became "criminalized"—even beyond the letter of the law. This dramatic change in discourse, which gathered momentum especially in the second PP legislature, became part of a new political and electoral strategy. To some extent, then, an almost symbiotic relationship seemed to develop between ETA and the PP, thus also breathing new life into the more radical strands of Basque nationalism.

The relationship between the central government and the Basque region thus evolved as follows. Attempts to bring all parties to the negotiation table had failed in 1999. For their part, the Basque nationalist parties and social groups and the MLNV (Movement for the Liberation of Basque Nationalism, headed by Batasuna) met in the Navarra town of Lizarra (Estella).[10] The meeting led to the establishment of a common front committed to bringing the central government to the negotiating table to advance toward Basque political self-determination. In September 1999 ETA announced a unilateral cease-fire. Faced for the first time in the post-Franco era with a united Basque nationalist front, the state reacted in the most negative terms. The ruling directorate of Batasuna was imprisoned on the charge of publicizing ETA's demands and thus collaborating with a criminal organization, following the passage in 2002 of a law outlawing certain political parties (discussed below).

The die was cast for a polarization of the Basque question. When a degree of pressure began to build within Spanish public opinion favoring some kind of talks, the government agreed to meet ETA members in Switzerland in 1999. The meeting took place, but shortly after, ETA's negotiators were arrested in France and deported to Spain. Six months later, ETA rescinded its cease-fire. The renewed killings quickly provoked a profound crisis within the Basque political system. On the one hand, after more than a year of peace, the vast majority of Basques were simply unwilling to accept a reversion to the status quo ante. ETA and its supporters, therefore, became even more marginalized within Basque society than had been the case during their waning popularity in the 1990s. On the other hand, the government embarked on an aggressive campaign not only against ETA but against all expressions of regional nationalism.[11] At this point, the PP became further emboldened by its majority control of Parliament following the 2000 election, pushing even further its aggressive rhetoric against expressions of regional nationalism.

In a parallel process, from 2003 the Basque nationalist party PNV embarked on a more radical rhetoric of self-government. This was ultimately manifested in the Ibarretxe Plan, which outlined a radically new relationship between the Basque country and the central government, pushing beyond the project for Basque independence in association with the Spanish state. The project was taken by the PP as an affront to the unity of the Spanish state, and although it was approved in the Basque Parliament, it was subsequently rejected by the Spanish Parliament under the PSOE government.

The counterterrorism laws described earlier were hardened considerably under the two successive PP legislatures. Throughout this period we can see, on the one hand, the introduction of a series of measures that toughened criminal procedures for suspected and convicted terrorists, and, on the other, the establishment of a political discourse by which protest politics and perceived dissidence or unconventional politics of any kind would be criminalized. To some extent the latter phenomenon expressed the return of a reactionary culture rooted in the Francoist authoritarian tradition (*franquismo sociológico*), which has resonance in a significant sector of society. In this regard, and in line with neoconservative ideology, there is a hardening of antiterrorist discourse in terms of greater social control, perceiving as enemies of the nation not only suspects of terrorism but also forms of political dissidence or opposition.

Thus the PP undertook a new legislative direction with the following elements: First, it introduced tougher sentencing for terrorism-related crimes. LO 7/2003 of June 30, 2002, increases the maximum prison sentence through accumulated crimes to forty years. Second, it made a stronger demarcation in sentencing between common criminal-justice cases and terrorist cases (regarding, for example, leniency and parole conditions). Third, it altered conditions of detention. LO 13/2003 of October 24, 2003, extends incommunicado detention to thirteen days, but does allow for the suspect to have a second forensic medical examination to be appointed by the judge (article 510.4). Fourth, a political party law was passed that made Batasuna illegal (LO 6/2002).

Finally, there seems to have been some level of politicization in certain judicial investigations. The most evident example was the 18/98 Sumario, which is still ongoing at the time of writing. This case seeks to criminalize some Basque civil-society organizations that are close to radical expressions of regional nationalism. The justification is that these organizations are creations of ETA or are sufficiently close to its objectives and members to be considered dangerous (ODHPV 2005). This is problematic for due process in that it casts suspicion of guilt simply by virtue of one's sharing certain political objectives with a terrorist organization. As of this writing, around 250 people have been charged, and search warrants have been issued for the offices of a number of mass-media centers in the Basque country. This has effectively criminalized a broad network of loosely connected social, cultural, and media associations, merely on the basis of their suspected connection or complicity with ETA.

In this polarization of the political discourse, all expressions of radical politics were included in the category of potential enemy of Spain. This included antiglobalization groups and other critical movements. The logic is very simple: radical political groups are natural allies of ETA because radicalism is also a constitutive element of the terrorist organization. This line of thought became more evident following 9/11 (Calle 2005: 155–70). Thus began a process of placing all kinds of perceived undesirables under the umbrella of "criminal." This has been detrimental to the consolidation of democratic values in what is still a relatively young democracy. Moreover, specifically in terms of the PP's political strategies, it led to an irresponsible politicization of antiterrorist discourse for electoral purposes.

However, this rhetoric of reaction (Hirschman 1991) had a boomerang effect. From this dynamic emerged one of the most important cycles of protest politics in the history of democratic Spain, which has taken the form of a series of huge peaceful demonstrations since the year 2000. These included antiglobalization demonstrations, pro-environment protests and the mobilization of the antiwar movement. It was in this context that the March 11, 2004, bombings by al Qaeda affiliates took place, and the PP's desperate attempts to establish links with ETA. The government ultimately offered no effective response to the bombings other than to deny the mounting evidence regarding al Qaeda involvement and to seek to trivialize popular sentiment and mobilization in protest of the government's politicized handling of the situation.

## The New PSOE Government, International Terrorism, and the "End" of ETA

The election of 2005 brought Jose Luis Rodriguez Zapatero, the PSOE candidate, into government, along with a new tone on antiterrorist policy. First, popular sentiment, in contrast to the United States following 9/11, did not express support for tougher measures or hard-line politics, but rather expressed a sense of relief following the immediate decision to withdraw Spanish troops from Iraq. Spanish involvement in Iraq was perceived as having been a contributory factor in heightening the risk of related terrorist attacks in Spain. Thus, Zapatero's more placatory rhetoric about constructing an "alliance of civilizations" was in direct contrast to the PP's alliance with the U.S. and UK's more aggressive foreign policy. At the same time, though, the new form of terrorist activity has unleashed new security measures, which have affected Spain's Muslim community. These include the regulation of Islamic mosques and the possibility of expulsion of foreign terrorist suspects (HRW 2005b: 8–9).

As regards existing antiterrorist legislation, there has been no significant change in the law. Indeed, hard-line sentencing has continued, as has the general application of criminal justice procedures (generally in accordance with the principle of due process). By contrast, there has been a change in the discourse of antiterrorism. The Zapatero government has sought to depoliticize the issue (in a partisan sense) and leave the matter in the hands of the police and the judiciary. At the same time, the government has built political bridges with the regional nationalist parties in the Basque country, Catalonia, and Galicia, in an endeavor to renegotiate relations between the central government and the regions, including the establishment of a new federal pact.

The change in political climate toward more conciliatory language has also created a more propitious environment for a new stage in the evolution of the ETA question. Meanwhile, ETA has been weakened in its operational structure and has decreasing popular support among the Basque population. All this has combined in a complex way to create the context for a declaration of a "permanent cease-fire" by ETA in spring 2006 (interestingly, using the very same terminology as did the IRA in 1994, preceding the Good Friday Agreement of 1998) (*El País*, March 20, 2006) The cease-fire seems to be the most promising move yet in the direction of a long-term solution to the problem. However, even in the best of scenarios, the definitive dismantling of ETA is likely to be a lengthy, complicated, and arduous process. In August 2006 official talks between the government and ETA were initiated in order to take the first steps toward a final peace settlement. For now the ETA cease-fire has made possible a process of political negotiations with the parties of the Basque country with a view to establishing a new framework of self-government. Overall, though, the process is beset by a number of obstacles. First, Batasuna's continuing "illegality" rules it out as a valid interlocutor in negotiations with other political parties. Second, the government is at pains to ensure that it does not appear to be entering a negotiation process that is from the outset "conditioned" by ETA (which, although no longer active, is still potentially threatening). In this regard, the unrelenting opposition by the PP to the possibility of a peace process is an added difficulty.

It is too soon to tell what the outcome of these events will be. It does appear that certain key factors have contributed to ETA's decision to seek a way out. First, the more effective police action in terms of dismantling ETA operations seems to have weakened the organization's logistical capacity. This has been aided by better collaborative relations with France in terms of antiterrorism police work. Third, the Irish peace process has become a point of reference for the Basque question. Finally, a new (and renewed) PSOE government, now distanced from the GAL episode, seems to create a more favorable context for negotiation than seemed possible under the Partido Popular. Zapatero's attitude in particular has been much more conciliatory toward demands for greater decentralization than was the Aznar government.

In any event, a serious public discussion has begun for the first time of the relationship between counterterrorism and democracy, with reference to principles of due process and civil liberties.[12] This is important for Spain's internal process of democratic consolidation. It is also related to events and normative debates at the international level, in the context of Abu Ghraib and Guantanamo, and CIA rendition flights in Europe with the complicity of EU member governments.

The Spanish case is instructive on various levels. First, it indicates the perils of "elite" pacted transitions. These carry the risk of leaving untouched the structures and habits of impunity within the public authorities, and in the use of force to the detriment of principles of due process and human rights. Moreover, it means that weak democratic values prevail.

Second, there are lessons to be learned regarding the importance of introducing measures of accountability and control over criminal justice procedures. Legal loopholes in criminal justice procedures became the Achilles heel of Spain's antiterrorist strategy. Moreover, the resort to "dirty" practices has had the boomerang effect of weakening the government's moral authority and boosting terrorist groups' sense of victimization. At the same time, there has been a learning process by which successive governments have learned that it is better to act within the law than outside it. The response, then, has been to toughen antiterrorist legislation. In the main, Spain thus has not deviated considerably from accepted international standards, except for some loopholes regarding conditions of detention. In recent times, the more problematic issue in terms of democratic values has been the hardening of antiterrorist rhetoric and the politicization of counterterrorism.

Third, the Spanish case points to the importance of democratic governments' paying attention to the symbolic and discursive dimension. Counterterrorism measures are best kept out of partisan politics, in order that all democratic forces can keep a common front against terrorist activity.

It is of interest that as Spain appears finally to face the possibility of the end of internal terrorist activity, it now confronts the perils of a new type of transnational terrorism, which creates a new set of challenges and questions about antiterrorist policies. At the same time, Spain's history and development create the potential for Spain to serve as a model for other similarly threatened liberal democracies. As Spain's prosecutor of ETA and Pinochet, Baltasar Garzon, critiqued U.S. counterterror tactics at an international conference: "I come from the country of the Inquisition . . . we had to learn from experience that torture, and mistreatment and degradation, do not work."[13]

# 8 Canada's Balancing Act

*Protecting Human Rights and Countering Terrorist Threats*

Howard Adelman



Before their political defeat by the Conservative Party of Canada, the Honourable Anne McLellan, deputy prime minister and minister of public safety and emergency preparedness, and the Honourable Irwin Cotler, minister of justice in the previous Paul Martin Liberal government, in their joint statement to the Special Senate Committee reexamining the Anti-Terrorist Act (ATA) in November 2005, claimed that "Canada is not immune from the threat of terrorism. We are a target."[1] Canada has never been directly attacked by *foreign* terrorists, though in a taped message released on November 12, 2002, Osama bin Laden explicitly named Canada as a target (C, *Securing*, 2004: 7). Canada had been used by terrorists for operational planning, reconnaissance, fund-raising, lobbying, and as a staging base for activities elsewhere.[2] On June 2, 2006, seventeen young Canadian Muslims were arrested as terrorist suspects. Some were charged with collecting ammonium nitrate fertilizer in a plot to create truck bombs to destroy the Toronto Stock Exchange, the offices of the Canadian Broadcasting Corporation, and CSIS, the Canadian Security Intelligence Service. Five were simply charged with belonging to a terrorist organization and attending a terrorist training camp but did not face weapons or explosive charges. Canada had become a direct target of radical Islamic terrorists.

Canada previously has been attacked by *domestic* terrorists. In the 1960s, Québec experienced a spate of terrorist bombings and kidnappings by members of the radical separatist movement the Front de Libération du Québec (FLQ), culminating in the abduction of British Trade Commissioner James Cross and the kidnapping and murder of Québec Labour Minister Pierre LaPorte; in response, the federal government introduced the War Measures

Act, rounded up and interned approximately 500 separatists, canceled all human rights protections, including habeus corpus, and sent military troops to occupy Québec. By the 1970s, the renowned Royal Canadian Mounted Police (RCMP), whose agents had infiltrated the FLQ, had become the most active terrorist organization in the country, as it ran amok torching separatist farms in Québec and the Praxis research headquarters in Toronto (MacDonald 1981).[3]

Canada has been a safe haven for terrorists who used Canada as a base for fighting battles "at home,"[4] including Sikhs fighting for the independence of the Punjab from India, and Tamils determined to have their own state in northern Sri Lanka. In 1984, Sikh extremists allegedly blew up Air India Flight 182 with 278 Canadians among the 329 who died. Two decades later, and two years after he was arrested, the court acquitted Ripudaman Singh Malik of charges of masterminding and financing the Air India bombing. Canada never managed to extradite the anti-Indian extremist Talwinder Singh Parmar, whom CSIS taped plotting to kill Rajiv Gandhi on a trip to the United States;[5] CSIS, in error, erased the tape. The Canadian government never solved the case of Tara Singh Hayer, the courageous Sikh journalist and outstanding leader in the struggle for human rights and freedom of expression who was to provide evidence in the Air India case; shot and paralyzed in 1988, he was assassinated in 1998.

Muslim extremist terrorists targeting the United States have also used Canada as a base. Ahmed Ressam was arrested crossing the U.S. border from Canada in December 1999 with explosive material that he admitted was intended for the destruction of the Los Angeles airport.[6] In his trial in Seattle, Ressam identified Samir Ait Mohamed, a fellow Algerian with whom he lived in Montreal, and whose refugee claim had been turned down by Canadian officials in 1998, as a fellow extremist planning to assist Ressam in the bomb plot against the LA airport. They also planned to blow up a tanker truck in Outremont in Montreal, which they believed was a Jewish neighborhood. After being arrested when he tried to cross the border into the United States on July 28, 2001 (before 9/11), Mohamed was held in a British Columbia jail on a security certificate for four and a half years based on the evidence provided by Ressam, but was never brought to trial even though the United States requested his extradition after charging him with conspiring to commit terror. On January 11, 2006, after agreeing to drop his fight against the outstanding deportation order, he was put aboard a Vancouver flight for an unknown destination.[7]

On the one hand, Canada fought the FLQ threat using radical legal methods that allowed for the suspension of human rights under the War

Measures Act, a legal method more radical than either the United States or the UK has ever employed. On the other, Canada has not used torture. Further, Canada eventually founded its security doctrine primarily on the conception of human security based on the responsibility of a state for satisfying the basic *needs* and *rights* of its members and others[8] (C, *Human Security*, 1999; Dewitt 2004: 579; McRae and Hubert 2001; Hampson 2002). Its essence is protection and "the primacy of the security of individuals ('freedom from fear and freedom from want')" (Dewitt 2004: 591). Perhaps this is why, in the parliamentary debate on the ATA, the most frequently raised issue was whether the measures infringed on the Canadian Charter of Rights and Freedoms and not the effectiveness of the provisions in combating terrorism.[9]

In 2004, Canada adopted its first National Security Policy, crafted to reflect the balance between the need for national security and the protection of core Canadian values of openness, diversity and respect for civil liberties (McLellan and Cotler 2005). In formulating its counterterrorism policies, the Canadian government does not stress the primacy of human rights but, rather, the proper *balance* between national or state security needs and the need for protection of basic human rights. The preamble of the ATA states that Canada will combat terrorism "while continuing to respect and promote the values reflected in, and the rights and freedoms guaranteed by the *Canadian Charter of Rights and Freedoms*" (Roach 2002).

This chapter examines the meaning and application of "balancing" in two legal cases involving national security, that of Mahmoud Jaballah and that of Maher Arar. Both the Jaballah and Arar cases involve torture and issues of inter-state cooperation to counter the threat of terrorism. Both also invoke very specific issues in balancing human rights and security issues, and the normative guidelines to achieve balance, as well as revealing the nature of the concept of balance employed in Canada.

In presenting these cases, this chapter focuses on only two institutions used to ensure accountability: first, a legal court, and, second, an independent commission. In regard to Mahmoud Jaballah I focus on the second court case under Justice Andrew MacKay that was concerned with the legality of a security certificate, the issue of deporting Jaballah back to Egypt, and the high risk that he would be subjected to torture. In regard to Arar, my analysis concentrates on the hearings and reports of the independent Arar Commission set up under Justice Dennis O'Connor, associate chief justice of Ontario, that was mandated to look into the role of Canadian officials in the deportation of a Canadian citizen by American authorities to Syria, where he was born and where he was imprisoned for almost a year and tortured before being allowed to return to Canada.[10] The Arar Commission was the first independent inquiry that touched upon post-9/11 security laws and practices.

## THE CONCEPTION OF BALANCE

The difficulty of reconciling principle with practice is that three alternative senses of the term "balance" are often confused, especially when applied to very different types and levels of balancing.

The first and most general meaning of balance—the "material model"—is that associated with weighing scales and teeter-totters. This sense of balance depends on a point of equilibrium. If this conception of balance is applied to the tension between human rights and security, where human rights and security concerns are on opposite sides of the teeter-totter, as the security situation gets worse, more threatening, and heavier, there are only two ways to maintain a balance. Conceivably, *greater* protections for human rights could be added as the threat to security becomes heavier and weightier—a practice not found even when this conception is invoked. In fact, there are usually fewer human rights protections to weigh down the other side. Alternatively, the fulcrum of the teeter-totter, the freedom of the individual, is shifted away from human rights toward the security end so that the balance can be maintained. However, if the freedom of the individual is defined in absolute terms as excluding indefinite detention or exposure to torture, then the fulcrum cannot be shifted in those cases and there is no way to find a balance.

The "metaphysical model" offers a second, very different method of achieving balance, distinct from the material model in that the two opposing forces exist as two realms within the same circle of reference. The most common depiction of the model is found in the yin-yang symbol. The yin-yang conception in the East is about balance as harmony between two complementary forces. Too much of one part—too many human rights protections (or too much fight) or too many threats to our security (or too much fright)—upsets the balance. Yin-yang is the avoidance of extremes. This model may implicitly be the conception of balance between protecting human rights and preventing security threats that the current executive branch of the U.S. government is using, except the yin and yang do not interact but are relegated to mutually exclusive enclaves. Human rights are viewed as the yin, feminine and passive but preserved for loyal citizens who support the regime and separated by a definite boundary line from the active and aggressive yang, where governance operates strictly from the perspective of power. Human rights are kept in balance and harmonized with security concerns by enclosing human rights in a separate and self-contained container, while threats to security are relegated to a different realm lacking human rights. Human rights and threats to security are contained within their separate and respective closed circles in which human rights are white and threats to security are black, unbound from human rights but kept in check by American security forces. Where the black forces exist, there are no human rights; where American innocents live in the realm of light, no abuses of human rights purportedly take place.

Finally, a radically different third form of balance is provided in the "matrix model," which in theory may be said to characterize the Canadian approach (though, as we shall see, very frequently not in practice), generally corresponding to the "human security" perspective. In the matrix model, balance is the variable rather than the constant. There are two forces, but instead of clashing, they travel in different directions at right angles to each other. Within each force there are two extremes: minimum (zero) and maximum (infinite or absolute). On one axis, we find zero to maximum protection against threat, on the other axis zero and maximum human rights protections. The object is to maximize both; balance is merely the effective result of where the two forces settle. Normality and maximum realization of the polity is achieved through a unitary combination of rights and freedoms that is diagonal, not a trade-off.

## SECURITY CERTIFICATES IN PRACTICE: JABALLAH

This section focuses on one specific government practice, the Canadian government's use of security certificates as "a rarely used mechanism for removing a person from the country . . . to ensure Canada's immigration laws are not misused by people who pose a threat,"[11] "to hold people in detention for indefinite periods rather than [rely on] on laws, policies, or institutions"[12]. Using a security certificate, the government can declare that person "inadmissible" to Canada, not only for "engaging in terrorism, or acts of violence that would or might endanger the lives or safety of persons in Canada," but because of suspicions that the individual *might be* a "danger to the security of Canada," or because (s)he belongs to "organizations that have engaged in or will engage in spying, subversion or terrorism," or simply "do not satisfy an officer of their identity."[13] A foreign visitor is then immediately subject to arrest and could be held indefinitely without bail, though, for a person with permanent resident status, a federal court judge must start a review within forty-eight hours (C, *Keeping*, 2004).[14]

Whether a permanent resident or a visitor is detained, by the seventh day of custody a federal court judge must *begin* a review of the government's evidence. If the judge finds the detention warranted, the permanent resident can be held without review for six months.

From 1993 to September 11, 2001, the CSIS provided information to detain twenty-two people in eight years. Since 9/11, CSIS used security certificates five times until twenty-one persons were detained in one action that turned into a farce. In another, more serious incident, seventeen suspects were arrested in summer 2006. The big difference after 9/11 is the access the detained person's lawyer has to evidence,[15] since security certificates may be based on information protected for national security reasons. Most significantly, neither the accused nor his lawyer is entitled to be present when the judge determines if further detention is warranted. Neither the accused nor his lawyer has the right to be present, let alone listen, object, question, or protest when the judge *and* government lawyers sitting together make the fundamental decisions about detention. Nor is the court under any obligation to share the evidence with the accused and/or his defense attorney.[16] There is a requirement that the court share a *summary* of the evidence at the initial thirty-day hearing, and, if the judge rules that providing that information does not risk national security, the detailed evidence. Only at the next hearing is the accused given an opportunity to be heard, but even at that time, (s)he or her/his lawyer may only have access to the summary evidence and the allegations. The judge assesses whether the issuance of the certificate was "reasonable." When the judge rules, the accused cannot appeal and can be quickly deported, *even to a country where he may be tortured*. A security certificate can be overturned when an individual has a hearing. On three occasions, a certificate has been overturned on review,[17] including the certificate against Mahmoud Jaballah.

Jaballah arrived in Canada in 1996 with his wife and four children, all Egyptian nationals (two children were subsequently born in Canada). Jaballah immediately claimed refugee status on the basis that he repeatedly had been arrested and tortured, and his wife had been detained and mistreated so that, on one occasion, she had a miscarriage (C, *Jaballah*, 2000: 1). If returned, he feared mistreatment by the Egyptian authorities. The family left Egypt five years earlier, ostensibly to go on a religious pilgrimage, but did not return. After staying in Saudi Arabia for three months, the family moved on to Pakistan. Subsequently Jaballah alone went to Yemen (1994–95) and Azerbaijan; he rejoined the family in Pakistan. After traversing Turkey and Germany, the family arrived in Canada with false Saudi Arabian passports.

On March 4, 1999, the Convention Refugee Determination Division (CRDD) of the Immigration and Refugee Board (IRB) denied refugee status both to Jaballah and his family. At the end of that month, he was arrested and held on a security certificate issued under the authority of the solicitor general and the minister of immigration. The Canadian government argued that Jaballah, a former principal of an Islamic school, was a high-ranking member of al Jihad, which had been named as a terrorist group; on that basis Canada wanted to deport him to Egypt. Justice Cullen quashed the security certificate in November 1999 (C, *Jaballah*, 2000: 1). Leave had been granted for judicial review of the negative refugee decision by the CRDD; rejection was also set aside on September 28, 2000, and referred back to a different CRDD panel on August 16, 2001. Meanwhile, the Canadian government issued a second security certificate and detained Jaballah on August 14, 2001, *a month before 9/11*, and kept him in solitary confinement in Toronto's Metro West Detention Centre. In 2005, Jaballah went on a long hunger strike in protest of the conditions of his detention, including quests for medical surgery on his knee and treatment for Hepatitis C that he allegedly acquired while in detention, as well as better visitation rights. During this time he took in only water, fruit juice, and broth. He was sent to the Etobicoke branch of the William Osler health centre, and was eventually released in September 2005.

Evidence pointed overwhelmingly to the high probability that Jaballah was a senior member of a very active global terrorist organization.[18] Yet Jaballah walks the streets of Canada today, under some restrictions about contacts and travel, because the Minister did not or could not provide a timely—not even a grossly delayed—response to the request for Canadian protection.[19] Procrastination replaced decision lest the minister be damned and subjected to a volley of criticisms for the failure to protect Canadians or to play a responsible role in the fight against terror if (s)he granted Canadian protection. If the minister rejected the claim and deported Jaballah, the decision would have been appealed on the grounds that the minister, in accordance with the *Suresh* decision,[20] had not made a reasonable decision to justify that the risk of torture to Jaballah was *less* than the risk to Canadians if Jaballah was allowed to walk the streets. The decision was, in effect, offloaded onto the courts.

Why was it virtually impossible, as Kofi Annan had stated, to balance the risk of torture if the detainee was sent back to Egypt with the risk to the security of Canadians? Did Jaballah's release move too far in the direction of protecting human rights and away from the protection of the security of Canadians?

## ANALYZING THE COURT'S BALANCING PROCESS

To examine the concept of balance employed in the Jaballah case, I cite three instances of balancing: (1) the determination that the court was legitimately entitled to hear the case, (2) the determination that the hearing officer had made a proper and reasonable decision in hearing the evidence, and (3) the determination that counsel for Jaballah had sufficient evidence without being given access to all of the evidence and thus was afforded a fair judicial review. A fourth potential balancing, namely the risk to torture to the individual versus risk to the security of Canadians, was never adjudicated by the court. I will discuss why not.

In deciding the court's legitimacy and the determination that it was not a kangaroo court, defense counsel charged that the court failed to observe traditional legal rules of fairness and neutrality in dealing with both the detained individual and his counsel. In a normal balancing process in this respect, the ideal is to be sufficiently forthcoming in the proceedings toward the counsel on each side to determine the issues, but not so close that one counsel has an unfair advantage over the other. The ideal is equal treatment for both and equal detachment from both. However, the law provided that in security cases, the counsel for government was to enjoy a decided advantage on the grounds of national security. That law had been upheld by Canadian courts. That court had not determined that the privileges granted to counsel for the government, compared to those granted to the counsel for the detainee, were so egregious that they so compromised the requirement of fairness that the court could not be presumed to be a just and fair adjudicator. Nor did counsel for the detainee provide that evidence or the arguments. Instead, counsel resorted to decrying the court. For the independence of the court had been assured by legions of other rules. The counsel for the detainee had not argued or demonstrated why the breach of fairness rules was so great in the differential access to the judge and in the different amount of evidence allowed by the court and law to the counsel on each side that they so offset the other rules protecting the independence of the court as to fundamentally violate principles of justice. The principle of balance used was neither a material model nor a metaphysical model, but a matrix model.

This determination was not decided in reference to the ideal, but on whether the norm of balance is so out of kilter with normal rules of judicial independence and fairness that justice could not be rendered. In the absence of evidence or argument, as distinct from oratory, the judge ruled that the distortion and imbalance was not so great in light of the laws of Canada and prior judicial rulings that the court had become an instrument of CSIS.

With respect to the evidence, there were two different balancing processes. Did the hearing officer proceed in a fair and judicious manner in considering the evidence? And in the appeal to the court, did counsel for the detainee have sufficient access to the evidence without compromising the risk to Canadian security?

With respect to the first, legal precedent had set clear guidelines for the fairness of the hearing. The evidence had to meet a standard of sufficient adequacy in the quantity and quality of the material presented, and what was presented had to meet minimum standards of relevance to the case at hand. There might have been far more evidence that was relevant but was not of sufficient quantity or quality to be presentable. There might have been good qualitative evidence, but it was not sufficiently relevant. Evidence had to be presented that met both standards and then a third process requirement. It had to have been appropriately and reasonably considered. No evidence or argument was presented that the evidence had not been appropriately and reasonably considered. The judge determined that, based on the evidence before him, the rehearing officer had dealt fairly with the issues. There had been no undue imbalance. Again, the principle of balance used was neither a material nor a metaphysical model, but a matrix model.

The remaining but key issue of balancing with respect to evidence was about the access to evidence by counsel for the detainee compared to the access available to the counsel for government. Amnesty International Canada (AIC), like many other human rights organizations, argued in reference to the Arar case (discussed later in this chapter), "It could be clearly unfair to reach findings on the basis of evidence that remains *in camera*."[21] If this principle applied to a commission inquiry, how much more apt it would be when applied to a legal proceeding concerning an individual's indefinite incarceration.

The matter was dealt with by adopting a matrix model of balancing. The rule governing access to counsel was that *sufficient* access had to be allowed to enable the detainee's counsel to understand the nature of the evidence going into the government decision without that evidence risking Canadian security. The government had set up a minimin rule governing the amount of evidence made available: as little evidence as possible would be provided but could be increased until it crossed a threshold of risk to Canadian security. At the same time, the test of sufficiency had to be met that allowed the detainee to understand the charges and the basis for them.

The most difficult balancing act would be between the risk of torture to the detainee versus the risk to the security of Canada. In fact, these are initially two different processes that have to be made as congruent as possible to achieve balance. Unfortunately, they are very incongruent. The government is faced with what turns out to be an impossible dilemma. In the process of determining the risk of torture, the ideal may be absolutely no risk, but in actuality the standard is *reasonable* probability that the detainee, if returned, will *not* be tortured. Somewhere (not articulated in this case) there is a probability of risk of torture that, once exceeded, would prohibit removal. Where that norm is set did not come up, because evidence points to the risk clearly being very high even if prior agreement between the two governments had been obtained that the returnee would not be subjected to torture. Given Canadian rules and requirements with respect to torture, the toleration of risk in this respect was low. In effect, the government in its hearing was weighing the risk of torture to the detainee if returned against the political risk. It is clear why the government was impotent to make the decision, since deportation breached all the government standards about risk of removal; yet allowing the individual to stay was politically unacceptable. The balance could not be struck. Again, the matrix rather than the material or metaphysical models was used, but in this case the criterion of balance could not be satisfied, leading to Jaballah's release in spite of deep concerns about the threat he potentially poses.

In answer to the question, "Can human rights be limited within a free and democratic society in the pursuit of counter-terrorist endeavors and, if so, to what extent?" (Conte 2002: 6), one method of adjudicating balance would entail distinguishing those human rights which can be compromised and absolute human rights that cannot, including unlawful arrest and detention without trial, the very outcome of issuing security certificates, and not exposing a person to torture. If Canada in its deep adherence to human rights is not to breach the absolute ban on torture, Canada cannot be complicit by deporting individuals back to states where they could be tortured. In not shipping them back, Canada cannot detain individuals indefinitely without bringing them to trial. Caught between a rock (the risk of the deportees being subjected to torture) and a hard place (the human rights provision prohibiting long detention without trial), Canada presumably must release individuals it suspects of terrorist links. Viewing that as a security risk and a risk to the public, Canada is confronted with a dilemma. If it sends the suspects home, it breaches one absolute right. If Canada detains the person for years, it breaches another absolute right. If the individuals are released, the government's responsibility to protect Canadians is perceived as being breached.

With respect to torture, Canada, as a party to international conventions banning its use, rejects the use of torture unequivocally. Deportation to face torture is *categorically* forbidden: "torture is so abhorrent that it will almost always be disproportionate to interests on the other side of the *balance* [my italics], even security interests" (C, *Jaballah*, 2003: 27). However, in the Canadian Supreme Court's *Suresh* ruling (2002), with respect to the minister's determining the risk to the returnee the court could only review whether the determination was made in a reasonable manner that the risk to national security outweighed any risk the person would face upon being returned. The principle of not being exposed to torture is absolute, but the practice of deportation where torture is a risk becomes relative. As the background paper for the Arar Commission on rights and freedoms put it, "in exceptional circumstances deportation from Canada to face torture might be constitutional under the *Charter* even though the right against torture is framed in absolute and non-derogable terms in ICCPR and CAT" (C, Commission, 2004b: 5; C, *Suresh*, 2002, para. 78). Ministers can deport persons who face a *risk* of torture, even if the risk of exposure to torture was relatively high but was not certain, presumably as long as there was evidence of an imminent great threat. It is incumbent on the minister to adjudicate this balance and present reasons and evidence for the determination made.

The balance drawn is between the risk to the security of Canada (very little if history is relied upon) and the risk of torture for the prospective deportee (relatively high if the past is used as a reference). If balancing those risks was the relevant frame, and if the model of balancing is a simple teeter-totter model, none of the people presently in detention would ever be deported or detained for indefinite periods. Either the principle of determination is not one of "balance" in this sense, or risk of torture and indefinite detention are not absolute prohibitions. Canada, an icon and a strong defender of human rights and international law, breaches "absolute" rights in favor of security concerns.

The guideline for settling the supposed "balance" is really not a weighing process, in the teeter-totter sense, but a reasoning process. Instead of a universal process norm in reference to the demands of necessity or weighing proportionality, the process gives the benefit of the doubt in actuality to the minister, as long as the minister goes through the motions of examining the evidence for risk to torture versus risk to Canadian security and calculating that risk. The courts do not second-guess whether the calculation is done in a *substantively* fair manner—unlikely given that risk to a collective self will almost always carry far more weight than the risk to the detained nonnative. In spite of the imperative under human rights norms to treat everyone as an individual who is equal, the *psychological* process of balancing favors state concerns.

## THE MAHER ARAR CASE AND INQUIRY

The Arar case raises a very different issue of the use of bureaucratic cooperation and possible complicity in allowing the rights of Canadians to be abused abroad in order to extract information from someone suspected of being involved in terrorism. More relevant to the Arar case, the deportation of Canadians to countries that practice torture may result simply from sharing information.[22] In Canada's 2004 national security policy statement (C, *Securing*, 2004), Prime Minister Paul Martin stressed the importance of an "integrated approach to national security" that entailed working with *key partners.* He did not address the question of which states were partners, nor the risks of such relations to the security of individual Canadians. The problem of a coordinated international response between and among states becomes particularly acute "when we seek to transfer the information obtained in one context to another, or between one state and another" (Rosenberg 2002: 4). The problem of inter-state cooperation is also complicated when cooperating states do not adhere to the principle of protecting basic human rights, but routinely practice torture, as is the case with Egypt and Syria. Some foreign governments may have fewer controls with respect to their security establishments and virtually no oversight. Canada is unlikely to be able to exercise any controls over the use of information provided to other states.

By and large, Canadians cooperate closely with Americans in the fight against terrorism. However, a number of practices introduced by the United States have disturbed Canadians. For example, following a U.S. decision at the end of October 2002 to photograph and fingerprint people born in Iran, Iraq, Libya, Sudan, and Syria who enter the United States, Canada issued a travel advisory suggesting that Canadians born in those countries not travel via the USA. However, other than actual torture lite (and sometimes evidently not so lite) of prisoners under American control (which American officials, including the president, have evidently condoned), the practice that has most affected and bothered Canadians has been "extraordinary rendition,"[23] after one of its citizens, Maher Arar, was widely, though incorrectly, believed to be the victim of this practice, and was then, correctly, believed to have been subjected to torture heavy.[24] The case set off a hue and cry in Canada and eventually a full-scale commission of inquiry into Canada's complicity in the practice.[25]

The overall outline of the story can be succinctly sketched.[26] Maher Arar, a Canadian telecommunications engineer born in Syria who came to Canada in 1987 at the age of seventeen, had been recalled from a family vacation in

Tunisia by his company to work on a project. En route to Montreal, he was detained at New York's John F. Kennedy Airport by U.S. Immigration and Naturalization officials on September 26, 2002, on allegations that he was linked to al Qaeda. Initially, the RCMP claimed that it believed that Arar simply would be denied entry into the USA (C, Commission, 2005, para. 12). On October 2, CSIS asked Washington to clarify the circumstances and reasons for Arar's arrest, and the following day CSIS received the RCMP report. Six days later, on October 9, CSIS learned from both the Canadian Department of Foreign Affairs and International Trade (DFAIT) and the RCMP that American authorities had deported Arar to Syria, even though American officials knew he carried a Canadian passport and Arar had expressed fears of deportation to Syria to a Canadian consular official.[27] Canadian officials were not notified about the deportation but had been involved in sharing information with the Americans and accessed the information when he was being questioned by Americans and by Syrians.[28] Further, the Syrians in their questioning of Arar seemed to have had access to the results of Canadian intelligence investigations.[29]

Canada provided the initial information to the United States that allowed the USA to target Arar.[30] The Canadian government celebrated the way it provided and shared information.[31] America, however, was the big boy on the block and it did not need or want Canada's approval generally or even specifically in how it treated a Canadian citizen. The American state department confirmed that Canada's "approval or consent (for the deportation) was not sought." It was precisely this process "without the proper caveats being attached to indicate the reliability of the evidence" and with "inadequate policies and safeguards to ensure information would not be shared with governments in ways likely to lead to human rights violations such as torture" that upset AIC (Amnesty International Canada 2005e: 10). Partly in response to Canadian public outrage, on October 16, 2002 Foreign Minister Bill Graham complained to the American government over the arrest and deportation. On October 22, 2002. DFAIT announced that Arar was being held in a Syrian prison. Arar's wife, Monia Mazigh, who holds a Ph.D. in economics, began a campaign for Canadian action to get her husband released and returned, a campaign that built momentum over the following twelve months.

In January, Canadians officials learned that Arar would be in prison for a long time and there was a possibility he could be sentenced to death (C, Commission, 2005a: para. 30); that spurred Canadian diplomatic efforts. Over six months after his deportation and incarceration in a Syrian prison, on April 30, 2003, Syria informed the Canadian government that Arar was to be charged with membership in a banned Muslim organization, the Muslim Brotherhood of Syria. A full ten months after the arrest, on June 27, 2003, Prime Minister Jean Chrétien pledged to Arar's wife that Canada would provide "all possible consular assistance" to get her husband released,[32] just when the Syrian Human Rights Committee (SHRC) based in London confirmed what had widely been suspected: Arar was being beaten and tortured in prison.[33] When in August 2003 Arar finally resorted to shouting to the Canadian consular official, Léo Martel, that he was being tortured, he was subsequently transferred to an investigative branch where he was tortured and forced to sign a "confession." Syria freed Arar on October 5, 2003, on the eve of the trial scheduled to be held before the state security court. Monia Mazigh credited Canadian "quiet diplomacy" for Arar's release. The next day, Arar returned to Canada, just a year after his deportation.

Initially, Solicitor General Wayne Easter rejected the appeals for a public inquiry, including an inquiry into whether the RCMP had played a role in Arar's arrest by the Americans. But the pressures increased when Arar held a press conference and informed the public that he had been mentally and physically tortured while in the Syrian prison and forced to confess that he spent time in Afghanistan though he had never been there. On November 5, 2003, in an effort to dissipate the rising pressures, Prime Minister Chrétien informed the House of Commons that the Canadian government had informed the U.S. government that its deportation of a Canadian to Syria was "unacceptable" and that Canada requested an "explanation." At the same time, the Prime Minister unequivocally insisted that there would be no independent inquiry into the case. However, he informed the House of Commons that the Canadian government was looking into whether Canadian intelligence officials played any role in Arar's deportation. On December 22, 2003, SIRC (the Security Intelligence Review Committee) announced its intention to look into CSIS's role in the Arar case, though it had been following the issue within a week of Arar's detention.

In 2004, a new Liberal government under Prime Minister Paul Martin took office. Represented by the Center for Constitutional Rights (CCR) in American courts, on January 22 Arar sued the U.S. government as well as then-Attorney General John Ashcroft, former Homeland Security Director Tom Ridge, former Immigration and Naturalization Services Commissioner James Ziglar, and FBI Director Robert Mueller for his deportation to a country that American officials knew practiced torture. This enhanced the pressure on the new Canadian government to hold an inquiry into Canadian officials' alleged complicity, but the decision to hold an inquiry had already been made. Irwin Cotler was the new Justice Minister. He had served as Arar's counsel and had supported holding a public inquiry. However, he recused himself from any official involvement in the case because of pressures that he was involved in a conflict of interest. Finally, four days after the announcement of Arar's suit against the American government, on January 28, 2004, Deputy Prime Minister Anne McLellan announced that there would be a public inquiry into the Arar case under Justice Dennis O'Connor to assess the actions of Canadian officials in Arar's deportation and detention. The mandate was given greater impetus just over a month later when the police chief of Ottawa informed the public that the force had been part of a joint operation investigating Arar. The Syrian and American governments both refused to cooperate with the inquiry.

## THE CONCEPT OF BALANCE IN THE ARAR CASE

The Arar case offers us the opportunity to examine the available relevant American records and examine the U.S. practice. What concept of balance does the United States government use in determining whether to send an individual back to a country that routinely practices torture? How does the United States assess, assuming that it does so sincerely, whether assurances that the person sent to a country that practices torture will not be tortured?

> The United States "does not transfer persons to countries where the United States believes that it is 'more likely than not' that they will be tortured. The United States obtains assurances, as appropriate, from the foreign governments to which a detainee is transferred. If assurances were not considered sufficient when *balanced* [my italics] against treatment concerns, the United States would not transfer the person to the control of the government unless the concerns were satisfactorily resolved."[34]

There are evidently three stages in making such a determination. In the first stage, the American government uses a "balance of probabilities" rather than denying the benefit of the doubt to countries with a record of practicing torture, or, on the other side of the equation, simply naïvely giving the benefit of the doubt to the country that practices torture. In other words, again assuming the U.S. is sincere that it actually uses such a criterion, it uses a material model of balance in which the fulcrum is placed in the center, and the United States itself calculates whether the government in question is likely to practice torture in this case. If the United States, on a balance of probability, calculates that the country is likely to practice torture, it does *not* decide *not* to send the individual to that country. Rather, the USA then seeks diplomatic assurances that the country will not practice torture. What measure does the United States use to assess whether such assurances can be regarded as reliable? Again, it uses a material model in which the weight of the assurance is balanced against the record of past practice. Presumably, if in the record of assurances in the past (and using a "balance of probabilities"), the country had practiced torture in *fewer* than half the cases in which assurances were given, then the USA would deport the person to that country. However, a third fallback position would then be put in place if that country had tortured returnees in more than half the cases where assurances had been given. The United States would then go through a third process and seek to "satisfactorily resolve" its concerns that torture would not be practiced. It is not clear what criteria would be used to assess whether the concerns could be satisfactorily resolved. Presumably the United States would seek more forceful assurances to allow the balance of probability judgment to shift sufficiently to the allow deportation to take place. From this procedure, it seems clear that, on objective grounds, in the vast majority of cases, individuals would be sent back to countries that routinely practice torture. By using a three-stage system of material balancing, overwhelmingly the outcome shifts in the direction of deportation of individuals to countries that practice torture.

What sense of balance was used by the Arar Commission in the tension between the disclosure obligation to reveal evidence to the public under the requirement of a right to know in a public inquiry the evidence on which an assessment is made, and the obligation to protect sensitive information relevant to the security of the country and its citizens? The commission determined that the onus of proof rests on the determination that there is a security risk, otherwise information should be released.[35] A second issue of balancing can be found in the balance struck between the obligation to protect one's own citizens from torture and the obligation to cooperate with allies (and others) in order to reduce the threat of terrorism, particularly when the closest ally to Canada is engaged in the practice of extraordinary rendition.

With regard to the first issue of balance, would all the evidence be made public? The Commissioner of the inquiry, the Honorable Dennis R. O'Connor, was pressured by Arar's supporters to publish all documents, but sensitive to the issue of national security and subsequently (June 16, 2005) explaining that lengthy court battles over the issue would create enormous delays for the inquiry, O'Connor opted instead to hold in-camera sessions to determine what evidence could be made public. Accompanied by a heavily censored classified report filed with the commission on September 14, 2004,

SIRC told the Commission that CSIS was *unaware* of U.S. plans to arrest and deport Arar to Syria.[36] Over 1,000 pages of censored documents were released by the commission on November 26, 2004, reinforcing this interpretation. However, the 2,300 pages of documents released by the commission on April 21, 2005, suggested that Canadian officials had possibly "encouraged" the interrogation of Arar, and wanted to and did access the results. As stated above, this latter point was confirmed in the final report.

In May 2004, Senator Pierre De Bané informed the commission that he had learned from Gar Pardy, a journalist writing for the Ottawa *Citizen*, that U.S. officials had offered to return Arar to Canada on the condition that Arar be incarcerated and charged; only after Canada refused, the U.S. deported Arar to Syria. So if the RCMP refused to accept Arar back and charge him, they had to know how serious the Americans were in wanting Arar arrested and should in any normal reasoning process at the very least have expected Arar's deportation to Syria. Such a conclusion was reinforced when Defence Minister Bill Graham, the minister of foreign affairs when Arar was deported to Syria, stated that he was "frustrated" by the lack of cooperation he received from Canadian police and security officials. One can draw the conclusion, though the principle is nowhere stated that I could find, that the commissioner released sufficient information to discern the story line of Canadian official complicity in the action, but not enough information to compromise Canadian security concerns and clearly, if it had free rein, would have released a great deal more.[37] A matrix model of revelation was used in which the targets were minimal exposure of security matters, but sufficient revelation to discern what happened through careful examination of the evidence thus far released.

Do we get any sense of the principle of balance used in determining how much to cooperate with allies in sharing information to protect Canadians from terrorism, versus the obligation to protect Canadians from being tortured? On June 2, 2005, Graham officially apologized and took a degree of responsibility for the long time Arar had been incarcerated in Syria. "Clearly we would've preferred he'd been gotten out earlier, and I'm very sorry that he was not, for obvious reasons."[38] However, his explanation suggested that the main reason for the lack of vigilant action on the part of the government was not moral guilt but ignorance, for he said that Canada would have conducted itself differently if the government knew then what it now knew.

Whether some Canadian officials knew that the U.S. planned to deport Arar to Syria, whether Canadian officials knew or should have known that Arar was being tortured in prison, whether Canadian officials did all they could to free Arar, and whether Canada could have pressured the U.S. to intervene in a positive and more forceful manner, the question seems to be about Canadian officials supplying information to both America and directly or indirectly to Syria that made Arar a suspect. And, as the Arar Commission concluded, the evidence clearly suggests that they did.[39] Once arrested after the Canadians supplied information that they deemed insufficient to prosecute Arar, did the officials de facto hand Arar over to the Americans for them to deal with the problem? Given American attitudes and practices that were already known at that time, it is difficult to believe that RCMP officials did not consider or expect that the Americans might hand Arar over to Syria, a country they knew routinely practiced torture.

DFAIT seemed to have been inhibited in insisting that RCMP put greater pressures on the USA (Amnesty International Canada 2004a: 7) and was not fully aware of the RCMP's approach to and attitude about the problem. Different Canadian departments and officials balanced security concerns with the absolute principle of protecting Canadian citizens from torture in a radically different manner, varying from the justice department's placing clear primacy on the rights of citizens, on the one hand, to the RCMP's apparent indifference to those rights.

While Amnesty International acknowledges that "intelligence sharing is a necessary intergovernmental function in today's world," it only supports such sharing if human rights are enhanced and the information sharing is not at the expense of human rights protection. "Among other benefits, effective and reliable intelligence sharing can help to prevent human rights violations and identify the whereabouts of suspected perpetrators of human rights" (Amnesty International Canada 2004b: 5). However, sharing uncorroborated or speculative information may lead other governments to draw unwarranted conclusions. And information shared with a purportedly "reliable" ally may be passed onto third, far less reliable and scrupulous parties in a "ripple effect" (Heyman 2002: 453).[40] However, this was not evidently a prime consideration of the RCMP.

In contrast to the RCMP, CSIS claimed that information is only disclosed to a foreign agency of a country in which there are human rights concerns after considering various issues. These issues include the potential use to which the foreign agency may put the information, especially if it concerns Canadians, and the degree of the threat that an affected individual poses to national security. In other words, as with the Americans, Canadian security concerns are balanced against the threat of torture to the Canadian. Further, CSIS then considers "the ability and willingness of the foreign agency to respect caveats and protect the information from public disclosure" (C,

Commission, 2005a: para. 29). Though CSIS was not as forthcoming in stating whether an assurance would be sufficient to share information, and CSIS did not indicate that it checked the track record of previous assurances, as the Arar Commission reported, CSIS did *not* share information with the Americans with respect to Arar. Thus, although I do not have sufficient evidence to indicate whether CSIS used a material, teeter-totter model of balancing or a matrix model, even if the material model was used, CSIS clearly had different criteria for balancing, and the fulcrum was likely set in the middle rather than skewed either towards defending the security of Canada, or, much worse, defending the reputation of a Canadian agency.

Perhaps the worst effect of sharing information, not mentioned by Amnesty or CSIS, is the demoralization of the victim of torture when that victim discovers that agents of his own government had to have provided information to the third-party interrogators given the questions they asked. During the inquiry, Maher Arar "was particularly disturbed by certain 'leaks' from sources allegedly inside the Canadian Government that cast him in a negative light" (C, Toope, 2005: 20).

Thus, in weighing the risk of torture following deportation versus risks to Canadian security, the Americans may have used a material, teeter-totter conception of balancing in which the fulcrum was clearly shifted well in the direction of favoring security concerns, but the RCMP was even worse. The criterion for assessment was not a security concern, but the reputation of the RCMP. With respect to the issue of releasing evidence versus the suppression of evidence lest security be compromised, it appears as if the commission used a matrix model and released sufficient evidence to allow readers to discern what happened without trespassing on minimal standards required to protect security. In the release of information, the commissioner balanced not only the right to know with security, but, more significantly, the right to arrive at conclusions expeditiously with the right of the public to know. It seems clear that the matrix model was used, as sufficient material was released without jeopardizing security concerns while allowing the commission to proceed without legal challenges. Further, in the release of the final report, the commission was unequivocal in asserting that the public's right to know was preeminent; the onus of proof on nonrelease rested on those making security claims to suppress the public release of information. In the case of the principle of balance used in sharing critical information with allies and countries that practice torture to defend security, and the need to protect Canadian citizens, Canadian law is clear in putting severe limits on sharing if Canadians are put at risk of torture. Since the RCMP could not strike that balance and even used an improper criterion, it erred not simply on the side of security, but on protecting its own reputation and displacing responsibility and accountability onto others.

Finally, in a very different example of balance, consider the balance between the use of public outrage versus quiet diplomacy in seeking to free Arar. Whereas Arar's wife, Monia Mazigh, commended Canada's use of quiet diplomacy, AIC criticized Canada for not striking the right balance between quiet and noisy diplomacy. Clearly here AI is using a teeter-totter model of balance and wants the fulcrum to be virtually fixed in spite of different situations and contexts. I can only suggest that AI is using both the wrong model of balance and a very rigid application of it. The matrix rather than the material model would be more appropriate.

What are the implications of the three different models of balancing examined here? The metaphysical model leads to ideological, "us" versus "them" dichotomies. The material model allows a fulcrum to be placed according to the bias of the official while maintaining the dispassionate rhetoric of balancing. It seems to guide the balancing practices of the U.S. government, though it is likely that the metaphysical model implicitly inspires its practices. The matrix model, which allows the balance to float in an effort to maximize two different outcomes, seems to be the model of balance that is both most useful and least conducive to manipulation. It has been used extensively by Canadian authorities.

When options to act are incongruent, when points of view or ways of looking at the world are so opposed that there is no possibility of finding a "balance," this simply means that it is incumbent upon politicians to come up with solutions that do not present such stark alternatives. The choice should not be between sending a person back to be tortured versus allowing a non-Canadian to roam Canadian streets while the government holds considerable evidence suggesting that the individual is a high-ranking member of a terrorist organization. When there seem to be only two opposing choices, it is easy for the practice of judicial and judicious balancing to degrade to the level of seesaws and teeter-totters, or even to operate in terms of a metaphysical model. In fact, in most contexts, the most appropriate model is the matrix, but in some situations even the demands of balance in that model cannot be met. When the matrix model is unable to strike a suitable balance, there is a danger of decision by delay or delegation.

# 9 Germany

*State Responses to Terrorist Challenges and Human Rights*

Wolfgang S. Heinz

Germany has suffered less direct threat than the other countries discussed in this book, and it has thus far maintained one of the most liberal and democratic counterterror policies, demonstrating that another way is possible. The fight against terrorism, especially in its initial stages, usually requires immediate, comprehensive, and stringent action by the state. Often in society there is a sense of shock and helplessness, which elites seek to overcome by resorting to both substantial and symbolic actions. They want to communicate, "We are not helpless and we will no longer be victimized." Often police and intelligence powers, and sometimes those of the military, are expanded, while state action is increasingly geared towards secrecy. Accountability—via Parliament, the judiciary, media, and NGOs—is resented and sometimes actively weakened.

From a human rights perspective, which includes a long history of learning from counterinsurgency wars and the repression of social movements and terrorist activities, the accountability of the democratic state must be safeguarded. Here we can distinguish between horizontal accountability,[1] which includes parliamentary, judicial, and opposition party activities, and vertical accountability. The latter includes international (including UN) and regional human rights norms and monitoring (in Europe, especially important are the European Convention on Human Rights and the European Court of Human Rights), critical reporting by neighbors and allies, and global civil society, including human rights NGOs and the international media. If these latter acted only on their own they would probably be relatively weak in comparison to the entrenched bureaucracy-to-bureaucracy contacts among police, intelligence, and diplomatic agencies. But taken together they can exert a certain pressure: governments rightly feel monitored by independent actors, they need to explain and justify themselves, and sometimes they need to restrain their action.[2] Germany has maintained these channels.

Germany's relative success affirms Alison Brysk's conclusion in Chapter 1 that "some cope better than others," and it follows the pattern of causal factors she lays out: the legal lessons of history, state and public perception of threat, and the influence of international norms. Germany's postfascist reconstruction as a highly accountable, transparent constitutional democracy helped it to mount a relatively liberal response to the terrorism of the 1970s, which provided an institutional toolkit of democratic counterterror. Germany's broader international commitments to the European community and international law have generally served to improve vertical accountability for human rights. However, in the framework of international and bilateral cooperation in the fight against transnational terrorism, Germany had to make decisions about whether to engage in or condone strategies such as extraordinary rendition, the deporting of terrorist suspects to countries where they might be tortured, or illicit intelligence-gathering.

States choose counterterror strategies according to their models of threat perception and resulting strategic doctrine. The German political scientist Gert-Joachim Glaeßner suggests three models of states fighting terrorism (2003: 235):

- In the first model, the state conceives terrorist acts as especially severe criminal offenses. The goal is the capturing and sentencing of the offender and fighting terrorism within the constraints of the rule of law. This has been the dominant current approach in Germany.

- The second model includes the U.S. "war on terror." In this model terrorism is a form of guerrilla warfare. The goal is to stop or eliminate terrorists, and the boundary between combatants and noncombatants is blurred.

- In the third model, acts of violence by terrorists are seen to operate in a legal grey zone between crime and politics, with the effect that the state's reaction always runs the risk of blurring these differences when "due process" and the rules of combat are replaced by the demands of "national security." An example is Germany in the 1970s: "Penal law and code of criminal procedure were changed to respond to the new situation" (ibid.: 238; author's translation).

But the long-term trend for Germany is captured by Peter Katzenstein, who noted that West Germany and Japan would not regard a "war against terrorism" as a viable option, since the identity of both states "simply does not leave open an almost automatic framing of conflict in terms of war" (Katzenstein 2001: 3). In his view, Germany's campaign against terrorism was proactive. Prevention was the goal, which made it necessary to weaken rights and increase police powers. He emphasizes that it was a domestic and hard campaign for the state, because the Red Army Faction received outside help from the PLO and from the German Democratic Republic.

This chapter looks at the political and legal context of state action against terrorism, followed by a brief characterization of the terrorist threat to Germany and an overview of its measures against the Red Army Faction during the 1970s, then the renewed threat and response after September 11, 2001. In the course of the chapter the comparative areas of state action regarding civil liberties, penal law and criminal trial procedures, prison conditions and torture, and foreign military and intelligence operations will be discussed. The final section will present some implications of Germany's liberal policies for international cooperation.

## THE GERMAN POLITICAL AND LEGAL BASELINE

In the aftermath of the massive human rights violations committed under Nazism, Germany's rule of law was constructed to ensure that a police state could never again arise. "The dignity of the Human Person is inviolable," says article 1, paragraph 1 of the German Constitution, also called Basic Law *(Grundgesetz)*. The Basic Law is "absolute" in the sense that it is the standard for any other law being promulgated; no balancing is possible here between security needs and constraints on the obligation of the state to respect and protect the dignity of the individual. Articles 1–19 codify fundamental rights whose basic content *(Kern)* cannot be legally changed even if all members of Parliament want to do so: this is the ironically named "eternity guarantee" (GG, article 19, para. 2). Moreover, judicial guarantees, including the prohibition of torture, are codified in articles 101–4 of the Basic Law, in the German Penal Code (StG3), and the Code of Criminal Procedure (StPO). Defendants must receive a judicial hearing within forty-eight hours of their arrest, and there is no exception for terrorist suspects (unlike Great Britain, for example, where Parliament decided that police may hold a suspect for four weeks, as Todd Landman's chapter in this volume discusses). Recently, a debate among legal scholars has started on what exactly constitutes human dignity, and some scholars argue for a more limited view of human dignity.

In 1968, the German Parliament adopted emergency legislation *(Notstandsgesetze)* that distinguished among disaster management, a state of tension, and states of internal and external emergency (a state of defense following an external attack) (Basic Law, articles 80a, 81, 115), which included some, but not comprehensive, derogations of civil rights. Strong protests against the new legislation took place, especially by students. So far, the provisions of this legislation have never been used by any government, neither against the RAF nor since September 11.

This strong unitary legal regime was tested in a domestic, nonterrorist situation of imminent peril in 2002 in what would come to be known as the Daschner case. After a child was abducted in the city of Frankfurt am Main, Deputy Police Chief Wolfgang Daschner ordered security officers to threaten a criminal suspect with torture in order to pressure him into giving information about the child's whereabouts. Daschner himself wrote a note about the case and sent it on the same day to the state prosecution, which later opened an investigation. It turned out that the suspect was indeed responsible for the crime, but that he had already killed the boy. A major debate about the case erupted in politics, the media, and society.

There were unusual reactions. Within a few days of the media reports about the case, a large number of high-ranking politicians—the federal minister of justice, politicians responsible for internal security and legal issues, state ministers—as well as representatives of professional organizations such as the president of the German judges' federation, the police federation, and human rights organizations, reacted with statements. Especially at the beginning, many demanded that Daschner should not be punished. Polls suggested that this was the majority opinion among the public. In the end, Daschner was convicted and sentenced to a very mild penalty: a fine only, to be paid in the event that he should commit such an act again.

The case was interesting because it was a nonterrorist "ticking bomb" scenario, unique so far in Germany. In Germany, this scenario was first discussed in a book by the conservative politician Ernst Albrecht, who was at the time prime minister of the state of Lower Saxony (Albrecht 1976). In the end, there was no support for a change in the law to allow leeway for state organs with respect to the absolute prohibition on torture.[3] Similarly, Supreme Court decisions after the 2001 security packages (discussed below) have restricted state limitations of civil liberties, affirming the fundamentals of the German legal regime.

Germany coped with a terrorist threat in two phases, a generation apart. While both the 1970s and 2000s resulted in modifications of legal norms, the specific issues resulting from the nature of the threat were different. During the 1970s response to domestic terror, changes in trial procedures and prison conditions resulted in debate on permissible restrictions of civil liberties and allegations of torture. By the 2000s incidence of transnational terror, the parameters of legal procedure had been resolved—but the boundaries of information-gathering, the rights of foreigners, and the implications of international cooperation emerged as key controversies.

## THE RAF IN THE 1970S AND 1980S
### *The Terrorist Threat*

During the latter 1960s and early 1970s, within the context of the "Extraparliamentary Opposition" (APO) movement and student movement more broadly, the question of violence was actively discussed in leftist political groups. When was it legitimate to use violence against things or people, for example, attacking policemen (without assassinating them)? Support for a militant, violent opposition came from the emerging "New Left" in the wake of the upheavals of 1968. In this context arose the Red Army Faction (RAF), a violent offshoot of the student movement that identified with liberation struggles in the Third World. Some activists distanced themselves from the RAF, while some practiced critical solidarity. However, very few chose the way of terrorism (Glaeßner 2001:240).[4]

The urban guerrilla, along the lines of the Tupamaros guerillas in Uruguay, served as a model at the time. The RAF's strategy was to provoke the state to overreact and use repressive measures against wider sections of society; they believed that this crackdown would lead in turn to broader support for the RAF. The use of violence had to be specific and defensible, and no terrorist bombing against the population was envisioned.[5] Internal debate arose subsequently over certain abductions and assassinations, such as the abduction of the president of the German employer's association, Hanns Martin Schleyer, and the assassination of his driver and three bodyguards during the abduction and, later, of Schleyer himself.

Acts of violence by the RAF were justified as reactive violence *(Gegengewalt)* to capitalism and especially American imperialism and its collaborators in the German government. The war in Vietnam was the single most important political event that radicalized many German youth, a war that was very visible in the media, especially the bombings. The RAF's strategy allowed for and demanded selective killings of leading representatives of the "capitalist-imperialist system" (Glaeßner 2003: 241 ff.). It included the assassinations of not only Schleyer but also the chairman of the board of the Deutsche Bank, Alfred Herrhausen; the banker Jürgen Ponto; Attorney General Siegfried Buback; the president of the Treuhandanstalt (a large state agency dealing with economic reconstruction in the former communist Germany), Detlef Karsten Rohwedder; Siemens board member Karl Heinz Beckurts; foreign ministry head of department Gerold von Braunmühl; and failed assassination attempts on the U.S. generals Frederick Kroesen and Alexander Haig. Killings of drivers and security personnel were not considered to be a moral problem, although they led to critical discussions among RAF supporters.

The RAF formed in the early 1970s with Ulrike Meinhof, Andreas Baader, Gudrun Ensslin, and Jan-Carl Raspe as its leaders. RAF members received military training in PLO camps in the Bekaa valley in Lebanon under Syrian control (Katzenstein 2001: 5). The RAF started with a command level of four people. By the 1980s about 15–20 members were active, supported by another 200 "illegal militants" and about 400 sympathizers (Baader-Meinhof-Report 1972: 129; Horchem 1990: 56). Especially in the initial phase, when attacks were more symbolic than murderous, security agencies were concerned that RAF could count on broad support and solidarity from youth, especially students and left-wing circles. In 1971, one out of four people interviewed by the poll institute Allensbach expressed "certain sympathies" with the RAF (cited in Peters 1991: 37). With the increase in deaths, the RAF rapidly lost any sympathies it might have had among radical youth. At first, RAF members were classified as normal criminals, and only later as terrorists. The government did not want to appear to validate the RAF's claims that it was becoming a repressive state.

Three generations of RAF members emerged (On the first, see Aust 1998; on the second, Wunschik 1997; on the third, Straßner 2001). The third RAF generation acted more "professionally"—and left almost no traces. It was much harder for the government to trace and catch terrorist suspects, especially because operations were much more transnationalized and involved Palestinian groups, Action Directe in France, the Red Brigades in Italy, and the PKK in Turkey. In the 1980s, the East German government provided ten second-generation RAF members with new identities, false papers, apartments, and jobs (Bästlein 2002: 254 ff.). On April 20, 1998, the RAF formally declared the end of its attacks and the dissolution of the organization.[6]

During the most eventful years, 1970–77, twenty-eight people died from assassinations and shootings; seventeen terrorists died. Two bystanders were killed by the police in shoot-outs. Between 1979 and 1993 thirteen assassinations or killings in shoot-outs occurred; eight terrorists died in various police actions, two in accidents, and one committed suicide (Aust 1998: 658–60). Between 1970 and 1997, thirty-four people were killed by the RAF; twenty people died who either belonged to the RAF or were in the scene around RAF (a total of 62 died and 220 were wounded; see Peters 2004).

TABLE 9.1  Counterterrorist Legislation in Germany

| Year | Description |
| --- | --- |
| 1970s | Penal Code: Amendments include prohibition of generally advocating violence, introduction of a new legal provision making it a crime to found or collaborate in a criminal or a terrorist group, even if the one has not committed a specific crime (StGB, articles 129, 129a) |
| | Code of Penal Procedure: Amendments include limiting the number of defense lawyers, body search for defense lawyers visiting their clients, incommunicado detention ordered by the government in case of a direct threat to the life of people legal recourse before a court of law was possible. |
| 1978 | Antiterrorism Act (Gesetz zur Änderung der Strafprozessordnung), April 14. |
| 1987 | Prevention of Terrorism Act (Gesetz zur Bekämpfung des Terrorismus), December 19. Article 129 of the Penal Code was amended to prohibit advocating violence and founding or collaborating in a criminal or a terrorist group even if the person him- or herself has not committed a specific crime (article 129, 129a StGB). Amendments to the Code of Penal Procedure include isolation of prisoners and denial of contact with legal counsel. |
| 2002 | Security Package I, January 1. Amends numerous security statutes to extend the powers of security authorities, enhance data exchange, prevent the entry of extremists and increase options for terminating residence, and extend and enhance surveillance powers across a number of sectors. Amends Law Governing Private Associations to allow for the banning of extremist religious or ideological groups regardless of nationality under certain circumstances. |
| | Prevention of Terrorism Act ("Security Package II"), January 1. Further limits the activities of extremist associations. |
| 2004–7 | Elements of Security Packages I and II declared unconstitutional in 2004, 2005, and 2007. |

Shawn Boyne stresses that RAF was not a threat to Germany's security, but a political threat. The state's counterterrorism strategy, however, consisted of the enactment of new legislation that infringed on civil rights. Databases profiled even left-leaning citizens, and loyalty screenings were used for citizens who applied for jobs in the public service. No reasonable suspicion was necessary to conduct an investigation. The state accumulated considerable power, but the response was within the existing framework of German and international law. Key elements were two broad antiterror packages that reformed existing laws and increased resources (see Table 9.1 for a summary). In the case of the RAF, no harsh interrogation methods bordering on torture were used. However, when it came to conditions of pre-trial detention and imprisonment after the verdict, regulations were extremely strict. Prisoners were isolated on the rationale that there was an imminent danger that new terrorist operations were being planned from within prisons. During the abduction of the Lufthansa flight "Landshut" to Somalia, total isolation measures (*Kontaktsperre*, the complete prohibition on contact) were rushed through Parliament and used on RAF prisoners. The government's justification was the prevention of new terrorist acts. Arrests were made publicly—no secret arrests took place, nor were secret detention centers used.

Against the backdrop of the assassination of a high-ranking judge, Günter von Drenkmann, and the death of the RAF member Holger Meins during a hunger strike (Aust 1998: 322), the German parliament adopted a law in December 1974 that sought to strengthen the hand of the prosecution (several defense lawyers had already been individually excluded from representing RAF prisoners). According to an amendment to the code of criminal procedure, lawyers could be excluded on the mere suspicion of their involvement in the crimes of the defendant. Another change in legislation prohibited the defense of several defendants by one lawyer. In addition, trials could now be conducted in the absence of the defendant if s/he inflicted conditions on him- or herself that prevented in-person court appearances. Clearly, this was a response to RAF hunger strikes.

In what became known as the "Stammheim" trial (1975–77) against the four first-generation RAF leaders (Baader, Meinhof, Ensslin, and Raspe), the defense lawyer Otto Schily attempted to demonstrate the close collaboration between the German and U.S. governments in the war in Vietnam. He formally asked the court to hear as witnesses the U.S. Secretary of Defense Melvin Laird, President Richard M. Nixon, and various high-ranking German politicians—all of which the court denied (Aust 1998: 385 ff.; for Schily's point of view, see Schily and Ströbele 1973). Schily later joined the Green Party, switched to the Social Democratic Party, and served from 1998 to 2005 as German minister of the interior.

After Schily discovered evidence that conversations between defendants and their lawyers had been tapped[7]—something absolutely prohibited under German law—he proposed to the Stammheim court on March 15, 1977 that the trial be suspended. Two days later, the state ministers of interior and justice for Baden-Württemberg acknowledged that surveillance had been introduced on two occasions to prevent new terrorist acts. They declared that they would do the same in similar circumstances. BfV and BND had installed listening devices in seven cells. The ministers stated that only prisoners had been listened to, not interviews with defense lawyers. The prosecution declared it had no knowledge of this operation, but the trial was suspended (Aust 1998: 541 ff., 546).

A particularly dramatic and peculiar approach was taken by a state agency in 1978 in the state of Lower Saxony. The State Agency for the Protection of the Constitution bombed the Celle prison in order to infiltrate an informer into the RAF group held there. Only many years later would this become public knowledge (Becker 1977).

## Allegations of Torture

In 1977, during the hijacking of the Lufthansa flight *Landshut* to Somalia, the federal government ordered a total prohibition of contact between RAF prisoners, and between prisoners and the outside world. The prohibition was justified as a way to prevent new terrorist acts. When defense lawyers challenged the decision before the courts, some courts declared the measures illegal. Notwithstanding such rulings, lawyers were denied access to their clients. When it became likely that lawyers would challenge the measure before the Federal Constitutional Court, the government introduced a law permitting the total isolation of prisoners (*Kontaktsperre*), which was approved in a record time of just a few days. It was justified on the basis of StGB article 34, which defines the justification of emergency *(rechtfertigender Notstand)*. This legal norm was meant to be used by an individual so that s/he could act if a threatened by an emergency situation where the state could not help him or her; here, however, it was used by the state against an individual. In the event of reasonable suspicion *(begründeter Verdacht)* that there was danger to the physical integrity, life, or liberty of a person, and that danger came from a terrorist group, it was now possible for the government to order the complete isolation of prisoners for up to thirty days; after two weeks courts had to endorse or change the decision (Aust 1998: 552–54).

One of the most difficult and emotional issues were allegations made by RAF prisoners and their defense lawyer that they were actually tortured by such isolation. To be sure, the courts and leading prison officials had clearly imposed a very strict, exceptional prison regime, motivated by the goals of preventing both escape and the planning and leading of RAF action from inside. Roughly ten hunger strikes took place, and prisoners were force-fed. As was noted earlier, one prisoner, Holger Meins, died. Authorities rejected these allegations of torture, which at least partially served to help radicalize supporters and attract new members.

Nonetheless, the physical and psychological situation of RAF leaders in Stammheim prison clearly deteriorated during their lengthy pretrial detention and hunger strikes. Authorities argued that prisoners were themselves responsible and therefore no state action was necessary (i.e., no change in prison conditions). When Amnesty International criticized certain aspects of imprisonment without accepting any allegation of "torture" (Amnesty International 1979–82), German government and other state officials reacted harshly.

During this time, anti-torture activists would come to university seminars to seek "solidarity with political prisoners," concentrating on criticisms of detention conditions (e.g., "isolation torture"). However, such activism raised the question of whether such demands of "solidarity" meant supporting demands regarding detention, or whether they might signal support for specific actions of the RAF or for armed struggle in general.

Finally, the Stammheim court asked independent experts to interview prisoners. In their reports—confidential, only for the courts—they stated that the prisoners' health had seriously deteriorated. Wilfried Rasch, director of the Institute of Forensic Psychiatry at the Free University of Berlin, suggested the establishment of encounter groups of up to fifteen RAF prisoners (see Rasch 1978). After the Schleyer and *Landshut* events, smaller groups were established in a few prisons. In public, a strong media campaign was initiated particularly by conservative and popular media, strongly criticizing what they saw as favorable conditions for murderers and terrorists[8].

The European Commission of Human Rights rejected applications by Ensslin, Baader, and Raspe that requested a decision that various standards of the European Convention of Human Rights had been violated by Germany, especially Article 3, which prohibits torture, and Article 6, the right to fair trial. The decision gives a good overview of all the state decisions and contains some criticisms of prison conditions.[9]

The introduction of new laws against terrorism and their discussion in Parliament were accompanied by an intense discussion in civil society. Civil rights organizations, academia, and the media were actively involved. A number of influential books were published; in particular, *Letters on the Defense of the Republic (Briefe zur Verteidigung der Republik)*, by Freimut Duve, Heinrich Böll, and Klaus Staeck, is a collection of public letters by mainly liberal and left-liberal authors on the necessity to respect civil rights even in difficult times (Duve, Böll, and Staeck 1977). While it is difficult to gauge their exact influence, the continuous critical debate probably contributed to a counterbalance of further far-reaching demands from the internal security community and their political supporters.

## DEVELOPMENTS SINCE SEPTEMBER 11, 2001

### *Characterization of the Terrorist Threat*

Four members of an al Qaeda cell in Hamburg were centrally involved in the attacks of September 11—Mohammed Atta, Ramzi Binalshibh, Marwan el Shehhi, and Ziad Jarrah. Peter Katzenstein wrote in 2001 that there is clear evidence that Germany was one of the major strategic staging areas for the attacks (Katzenstein 2001: 15), a view which is now outdated because we now know that planning took place largely in Afghanistan (9/11 Commission Report 2004: 155 ff., 160 ff.). So far, there has been no terrorist attack in Germany since 9/11, but fourteen Germans were among the nineteen victims who died in the bomb attack on a synagogue in Tunisia on April 11, 2002, attributed to al Qaeda.[10]

Germany, in cooperation with other European countries and with international institutions (such as the United Nations, the European Union, and the Council of Europe), has focused on the international fight against terrorism. Its main goals are to prevent terrorist attacks in Germany, as well as in other European and partner countries around the world. After the bomb attacks in London in 2005, attention has increasingly focused on the terrorist potential within the country among foreign extremist groups.

### *The State's Counterterrorism Strategy*

Central to the German state's counterterrorism strategy are the two security packages, I and II, that entered into force on January 1, 2002.[11] "Security Package I" includes amendments to numerous security statutes in order to, inter alia, extend the powers of security authorities in the interest of preventing terrorism, enhance necessary data exchange between authorities, prevent terrorists from entering Germany, enhance the identification of extremists who have already entered the country and increase the options for terminating their residence, enhance identification measures in visa procedures, facilitate the deployment of armed air marshals on German aircraft, enhance border control facilities, enable security checks on staff employed in essential facilities and facilities that are vital for defense, create the legal basis for integrating biometric data into passports and identity documents, limit the right to use firearms onboard civilian aircraft to police officers, and take swifter measures to ban the activities of extremist associations of foreigners in Germany.

The Law Governing Private Associations was amended to cover religious communities by deleting relevant exemptions. Now extremist religious or ideological groups can also be banned, regardless of the nationality of their members, if their goals or activities are directed at committing criminal offenses, if they oppose the constitutional order, or if they are directed against the concept of international understanding.

When the Prevention of Terrorism Act (Terrorismusbekämpfungsgesetz) also went into force on January 1, 2002 (it is also referred to as the Anti-Terror Act or "Security Package II"), the activities of extremist associations of foreigners were limited more effectively by extending the grounds for imposing bans or limiting activities (see article 9, "Amendments to the Law Governing Private Associations"). Sections 14 and 15 of the Law Governing Private Associations regulate the banning of associations of foreigners or their activities, insofar as their purpose or activities (1) promote activities outside the Federal Republic of Germany whose goals or instruments are incompatible with the basic values of a country that respects human dignity; (2) support, advocate, or solicit the use of violence; or (3) instigate, support, or threaten to launch attacks against persons or property. In this way the instruments relating to the *collective* activities of foreigners have been aligned with the instruments limiting the political activities of *individual* foreigners as set forth in section 47 of the Residence Act. EU foreigners (EU citizens) are not affected by this; the amendments regarding associations of foreigners only apply to associations of third-state nationals from non-EU countries (Germany 2002).

In 2004 and 2005, the Federal Constitutional Court declared unconstitutional three laws that all had been introduced at least partially to strengthen the national and international fight against terrorism. They are (1) the law to improve the fight against organized crime (enhanced powers of surveillance were under criticism; 1 BvR 2378/98, March 3, 2004), (2) a Lower Saxony law on public security and order (powers of preventive wiretapping were under criticism; 1 BvR 668/04, July 27, 2005), and (3) a national law transforming the EU European Arrest Warrant, the law whose safeguards for the rule of law were considered too weak (2 BvR 2236/04, July 18, 2005). In 2007, the court declared unconstitutional the law on air security, which had empowered as *ultima ratio* the minister of defense to order the shooting down of a civilian plane if s/he considers it would be used as a terrorist weapon.

Other significant developments in the state's security strategy involve the use of an electronic "dragnet," the deportation of aliens, and foreign military and intelligence operations.

*The* Rasterfahndung *(dragnet) after 9/11.* Considerable changes were made in the cooperation between intelligence and police organizations. In a federal state, police functions were mainly the responsibility of the sixteen German states (the federal state disposed of a border security force that was renamed "federal police" in 2005, but with much more limited powers than, say, the FBI). This was a conscious reaction to the Nazi dictatorship and the mass abuses committed by a highly centralized police force. One main government instrument in the search for terrorists, however, was a large-scale data comparison system, a "dragnet" *(Rasterfahndung)*. It was developed by the Federal Crime Office (BKA) under its president, Horst Herold (Aust 1998: 211 ff.; Hauser 1997). Although it received a lot of political support and positive reports in the mass media, its results were marginal; very few terrorists were captured despite an enormous investment of resources. After September 11, 2003, dragnet operations were used against 8.3 million people, approximately 10 percent of the German population, to discover so-called al Qaeda sleepers. An internal BKA report leaked to the public concluded that its goal could not be reached. From the point of view of data protection, specialists have criticized the dragnet methodology as a violation of privacy rights (Kant 2005: 13).[12]

*Deportation of aliens.* Operations and legislation after September 11 were directed specifically against suspected aliens. In addition to the dragnet, after the Madrid and London bombings in 2004 and 2005, respectively, Minister of the Interior Otto Schily suggested the introduction of preventive detention for suspected foreign terrorists without charge or trial on more than one occasion (he suggested that such an executive decision by the minister could be appealed to only one court).[13] But this proposal did not receive strong support in Parliament. However, in the new law on the integration of foreigners *(Zuwanderungsgesetz),* in force since January 1, 2005, the conservative opposition successfully put pressure on the government to include security aspects. Essentially, suspected aliens can now be deported based on a suspicion that must be supported by facts. There must be a prognosis of the danger these aliens present for German internal security (for a critical review, see Pelzer 2005). In 2003, the Council of Europe's Committee for the Prevention of Torture criticized German border police for using unnecessary violence when deporting foreigners (Deutsche Welle 2003).

*Foreign Military Operations.* Issues of human rights standards are also increasingly discussed with regard to foreign military operations, for example, in Afghanistan. German military operations always take place in a context of multinational operations—EU- or NATO-led operations. Given the large number of countries with their own rules of engagement, it is important to develop and approve, beyond humanitarian law applicable in armed conflict, common human rights standards for all national contingents on issues such as house arrest, detention without charge or trial, prison conditions, and the use of lethal force. Here, the issue of extraterritorial application of human rights treaties comes to the fore, such as the UN International Covenant in Civil and Political Rights of 1966 and the European Convention on Human Rights of 1950. The German Institute of Human Rights has formulated ten recommendations to the government and Parliament for German participation in the international fight against terrorism which focus on foreign and military policy (Heinz and Arend 2005).

*Foreign Intelligence Operations.* Foreign intelligence operations are largely invisible to the public because they are kept secret. In Europe, and in Germany in particular, some operations linked to antiterror measures became known in 2005. Though the cases of Kurnaz and Zammar (see below) were reported in 2003 and 2004 by the weekly *Der Spiegel*, no reaction could be noted by the government, Parliament or other political or police circles at the time. This changed with the publication of an article in the *Washington Post* on November 2, 2005, focusing on the U.S. policy of extraordinary renditions and CIA flights in Europe.[14] A major discussion ensued, which included statements by government ministers and debates in Parliament and in the media. So far, very few cases of questionable interrogations by German government agents abroad have become known, but those which have are interesting from a civil and human rights perspective.

### Individual Human Rights Cases

*Mohammed S. and Ihab D.* In autumn 2002, an official of the BKA sought and received the cooperation of Lebanese military intelligence in interrogating a terrorist suspect as part of an investigation of the German attorney general's office. On a visit to Beirut in October 2002, a BKA official was surprised how quickly he got answers to the questions he had handed over to his intelligence counterpart. He had the suspicion that the prisoner might have been tortured and stated, "in the BKA it was clear to everybody that there was torture." The official was also investigated for alleged private uses of his official cell phone. The German attorney general rejected this assertion, commenting that in such a case, interrogation would have been immediately terminated. Moreover, the BKA leadership rejected the official's criticisms, stressing that he had not informed them about his observations during his visit, only much later in the process. Though Lebanon is known to torture prisoners, no questions seem to have been asked, nor was there any follow-up to a prisoner's statement that he was ill-treated.[15] At the end of October 2002, two BKA officials were able to talk personally to two prisoners, Mohammed S. and Ihab D,; the latter complains that he was violently coerced into signing his statements.

*Murat Kurnaz (Turkish national, resident in Germany).* Minister of the Interior Schily and Minister of Justice Zypries have both publicly criticized the U.S. government for creating at Guantanamo a prison island free of legal and other controls. Nevertheless, in 2002 German officials from the BKA and BND visited Guantanamo and interviewed two prisoners, one of them Murat Kurnaz, a Turkish resident in Germany. These visits were subsequently criticized in the German media.

In March 2006, new information was published in *Der Spiegel*, reportedly based on evidence from German intelligence services. According to this source, the U.S. government and German intelligence had already established in 2002 that Kurnaz was simply in the wrong place at the wrong time and had nothing to do with al Qaeda. The U.S. government is reported to have offered in 2002 to the German government to take him back. But due to a strong negative reaction by the BfV, the German government declined the offer. There was a fear of creating domestic security problems and that perhaps he could be seen as a martyr. Later, the U.S. government stonewalled. The article claimed that the German government sought Kurnaz's release and return to Germany, although it declined to comment.[16] Kurnaz was released from Guantanamo and returned to Germany in autumn 2006.

*Mohammed Haider Zammer (Syrian–German dual nationality).* Zammar, a terrorist suspect, was transferred on U.S. initiative at the end of 2001 from Morocco to Syria. He was kept in an underground prison cell of the Syrian Military Intelligence agency and actually "disappeared" after he was brought to Syria because its government claimed for a time it did not have him. According to Amnesty International, he was tortured. German police and intelligence officials (both BKA and BND) visited Zammar in November 2002.[17] It has now become apparent that security agencies had already been informed by their U.S. counterparts. While the ministry of foreign affairs explained to the Zammar family's lawyer that it could not get access to Zammar, a German citizen, German intelligence officials were able to visit him. Zammar continues to be held prisoner in Syria, without charge or trial.

*Khalid El-Masri (German national of Lebanese descent).* At the end of 2004, while on a visit to Macedonia, El-Masri was detained by police and handed over to CIA agents who flew him to Afghanistan (there is an ongoing criminal investigation about the case by prosecutors in Munich). There he was interrogated for five months by, among others, an agent known as "Sam" who spoke German fluently. CIA interrogators told El-Masri, "You are here in a country without laws. Nobody knows that you are here and nobody cares what happens to you" ("Kronzeuge gegen die CIA," *Der Spiegel,* December 13, 2005, author's translation). El-Masri was flown back to Albania where he was released. It seems there was a mix-up of names of terrorist suspects on the wanted list.

To this day, the U.S. government has not officially recognized this "extraordinary rendition," or abduction. Chancellor Angela Merkel raised the case in her conversation with Secretary of State Condoleezza Rice in January 2006. Merkel said the U.S. government accepted that a mistake was made, but she was rebuffed by the U.S. state department immediately after this remark. In summer 2005, the U.S. ambassador to Germany, Dan Coats, informed Minister of the Interior Schily confidentially and in general terms about El-Masri's case after he was released. The minister kept the conversation confidential at a time, when El-Masri's lawyer formally requested the assistance of the ministry of foreign affairs. The ministry responded that it did not know anything. Later, at the end of 2005, the government informed the public that it first heard about the case through the letter by the lawyer to the foreign office. According to El-Masri, he was drugged during his transport to Afghanistan and beaten in custody.

## Investigations

In the German Parliament, the *Bundestag,* these cases, together with the revelations about CIA flights and reports about two BND agents' activities in Baghdad, led to increasing pressure on the government in winter 2005 and spring 2006. Demands concentrated on a comprehensive explanation from the government about what happened and what its future policies might be. (In autumn 2005, the government had changed from a Social Democratic-Green coalition to one formed by the Christian Democratic and Social Democratic parties.)

In Parliament, a special committee was mandated with overseeing the three German intelligence agencies (BfV, BND and MAD), the parliamentary control body *(Parlamentarisches Kontrollgremium,* or PKG). The official government justification was, of course, that the work of the intelligence agencies should not be endangered, and that foreign agencies would limit their cooperation if too much information was revealed. Since the meetings are very confidential and the committee rarely addresses the public, the scope and depth of control is not transparent to the public and has often been criticized by the media, as well as by some members of Parliament. In practice, most of the time the media discover critical cases (e.g., surveillance within Germany by the BND of an author critical of BND activities in the mid-90s),[18] and then the committee deliberates secretly. Real information is often absent from public discourse.

In 2006, however, the government handed over to the PKG a confidential, 300-page report covering the Baghdad BND case,[19] and the El-Masri, Kurnaz, and Zammar cases. A redacted version of 200 pages was distributed to all members of Parliament, and a 90-page version was published—an unusual step so far. The public report left out, however, specific case material on the recommendation of the Federal Commissioner on data protection (Germany, Bundesregierung, 2006).

In its report, the government argued that it must have the right to question suspects abroad, including in nondemocratic countries (ibid.: 81–84). Only if evidence emerges that the person interviewed was tortured would the interrogation be suspended. It is not clear, however, how such a conclusion would be made, especially in the light of the often-heard argument by security agencies (not the least in the United States regarding prisoners at Guantanamo) that suspects are likely to say that they have been tortured to enhance their defense. The government stated that in the future, the federal crime office should not be involved in questioning, only intelligence agencies.

The government had probably hoped that through the report it would be possible to silence voices who demanded a parliamentary investigation committee. A number of open questions had been answered by the government in the report. But after some difficult discussions among the three opposition parties (liberal, left, and green) because of diverging objectives, all agreed to join hands to push through an investigation committee that at the time of writing is being formed (this is possible with 25 percent of all members of Parliament). It will also look at the last three cases mentioned (omitting the Baghdad case).

## CIA Flights: Debates on the European Level

The Council of Europe (the Parliamentary Assembly and Secretary General) and the European Union (European Parliament) set up investigations on the CIA flights in Europe, separate from national investigations in various countries.

While only limited new information was provided in the final report— it is not clear which and how many terrorist suspects have been transported on which flights. The Council of Europe's secretary general, Terry Davis, presented the following key recommendations in February 2006. He called for national definition of such acts as aiding criminal offenses, official recognition of sites of detention, a regulatory framework for foreign secret services, and greater supervision of air traffic (Council of Europe 2006: 21)

Dick Marty, the Swiss parliamentarian and rapporteur of the Parliamentary Assembly of the Council of Europe, and the Secretary General delivered their final reports on June 2006. Marty acknowledged that there is no formal evidence of the existence of secret CIA detention centers in Poland, Romania, or other member countries. But he is convinced that serious indications continue to exist and grow stronger. He talks about a global "spider's web" that was established by the CIA and distinguishes four categories of aircraft landing points, which indicate different degrees of collusion on the part of countries concerned, stopover points, staging points, one-off pickup points, and detainee transfer and drop-off points (PACE 2006: 8, 13). In his report, fourteen member countries are identified, among them Germany (in the category of staging points). The majority of the Parliamentary Assembly supported his analysis and recommendations.

## THE IMPACT AND PERILS OF SECURITY COOPERATION

German state reactions to the Red Army Faction and post-9/11 developments have been influenced by three key factors: a legacy of state crimes committed under National Socialism that requires that rule of law standards had to be upheld, a much stronger control of executive action by Parliament and the judiciary than in most other Western countries, and an acknowledgement that German measures against terrorism had to be part of international cooperation, especially among Western states. All of this favored a general commitment to national and international human rights norms, even in situations bordering on national emergency. It also might have required some compromises in the practical field regarding international cooperation.

Fundamentally, Germany chose a criminal law approach to fight terrorism. Changes of legislation and some state practices on a few occasions transgressed fundamental rule of law principles (for example, incommunicado detention and prison conditions). The situation regarding a few post-9/11 cases has not yet been sufficiently clarified.

To summarize, the main continuities included that no special legal regime beyond harsh criminal-law measures was instituted in either the 1970s or after September 11. Even so, legal norms were changed so that the state was able to react more effectively against now-transnational terrorist threats. Changes in the 1970s mainly concerned penal law and criminal procedural standards, especially regulations on the defense lawyers for terrorist suspects. After 2001, the two antiterror law packages concentrated on facilitating contact, exchanging information and action between police and intelligence agencies, and allowing the state to ban national chapters of internationally acting foreign terrorist organizations (StGB, article 129b).

While there were and are risks in terms of the negative impact of counterterrorist measures on civil rights, no development toward a legal grey zone or shadow-state apparatus took place. Fairly lively debates about these issues continue to take place, not necessarily in the general public but apart from government and Parliament among interested circles of academics, media professionals, and NGOs.

After September 11, 2001, cooperation between states played a much bigger role than in the 1970s. Indeed, international cooperation is undoubtedly key in fighting transnational terrorism effectively. Three of the key questions to emerge were, Along which political-military dimensions should the fight develop, and according to which legal norms? And what could and should states do that might differ from the overall strategy, norms, and practices of the most important player, the United States?

While there was a strong sense of solidarity with the United States as victim of terrorist attacks in 2001, differences of opinion on strategy and tactics with some European countries came to the fore rather quickly, especially on Guantanamo. There was increasing concern regarding the excessive emphasis on military aspects of the counterterrorism strategy. In almost every European country, the main responsibility for the fight against terrorism lies with the ministries of the interior and, secondly, of justice, with a rather marginal role for the defense ministry. The obsession with the war metaphor—the most recent being the "long war" (see, e.g., Carafano and Rosenzweig 2005)—bolsters the military part of foreign policy and strategic thinking as well as the Pentagon among the U.S. bureaucracy in turf battles, but it has not found any substantial echo in any of the member states of the European Union.

The nexus between international cooperation and the protection of human rights was and is relevant with regard to the extradition or expulsion of foreigners to the United States, with a view to the death penalty and the possibility of a trial before a military commission in Guantanamo that lacks fairness (including the issue of whether in these cases evidence should be furnished to U.S. courts). In the EU and German extradition treaties of 2003, an assurance that no death penalty will be passed has been included. In the German legal assistance treaty of 2003, the government can—but does not have to—refuse extradition if evidence furnished is being used by special courts in an emergency situation *(Ausnahmegerichte)*. Similarly, German law impedes the expulsion of foreigners according to immigration laws to their home country where they might be subject to torture, other inhumane treatment, or severe human rights violations. As far as cooperation among foreign intelligence (and perhaps police) agencies, a key question has been whether the German government should use information generated in an unclear interrogation context, i.e., when a person might have been tortured, in order to prevent new terrorist acts? The German minister of the interior, Wolfgang Schäuble, responded affirmatively and was criticized by some politicians and supported by others.[20]

The issue of a legal grey zone and shadow-state apparatus is here very much in the public debate. So far, both political elites and society would not tolerate such a development in Germany or in international cooperation. At the beginning of January 2006, before her visit to the United States, the conservative chancellor of Germany, Angela Merkel, told the press, "An institution like Guantanamo in its present form cannot and must not exist in the long term. We must find different ways of dealing with prisoners. As far as I'm concerned there's no question about that."[21]

The alternative path followed by Germany may inform the wider debate among liberal democracies and the Western alliance—even the United States itself. Coming back to the U.S. experience that began this volume, as the former FBI agent John German observed with respect to the United States, "Terrorism will never go away, and free and open societies will always be especially vulnerable. But we do not win by coming less free and less open. Ironically, al Qaeda does not have the power to destroy the United States. But we do. By playing into a script written by the terrorists we have indeed squared the error" (German 2005: 16).

# 10 Conclusion

*Human Rights in Hard Times*

Gershon Shafir, Alison Brysk, and Daniel Wehrenfennig

This volume makes the case for human rights in hard times, when violent enemies of the state threaten the lives of large numbers of citizens. We compare the experience of the U.S. trade-off of human rights with most similar systems like the UK and Canada, which have stayed closer to democratic and international standards, to show that threatened democracies have better options. Like Michael Ignatieff, we adopt a comparative and historical perspective to show that this threat is not new—but the lessons we draw from history involve protection of the greater good from the politics of fear, not necessary adjustment to the lesser evil. We compare current threats and responses to commonly invoked security "role models" like Israel and Northern Ireland to independently analyze the import of their experience, and find that their trade-offs were not sustainable. Tracing the paths of cases like Germany and Spain shows how historical learning helps set the template for the current debate in those countries, and expands the menu for counterterror policies.

Democracy is necessary but not sufficient to protect human rights in hard times, and human rights are the necessary basis for a legitimate response to terrorism. Democratic rule of law, transparency, and participation must be maintained; they can mitigate some abuses against citizens within the national territory, and provide some retroactive accountability. But contesting the politics of fear that underlies the design of military policies, abuses abroad and against noncitizens, shadow states, and the unilateral abrogation of international law requires reframing national security as human security.

Moreover, liberal democracies must also strive to exercise cosmopolitan self-determination, in which leaders construct national interest in accordance with the needs of their own citizenry, guided by accountability to internalized universal principles—rather than by hegemonic aspirations. A democracy must be more than an elected Leviathan; rather, a democratic state is a political community constituted to protect its citizens from the range of threats to their life, liberty, bodily integrity, and human dignity. It must remain so even against the threat of unlawful and indiscriminate violence. This is the mandate and limit of state security policy.

## HUMAN RIGHTS AS HUMAN SECURITY

While it is clear that human rights protect the individual from state violence, it is useful to rehearse how the state's respect for human rights also contributes to the defense of the members of the political community from terror. One goal of terrorism is to create disruption and fear in a target society to produce major change in military policy, alliances, regime type, or even sovereignty. Another is to provoke the kind of excessive and indiscriminate repression that will make the discontented welcome the terrorists as their champions. In order to defend democracies from these threats, target states need reliable information, sophisticated understanding of structural causes and the global context, effective options for the control of violence, and international support. None of these alone will avail, and even together they may not eliminate illegitimate violence—but these are the responses with the best chance of decreasing the human and institutional damage. In the long run, respect for human rights contributes to informed and proportional policy making, democratic legitimacy, social cohesion, and international cooperation.

Many of the worst violations are pursued in the name of securing information, yet torture and illicit detention have not proven an effective source of intelligence for counterterror as an overall strategy. On the contrary, the historical and comparative pattern of counterinsurgency suggests that disproportionate and inappropriate tactics lead to a cycle of mutual escalation between insurgents and government forces, which ultimately "destroys the village in order to save it"—in the U.S. military's classic defense of scorched earth tactics in Vietnam, America's first major defeat. Beyond this, the effects of torture and abuse spread from degradation of the victims to corruption of the perpetrators to a systemic crisis of values that undermines the cohesion of democracies. A state that violates universal principles calls into question its own national identity, diminishing public support for security sacrifices in the name of that identity, alienating alliances based in part on common values, and blurring the distinction in international public opinion between terrorist violence and defensive "state terror" (Pfaff 2005).

The link between respect for human rights and international cooperation is expressed by the German Parliament's March 2004 resolution, an allied state which has felt unable to extradite certain suspects to the U.S. and failed to convict an indicted terrorist leader due to U.S. restrictions and interference with German legal standards of evidence.

> [I]t constitutes a blatant contradiction when, of all people, those who justify the fight against terrorism with the need to protect rights and the security of the people undermine this protection by the very methods they choose for this fight. It is therefore not only by international law that the USA, as the largest and strongest democracy in the world, is bound to respect the fundamental rights of even the most dangerous terrorists. This is all the more true as the USA expects and demands strict compliance with these rights and principles from others. International legitimacy is an important resource in the fight against international terrorism. One of the sources of legitimacy is the transparency of proceedings. (Heinz and Arend 2005: 42)

Similarly, the Spanish judge Baltasar Garzon, known equally for his decades of prosecution of terrorists in Spain and the landmark human rights case requesting the extradition of the former Chilean dictator Augusto Pinochet from Britain, has demanded the closure of Guantanamo and discussed how U.S. secrecy has constrained his own prosecutions of al Qaeda suspects in Spain (Sciolino 2006). In July 2006, the twenty-five nations of the European Union formally demanded that President Bush close the Guantanamo prison.

## BEST PRINCIPLES AND PRACTICES FOR SUSTAINABLE NATIONAL SECURITY

Sophisticated understanding and policy alternatives are best achieved through democracies' characteristic commitments to open debate, pluralism, and participation—not a militarized politics of fear. The first thing liberal democracies need to stay liberal is a democratic national security process. In addition to the classical role of checks and balances like parliamentary debate and judicial review to safeguard the rights of suspects, a transparent and pluralistic national security policy process protects citizens from misguided or ill-informed policies made by a narrow or self-serving elite. The road to Abu Ghraib was paved with discarded memos from dissident lawyers within the Bush administration who were systematically excluded from policy making (Golden 2006), while the veil of secrecy over Guantanamo produced international condemnation rather than actionable intelligence—as silenced FBI interrogators had warned.

The rule of law is what separates liberal democracy from populist caprice, which is at special risk in times of threat. This book shows that states can maintain the rule of law with even a derogatory legal regime such as the UK, but dualistic or parallel zones of illegality undermine democracy and grow to contaminate even its theoretically protected members and practices. The Landau Commission was convened in the wake of the coerced confession of an Israeli citizen, whereas Canada's unitary regime has renegotiated its detention policies for noncitizens.

Comparative and historical analysis indicates that terrorism may be temporarily suppressed by military campaigns, but ultimately diminishes only when there is some viable political response to the grievances of the supporters of violent outsiders. This does not mean that violence will disappear with attention to "root causes," only that in the long run, a more just and democratic world order will be relatively more stable and peaceful. One implication of this understanding is that human security must include human rights education in the broadest sense; an active promotion of a democratic and cosmopolitan national identity that interprets unavoidable losses as honorable sacrifices for common values supported by a compassionate political community, rather than fear-provoking threats to the existence of the nation (see below).

It also means that democratic societies will always need effective and legitimate options for the control of violence, alongside long-term political and ideological reconstructions. Generally, our comparisons show that in most instances police rather than military forces will be more appropriate and internationally legitimate to counter terror. Respect for human rights in the conduct of police campaigns works logically and historically to increase their effectiveness. Discriminatory measures such as racial or religious profiling tend to reduce community cooperation with the police and reduce immigrants' integration, especially in vulnerable immigrant communities that may have information on transnational terror networks. On the other hand, strong social cohesion and participation rooted in common community values contribute to effective policing in international as well as domestic conflicts.

Finally, our work supports the notion of meaningful multilateralism as a "best principle" of sustainable human security. EU membership did more for Britain than set a standard of international legal accountability—multilateralism actually contributed to a framework for resolving the underlying conflict. Similarly, Spain became a more liberal democracy in the EU context, with positive effects on security policies and increased scope for self-determination.

TABLE 10.1  Best Practices for Human Security

| *Horizontal Accountability* | *Actors* | *Best Practices* |
| --- | --- | --- |
| Parliamentary control | Elected representatives | Monitoring and review of military and executive (Heinz, Forsythe, Adelman, Campbell) |
| Judicial control | Judges, lawyers | Courts review laws and policies; lawyers represent noncitizens (Heinz, Landman Shafir) |
| Opposition | Political parties, designated group representatives | Contest policies, discrimination and definition of national interest (Heinz, Adelman, Forsythe) |

| *Vertical Accountability* | *Actors* | *Best Practices* |
| --- | --- | --- |
| International organizations | United Nations (UN), Council of Europe | Conventions, reports, silent diplomacy, membership pressures (Heinz, Campbell, Martí et al.) |
| International law | European Court of Human Rights (ECHR), Intl. Criminal Court (ICC) | Judicial review (Campbell, Landman) |
| Allies | Allied countries, NATO | Critique (Heinz, Falk); resistance (Adelman, Martí et al.) |
| Global civil society | International NGOs (ICRC, AI), public opinion, media | Information, mobilization (Martí et al., Heinz, Forsythe) |
| Public Opinion | Civic groups, private citizens, educators, schools | Surveys (Adelman), symbolic actions (Martí et al.), debates publications (Campbell, Shafir, Brysk) |

| *Alternatives* | *Actors* | *Best practices* |
| --- | --- | --- |
| Legitimate social control | Police, peacekeepers | Community-based policing, weapons control (Landman) |
| Transnational support | IGOs, esp. regional | Information and judicial cooperation (Heinz) |
| Political Solutions | States, rival groups, hegemons | Conflict resolution, power sharing (Campbell) |

The best practices that flow from these best principles can be summarized as horizontal accountability, vertical accountability, and alternative modes of national security. Horizontal accountability comprises the checks and balances of democratic institutions for transparency, participation, and legal control of national security policy. Vertical accountability consists in the pressures from above and below to incorporate universal norms in state practices. Alternative pathways to human security provide long-term reduction of threat, and sustainable responses to nonstate violence. Each of our cases demonstrates a combination of these factors; some notable illustrations of particular best practices are indicated in Table 10.1.

## EXPORTING ILLIBERALISM: "WORST PRACTICES" OF THE WAR ON DEMOCRACY

The U.S. export of illiberal models of counterterror has distorted national debates on the appropriate balance between rights and security. Cosmopolitan global influences can contribute to humane security policies—but other modes of international exchange are part of the problem this book seeks to address. Governments import and export counterterror models and legislation, and scholars and the public study and discuss them. Examining three countries not profiled in this volume, Turkey, India, and Australia, will further demonstrate the uses and abuses of foreign laws and models in the context of fashioning counterterror policies that protect human rights in threatened democracies beyond the Atlantic alliance.

The Turkish counterterror law that took effect in 1991, developed as part of its struggle against Kurdish separatism and terror, defines terrorism based on its purpose or aims rather than referring to specific criminal acts. The government of Prime Minister Recep Erdogan, however, is attempting to bring Turkish human rights laws into line with EU standards. As part of this process Turkey has improved its civil rights legislation for its citizens and granted cultural and linguistic rights to the Kurdish minority, though its practice still lags considerably. Its antiterror law was also purged of infamous restrictions on the press and the freedom of speech as part of the EU-inspired reforms. But after a five-year lull, violence against both civilians and military forces has been on the rise since June 2004, when the PKK announced it was resuming its attacks. In addition, Turkish targets were attacked by international jihadists. Searching for a way to reconcile national security with human rights, the Turkish cabinet has been studying the stiff antiterrorism legislation passed in Britain in the wake of the July 7, 2005, bombings in the London tube. The new Turkish legislation might include broad definitions of both terrorism and its supporters ("Turkey Seeks Tougher Anti-Terror Measures" 2005). Turkey's desire to join the EU has been counterbalanced by the resurgence of ethnic terror and U.S. influence, in a classic example of Adelman's negative concept of balance.

India suffered grievous terrorism from its inception over control of parts of Kashmir and Jammu. In 1995, its Terrorist and Disruptive Activities Prevention Act, under which tens of thousands of individuals were detained but never charged, was allowed to lapse by the Indian Parliament. The Bharatiya Janata Party-led government proposed a new antiterrorism bill in 2000 but, under criticism from human rights groups and the Congress Party, it failed to win approval. In late October 2001, drawing upon "new antiterrorism legislation in the United States and Britain to justify the new Indian law," a new Prevention of Terrorism Ordinance was enacted (Sidel 2004: 163). It allowed for up to 180-day detention of suspects, broadened the definition of terror-related crimes, and increased their punishment. But the Indian antiterror legislation went beyond the initial U.S. and UK responses—the Patriot Act and the Anti-Terrorism Act—and opponents were able to use this disparity to scale back the law's stringency. In fact, it was passed only after the December 2001 attack on the Parliament in Delhi and the convening of a special session of both houses of Parliament (Sidel 2004: 165–66). The new coalition government under Congress Party leadership, however, repealed this legislation in 2004. It is obvious that while the example of the United States allowed one Indian government to promulgate sweeping counterterror legislation, its legitimacy remained in question.

Similarly, Australia, which had no direct experience of terrorism, introduced a series of counterterror legislation in 2002, among others the Security Legislation Amendment (Terrorism) Bill to expand government authority. These new laws generated public opposition—and special umbrage was taken at the attempt to pass legislation that went further than U.S. and UK counterterror legislation—until it was softened. When Australians were the victims of the bombing of tourist sites in Bali on October 22, 2002, the tougher measures were adopted (Sidel 2004: 156–62). As in Turkey, the balancing process shifted towards a politics of fear.

"Learning" from foreign examples without democratic debates and constraints was most clearly demonstrated in regard to the use of torture, along with cruel, inhumane, and degrading treatment of detainees. The "French School" of counterinsurgency born in Indochina and Algeria, which employed torture as its principal weapon, was exported to Latin America, especially Argentina, "leading to an epidemic of torture," and again back to Vietnam by the United States (Robin 2005: 44, 49–53). It has been strongly suggested that the British practices of coercive interrogation in Northern Ireland played a role in the development of Israeli methods used against Palestinian terror suspects in the occupied territories. Israel itself provided an example or even served as an explicit model to the United States in developing its coercive interrogation tactics during the post-9/11 Afghan and Iraqi wars. The hegemonic stature of the United States magnifies the contravention of international humanitarian law it emulates by projecting it globally.

Although the coercive interrogation methods, models, and examples mentioned provided short-term relief and possibly thwarted specific attacks, they proved to be colossal policy failures. Effectiveness does not seem to have served as the yardstick of torture. France and the United States are long gone from Vietnam, the military dictatorships in Latin America have been replaced with democratic regimes, and Israel is now embroiled in seemingly irresolvable structural conflicts in the West Bank and Lebanon, in which military might does not provide sustainable security. The bitterness and shame they left behind, however, are slow to abate.

In speaking of nondemocratic regimes, the Egyptian sociologist and human rights activist Saad Eddin Ibrahim observed, "every dictator in the world is using what the United States has done under the Patriot Act and other derivative measures to justify their past violations of human rights, as well as declaring a license to continue to abuse human rights at present and in the future" (*Human Rights Defenders* 2003). The use of hegemonic Western models works differently in liberal democracies that are constrained by parliamentary opposition and human rights organizations. Overall, the counterterror legislation of the hegemonic powers—the U.S. as well as the UK—not only offered the model but also set the parameters for the legitimacy of legislation, the extent to which human rights may be sacrificed in the service of the war on terror. As the Australian justice Michael Kirby stated to the Australian Bar, "the countries that have done best against terrorism are those that have kept their priorities, retained a sense of proportion, questioned and addressed the causes of terrorism, and adhered steadfastly to constitutionalism and the rule of law" (Kirby 2001: 32–35).


NATIONAL INSECURITY AND THE POLITICS OF FEAR

We found particularly counterproductive and worrisome the loss of that sense of proportion, most specifically in the designation of U.S. counterterror policy as the "War on Terror" or our era as the "Age of Terror." Our objection is not to the designation of the enemy as terrorists or to the goal as the delegitimation and eradication of their means—indiscriminate violence aimed at civilians. Rather, we question the metaphorical use of the term war as its counter-means. We are concerned that the boundaries of this "war" are amorphous and its duration open-ended. Even more, we are troubled by its use as the idiom for our age as, for example, Ignatieff chose to subtitle his volume. Such narrow focus not only ignores or backgrounds other pressing issues and concerns, but courts the hazard of what sociologists and criminologists have described as moral panic.

In Stanley Cohen's apt description:

> Societies appear to be subject, every now and then, to periods of moral panic. A condition, episode, person, or group of persons emerges to become defined as a threat to societal values and interests; its nature is presented in a stylized and stereotypical fashion by the mass media; moral barricades are manned by editors, bishops, politicians and other right-thinking people; socially accredited experts pronounce their diagnoses and solutions; ways of coping are evolved or (more often) resorted to; the condition then disappears, submerges or deteriorates and becomes more visible. Sometimes the object of the panic is quite novel and at other times it is something which has been in existence long enough, but suddenly appears in the limelight. Sometimes the panic passes over and is forgotten, except in folklore and collective memory; at other times it has more serious and long-lasting repercussions and might produce such changes as those in legal and social policy or even in the way the society conceives itself. (Cohen 2002: 1)

Examples of such panics in the past ranged from witchcraft, through Prohibition and juvenile delinquency, to McCarthyism. All four were moral panics in that they were viewed as a threat not just to their victims but to the social order itself. Though analysts of moral panics have at times pointed out that they may be emotional, irrational, or the sublimation of deeper concerns, this does not have to be so. The threat of global terrorism is concrete and real, and in an age of weapons of mass destruction can lead to particularly devastating results. And yet, while the term WMD during the Cold War referred almost exclusively to nuclear weapons, since then this phrase has been expanded to include biological and chemical weapons as well, though the effects of the three types of weapons vary greatly (Mueller 2005: 217–20). In fact, most scholars who studied the incidences of such panics share the view that moral panics trade on fears and generate it in a disproportionate measure (Goode and Ben-Yehouda 1994: 36–38, 43–45).

Our own question is how to prevent reasonable fear from turning into moral panic, into a feeling of national insecurity? Terrorism is unique, and distinct from other sources of moral panics, precisely in this sense: its goal is to terrify the public. A pervasive and exaggerated sense of insecurity plays directly into the hands of terrorists by creating the panic that they seek to unleash but are unable to create on their own.

Alarmism and the politics of fear that generate moral panics are also liable to make analyses required in a struggle against terrorists and the responses to them flawed. Moral entrepreneurs and crusaders play a crucial role in inflating the level of threat so as to demand the tightening of legislation, adding new rules and, on occasion, justifying the breaking of laws in the fight against threats. Political leaders in the U.S. have extended the "war on terror" into Iraq or, as in Spain, attributed terror attacks to erstwhile opponents, thus misrepresenting enemies to advance political agendas that might be only tenuously related to the original threat (Cohen 2002: 90–92; Goode and Ben-Yehouda 1994: 79–82). Shadow-state apparatuses, grey zones of counterterror law, and even policies which simply weaken due process protections illicitly expand definitions of terror, executive power, and targeted suspects—thus falling into the provocation trap that has been a hallmark of terrorists. Successful provocation, after all, requires the distinct interaction of two parties: the provocateur and, not less importantly, the provoked.

Al Qaeda and other terrorists commonly justify their methods by reference to criteria of necessity and proportionality. Terror, they hold is the tool of the weak in asymmetrical warfare. They contend that attacks on Muslims around the world, which they view as interconnected and systematic, have taken such horrific toll that they justify the worst excesses of al Qaeda's own "counterterror" (Gerges 2005; Wiktorowicz 2006: 221–22). In short, terrorists are the true masters of generating moral panic with the intention of lowering or demolishing moral barriers so as to justify "collateral damage." But their use of these principles is unmoored from international humanitarian law, in particular the four Geneva Conventions of 1949. The obligations of necessity and proportionality that were refined in those documents were accompanied by additional fundamental principles: civilian immunity, distinction between civilian and military targets, and above all humane treatment, namely the prohibition of torture, inhumane and degrading treatment of prisoners and civilians. These principles form a cluster or concord, and in fighting terrorism they are the values around which the battle is waged. In defending them, liberal democracies defend themselves. In defending themselves, they defend and are protected by human rights and international humanitarian law.

Fighting the moral panic that legitimates terrorism requires that we not succumb to it ourselves. Whereas the media may be competent in assessing risk and comparative probabilities in the economy and sports, both the media and political leaders have contributed to an excessive feeling of vulnerability when it comes to international terror. The best antidote to moral panic is education. This book seeks to contribute to that education by showing how democracies can move from national insecurity to sustainable protection of the rights we are fighting for.

# Notes

## 1. BRYSK, HUMAN RIGHTS AND NATIONAL INSECURITY

1. We do not consider the important and related but distinct question of the conduct of foreign military operations, which is generally treated as a question of international humanitarian law or laws of war rather than human rights standards strictly speaking.

## 2. FALK, ENCROACHING ON THE RULE OF LAW

1. For an attempt in this direction, see Falk 2005a.

2. For useful discussion of this observation, see O'Donnell 2005. On the American tendency to absolutize its goals in wartime, see the influential study by Tucker (1960).

3. See Falk 2007.

4. This history is narrated persuasively in McCoy 2006.

5. For a depiction in the setting of the Vietnam War, see Falk, Lifton, and Kolko 1971.

6. The report offers strong criticisms of President Bill Clinton's economistic approach to world order and provides a blueprint for a much more militarist foreign policy. The report was signed by many who would become core members of the Bush entourage of advisers and is notable for three reasons: its stress on the importance of regime change in Iraq, its failure to relate American strategic priorities to counterterrorism, and its recognition that its recommendations could not be operationalized without a change in the political climate that would mobilize the American people for war.

The acknowledgment of this last point in the PNAC report, together with the U.S. government's many failures to heed warnings about a terrorist attack on American targets, as well as mystifying oversights in the face of the attack itself, have fueled suspicions about some level of official complicity with respect to the 9/11 events, at least a willingness to allow something to happen that might have been prevented. The most responsible and comprehensive critique of the official version of 9/11 can be found in two books written by a highly respected philosopher of religion, David Ray Griffin (Griffin 2004, 2005).

7. Merillat 1964; Moore, Tipson, and Turner 1990. Perhaps the most penetrating exploration of this issue is to be found in the jurisprudential approach of McDougal et al. (1960).

8. See Goldsmith and Posner 2005 for a highly intellectualized argument for the subordination of international law, which means generally subordinating the rule of law to the extent that it is structured by reference to international standards; for highly unprecedented arguments favoring presidential unaccountability in wartime, see Yoo 2005. For a critique of Yoo, see Cole 2005. For useful defenses of legality as the basis for foreign policy, see Sands. 2005; Bartholomew 2006. On the resistance of some government lawyers to the neoconservative assault of legality, see Hajjar 2005: Bilder and Vagts 2004.

9. See the useful range of interpretations in Ignatieff, ed., 2005. For a neoconservative approach to this issue of a distinctive American role that is less law-oriented than that of Western European liberal democracies, see Kagan 2003.

10. I originally shared this sense of plausibility, justifying the recourse to war against the Taliban regime in Afghanistan as the appropriate response to the sort of continuing threat that seemed to be posed by al Qaeda. See Falk 2003.

11. This strategic posture was initially depicted by President Bush in his address to the graduating class at West Point on June 1, 2002. It was authoritatively set forth in *National Security Strategy of the United States of America,* White House, September 2002, Section V, and has been restated in the sequel document, *National Security Strategy of the United States of America,* White House, March 16, 2006, pp.18–24.

12. Israel's attack on the Iraqi nuclear reactor at Osirak in 1981 was premised on such a preventive rationale, but not as associated with a terrorist threat. The attack exhibited an overall unwillingness to allow any neighbor to become a potential challenger to Israeli military dominance in the region.

13. On the role of A. Q. Khan, see Seymour M. Hersh, " 'The Deal': Why Is Washington Going Easy on Pakistan's Black Marketers?" *The New Yorker,* March 8, 2004.

14. There are various relevant legal memoranda by government lawyers, especially Jay S. Bybee, Alberto Gonzales, and William J. Haynes, II; the main documents are listed in Bilder and Vagts 2006, n. 1. For the main official texts, see Greenberg and Dratel 2005; Greenberg 2006. The most authoritative political defense of U.S. government practices was given by President Bush: "President Discusses Creation of Military Commissions to Try Suspected Terrorists," White House, September 6, 2006.

15. See the exhaustive assessment of this position in Luban 2006. For a notorious scholarly argument favoring "legalized" torture, see Dershowitz 2002. Also see Scheppele 2005.

16. John Major and Kim Campbell, "Terrorism in Democracies," IXXI breakfast conversations, London School of Economics, December 1, 2005.

17. Condoleezza Rice did raise these issues in a widely quoted talk given in Cairo on June 20, 2005, but it did not result in any visible change in policy. Her essential message was as follows: "For 60 years, my country, the United States, pursued stability at the expense of democracy in this region here in the Middle East—and we achieved neither. Now, we are taking a different course. We are supporting the democratic aspirations of all peoples." "Remarks at the American University of Cairo," http://www.state.gov/secretary/rm/2005/48328.htm.

18. Indeed, the 2006 Quadrennial Defense Review highlights its extensive review of American defense planning by reference to what it describes as "the long war" for which it posits no benchmarks for an eventual outcome. *Quadrennial Defense Review Report,* February 6, 2006, especially the section entitled "Fighting the Long War," pp. 9–11.

19. See the useful study focused on the World War II experience by O'Donnell (2005).

20. See *Korematsu v. United States* 320 U.S. 214 (1944); also *Hirabayashi v. U.S. 320* U.S. 81(194). See O'Donnell 2005: 271–93.

21. See *Hamdi v. Rumsfeld, 296 F.3rd 278 (2002)*; further upheld in *Hamdi v. Rumsfeld,* 542 U.S. 507 (2004); also *Jose Padilla v. Donald Rumsfeld,* 243 F. Supp. 2d 42 (2003). The United States Supreme Court later reversed, affirming Hamdi's right to habeas corpus, a result now overridden by the Military Commissions Act that deprives alien detainees of habeas corpus.

22. See the memorandum of William H. Taft IV, legal advisor to the Department of State, "President's Decision about the Applicability of Geneva Conventions to al Qaeda and Taliban," March 22, 2002, in Greenberg 2006: 283–316. A conservative rationale is to be found in Lee A. Casey and David B. Rivkin, Jr., "Rethinking the Geneva Conventions," in Greenberg 2006: 203–13.

23. For a relevant overview of tendencies toward "new wars" and their implications for domestic political order, see Kaldor 1999.

24. "President Discusses Creation of Military Commissions to Try Suspected Terrorists," White House, September 6, 2006.

25. See especially the views presented in Greenberg, n. 13; also Roth and Worden 2005. See also the special issue of *The Nation* entitled "The Torture Complex," December 26, 2005, pp. 11–42.

26. This argument is developed in the most nuanced form by Ignatieff (2004). For a shorter, chastened statement, one made after the Abu Ghraib disclosures and hence less deferential to the rationales put forward by the U.S. government, see Ignatieff 2005. A broader exchange of views can be found in Levinson 2004.

27. John Bolton has been the most outspoken neoconservative voice on the proper view of international law and authority of the United Nations. In his own words, "It is a big mistake for us to grant any validity to international law even when it may seem in our short-term interest to so—because, over the long-term, the goal of those who think international law really means anything are those who want to constrict the United States." For this and related assertions see "John Bolton: An Unforgivable Choice as UN Ambassador," Council on Hemispheric Affairs, March 10, 2005; available at http://www.coha.org. Jack

Goldsmith and especially John Yoo have been the most influential academic supporters of the approaches to legal issues taken by the Bush presidency.

28. United Nations, Economic and Social Council, Commission on Human Rights, 2006.

29. Pub. L. No. 107–40, 115 Stat. 224 (2001).

30. "On NSA Spying: An Open Letter to Congress," *The New York Review of Books*, February 9, 2006. http://www.nybooks.com/articles/18650.

31. For text of Geneva Convention relative to the treatment of prisoners of war, see *The Geneva Conventions of August 12 1949* (Geneva: International Committee of the Red Cross, undated, pp.75–134, at 75–78). Article 5 is particularly pertinent as it confers prisoner of war status on any person detained as a combatant until such time "as their status has been determined by a competent tribunal."

32. See 10 U.S. Code §§821, 836 (2001); and Public Law No. 10740, 115 Statute 224 (2001).


## 3. FORSYTHE, THE UNITED STATES

1. See especially Tim Golden, "After Terror, A Secret Rewriting of Military Law," *New York Times*, October 24, 2005; John Barry, Michael Hirsh, and Michael Isikoff, "The Roots of Torture," *Newsweek*, May 24, 2004. See also Mayer 2006: 32–42. Alberto J. Mora, who fought the policy of abuse from inside the Bush administration, had a military background but was a civilian political appointee at the time of his determined dissent.

2. This was suggested diplomatically in establishment circles. Bilder and Vagts. 2004.

3. For a short and readable overview, see Jordan Paust, "The Common Plan to Violate the Geneva Conventions," *Jurist*, May 25, 2004, http://jurist.law.pitt .edu/forum/paust2.php.

4. It is reasonable to characterize Afghanistan during 2001 and 2002 as manifesting an internal armed conflict between the Taliban government and the Northern Alliance, over which was imposed an international armed conflict between the United States and the Taliban government.

5. See United Nations, Economic and Social Council, Commission on Human Rights, 2006, para. 9. This is a report by five independent experts appointed to various duties by the UN Human Rights Commission. The key legal point is contained in 1977 Protocol I, additional to the 1949 Geneva Conventionss, Article 75, parts of which apparently the United States has accepted as part of international customary law. For a short and readable review of this issue, plus notation of its importance, see Adam Roberts, "Keeping the Unlawful Combatants out of Legal Limbo," *Washington Post*, Outlook, February 3, 2002.

6. Some of those detained at Guantanamo were of various nationalities and seized in Bosnia or Macedonia or Pakistan or some other place outside of Afghanistan, and whose legal status was clearly different from Afghan nationals.

7. In fact, during the Vietnam War, the United States detained North Vietnamese and Viet Cong irregular fighters in a special prison regime supervised by the International Committee of the Red Cross (ICRC). As long as these enemy fighters could be distinguished as such by carrying arms openly rather than secretly planting bombs, inter alia, the United States created for them a supervised humanitarian quarantine in keeping with IHL principles—all the while denying them the official status of prisoners of war. "Terrorists" were treated otherwise.

8. There is no clear scientific or legal distinction between torture and lesser forms of mistreatment. Case law over time might clarify the difference, as per the European Court of Human Rights or the Israeli Supreme Court. But given that the international legal definition of torture hinges on the intentional infliction of *intense* pain, physical or mental, the dividing line is subjective.

9. Dana Priest, "CIA Holds Terror Suspects in Secret Prisons," *Washington Post*, November 2, 2005, A1.

10. Unpublished source, January 2006, in the possession of the author.

11. Douglas Jehl, "White House Has Tightly Restricted Oversight of C.I.A. Detentions, Officials Say," *New York Times*, April 6, 2005, A19.

12. For a particularly good analysis of U.S. ties with Uzbekistan on this matter, with confirmation from British diplomatic circles, see Don Van Natta, Jr., "U.S. Recruits a Rough Ally to be a Jailer," *New York Times*, May 1, 2005, A1 and A12. Also, an Australian security official confirmed that another person was picked up in Pakistan, then transferred to Egypt, then sent to Guantanamo. *New York Times*, February 16, 2005, A9. U.S. officials had previously denied all this. See also Mayer 2005a, starting at 106.

13. Michael Scheuer, "A Fine Rendition," *New York Times*, March 11, 2005, A23. The author is a former CIA official.

14. *Hamdan v. Rumsfeld*, no. 05-184, decided June 29, 2006.

15. Initially, under Baccus and Dunleavey, particularly the military police at Guantanamo operated according to the rule book of the Geneva Conventions. Interview with Rick Baccus, "The Torture Question," *Frontline*, PBS, http://www.pbs.org.wgby/pages/frontline/torture/interviews.

16. This essay has more on the ICRC later. The FBI memos were obtained and published by the ACLU on its Web site. The interrogator's book is Saar with Novak 2005; the chaplain's is Yee 2005.

17. Amnesty International 2004. For another summary, see Human Rights Watch 2004c. For yet another reliable report, see Bob Herbert, "Stories from the Inside," *New York Times*, February 7, 2005, A27. And see especially Margulies 2006, based on prisoner interviews.

18. Lelyveld 2005; Ignatieff, 2004.; Felner 2005. See also Chapters 4 (Campbell) and 6 (Shafir) in this volume.

19. Douglas Jehl, David Johnston, and Neil A Lewis, "C.I.A. Is Seen as Seeking New Role on Detainees," *New York Times*, February 16, 2005, A16. Porter Goss, the CIA's new head, told Congress he could not confirm that all past agency practices had been in keeping with federal laws that prohibited torture.

Douglas Jehl, "Questions Left by C.I.A. Chief on Torture Use," *New York Times,* March 18, 2005, A1.

20. Saar 2005. His account on this point was later confirmed by other sources.

21. James Fallows, "Blind into Baghdad," *Atlantic Monthly,* January–February 2004; and Michael R. Gordon, "How the Postwar Situation in Iraq Went Awry," *International Herald Tribune,* from the *New York Times,* October 29, 2004. See also Diamond 2005; Galbraith 2005.

22. See the Schlesinger report, reprinted in Greenberg and Dratel 2005 and elsewhere. An internal military investigation of Miller at Guantanamo recommended a reprimand, but this did not occur. David S. Cloud, "Guantanamo Reprimand Was Sought, an Aide Says," *New York Times,* July 13, 2005, A16.

23. Douglas Jehl, "C.I.A Order on Detainees Shows Its Role Was Curbed," *New York Times,* December 14, 2004, A13.

24. Reuters, "Harsh Tactics Were Allowed, General Told Jailers in Iraq," *New York Times,* May 30, 2005, A8. The Bush administration forced General Sanchez into retirement, rather than try to promote him and have him testify in Senate confirmation hearings. There was a fear that he would testify that higher authorities pressed him for more intelligence from prisoners, even if he had to violate military rules. See Kelley 2006.

25. A UN rapporteur on Afghanistan for the Human Rights Commission, M. Cherif Bassiouni, who teaches at Depauw University in the United States, compiled a damaging report on prisoner treatment in Afghanistan, whereupon his tenure was not renewed by his parent body. For the report see UN Doc. E/CN.4/2005/122. See also Warren Hoge, "Lawyer Who Told of U.S. Abuses at Afghan Bases Loses U.N. Post," *New York Times,* April 30, 2005, A6; and "UN rights investigator removed from Afghan post after report critical of US," *The Jurist,* April 25, 2005, http://jurist.law.pitt.edu/paperchase/2005_04_25_indexarch.php.

26. "Command Responsibility: Detainee Deaths in U.S. Custody in Iraq and Afghanistan," *Human Rights First,* February 2006.

27. See the online reports of Human Rights Watch available at http://www.hrw.org/doc/?t=pubs.

28. On ghost detainees in Afghanistan, see Eric Schmitt and Tim Golden, "Details Emerge on Terror Suspects' Afghan Jailbreak," *International Herald Tribune,* December 4, 2005, http://www.iht.com/bin/print_ipub.php?file=/articles/2005/12/04/news/bagram.php. On CIA use of cold cells and waterboarding, see Human Rights First, "US Law and Security Digest," issue 74, December 2, 2005.

29. It is relevant to recall that given the tenor of the times, American citizens seen as lending support to "the enemy" were treated badly when detained. James Yee, an Islamic chaplain at Guantanamo, was given harsh detention conditions, including prolonged isolation, before all charges were dropped. John Lindh, captured while fighting for the Taliban in Afghanistan, was treated illegally and coercively before legal proceedings and plea bargaining led to his twenty-year jail

term. For receiving a shorter sentence than the law allowed, he dropped his charges about mistreatment. Jose Padilla was declared an enemy combatant and stripped of his constitutional rights for about a two-year period. He subsequently claimed he was tortured in various ways; see AP, "Padilla's Papers Detail Charges of Mistreatment," *New York Times,* November 2, 2006, A19.

30. Again, the pertinent memos are reproduced in Greenberg and Dratel 2005. U.S. policy was similar to Israeli policy in occupied territory at least up to 1999: the rejection of the formal application of IHL, promise to treat humanely, but actual abuse of prisoners.

31. See Amnesty International 2004.

32. Neil A. Lewis, "U.S. Spells Out New Definition Curbing Torture," *New York Times,* January 1, 2005, A1.

33. Various sorts of semantic games by governmental spokespersons tried to convey that "sleep management" and "stress positions" did not add up to abuse, humiliating treatment, degrading treatment, ill treatment, or, in combination, torture. See Adam Hochschild, "What's in a Word? Torture," *New York Times,* May 23, 2004, Op-Ed, 11.

34. Josh White and John Mintz, "Red Cross Cites 'Inhume' Treatment at Guantanamo," *Washington Post,* December 1, 2004. A10. See also Anthony Lewis, "Guantanamo's Long Shadow," *New York Times,* June 21, 2005, A23, reacting to a statement by Vice President Cheney. See also the statement by Secretary of Defense Rumsfeld, denying that any abuse at Abu Ghraib was related to interrogation. Eric Schmitt, "Rumsfeld Denies Details of Abuses at Interrogations," *New York Times,* August 28, 2004, A1.

35. David Johnston and Thom Shanker, "Pentagon Approved Intense Interrogation Techniques for Sept. 11 Suspect at Guantanamo," *New York Times,* May 21, 2004, A10; and Agence France-Presse, "Pentagon Gives No Excuses for Suspect Treatment: Senators Aghast," Yahoo! news, June 13, 2005.

36. A German national was seized by the United States in the Balkans and then transferred to Afghanistan, where he was abused. It was a case of mistaken identity, and NSC Adviser Rice intervened after some months to get him released, with involvement by the German government. "Ghost detainees" could be "rendered" almost anywhere in this secret, unaccountable process. Apparently the prisoner was bound in painful positions, beaten, and injected with drugs. David Johnston, "Rice Ordered Release of German Sent to Afghan Prison in Error," *New York Times,* April 23, 2005, A3.

37. For one concise overview, see Kelley 2006.

38. She claims in her book that she was used as a scapegoat, having neither the authority nor the resources to have been responsible for abuses at Abu Ghraib (Karpinski 2005).

39. UPI, *Washington Times,* May 26, 2004, reporting on Pappas's comments to Major General Taguba. See also Douglas Jehl, "Officers Say U.S. Colonel at Abu Ghraib Prison Felt Intense Pressure to Get Inmates to Talk," *New York Times,* May 19, 2004, A21.

40. The Church report was widely seen as a whitewash of the issues. Among

many typical press reports, see Tom Squitieri, "Pentagon Report on Prisoner Abuse Met with Skepticism; Probe to Go On," *USA Today*, March 11, 2005.

41. Among many sources, see Holtzman 2005; UPI, "Report: General Urged Dogs for Abu Ghraib," *Washington Times*, May 26, 2004; and Kelly 2006.

42. See Mandelbaum 2003: 93. A public opinion poll conducted at the University of Maryland in summer 2004 found that the American public opposed almost all forms of torture, even when faced with possible terrorism (cited on PIPA mailing list, listserv@americans-world.org).

43. John Tierney, "Hot Seat Grows Lukewarm under Capital's Fog of War," *New York Times*, May 20, 2004, A14. For a general overview of the lack of congressional oversight of the Bush Administration's policies, stemming from the fact that a Republican Congress was disinclined to review a Republican President, see Ornstein and Mann 2006.

44. E.g., a cover story on torture with a picture of John McCain by *Newsweek*, November 21, 2005.

45. Eric Schmitt, "Senate Moves to Protect Military Prisoners Despite Veto Threat," *New York Times*, October 5, 2005, A1.

46. The vote was 308–122.

47. Eric Schmitt, "Exception Sought in Detainee Abuse Ban," *New York Times*, October 25, 2005, A 17.

48. "President's Statement on signing of H.R. 2863, the 'Department of Defense, Emergency Supplemental Appropriations to Address Hurricanes in the Gulf of Mexico, and Pandemic Influenza Action, 2006'" at http://www .whitehouse.gov.news/releases/2005/12/print/200t1330-8html. See especially para. 6.

49. For a concise overview, see R. Jeffrey Smith, "Many Rights in U.S. Legal System Absent in New Bill," *Washington Post*, September 29, 2006, A13; and the editorial "Rushing Off a Cliff," *New York Times*, September 28, 2006, A22.

50. There were repeated efforts to discredit the ICRC. Editorials, op-ed pieces, and one Republican "study" attacked the organization, using false statements and misrepresentations. Given some of the allegations, it was probable that some executive officials were involved behind the scenes. See, for example, Republican Policy Committee, "Are American Interests Being Disserved by the International Committee of the Red Cross?" June 13, 2005.

51. *Rasul v. Bush.*

52. Detainee Treatment Act of 2005, section 1005 of the DOD Appropriations Act of 2006.

53. For a short, readable review of the options available for legally processing suspected terrorists, see Benjamin Wittes, "Justice Delayed," *Atlantic Monthly*, March 2006, 36–37.

54. See the review of the *Hamdi* and *Rasul* cases, as well as the matter of military commissions, in the *American Journal of International Law* 99(1) (January 2005), 261–62.

55. In 2005, a poll of citizens found that in Britain and France, China rated more favorably than did the United States. Favorable views of the U.S. were 38

percent in Indonesia, 23 percent in Pakistan, and 23 percent in Turkey. Will Lester, for the Associated Press, in *The Lincoln Journal Star*, June 24, 2005, A4.

56. Brian Knowlton, "EU Warns Members on Secret U.S. Camps," *International Herald Tribune*, November 28, 2005.

57. See Human Rights Watch, "UK: Promises on Torture Don't Work," October 6, 2004; http://hrw.org/english/docs/2004/10/06/uk9459.htm. For an analysis of Canadian rendition, see Clifford Krauss, "Evidence Grows That Canada Aided in Having Terrorism Suspects Interrogated in Syria," *New York Times*, September 17, 2005, A6. Regarding Swedish rendition and cooperation with the CIA, see Craig Whitlock, "New Swedish Documents Illuminate CIA Action," *Washington Post*, May 21, 2005, A1. One report named seven countries engaging in rendition: the United States, Canada, Britain, the Netherlands, Germany, Austria, and Sweden (not a NATO member). Thalif Deen, "Rights: U.S. Practice of 'Outsourcing Torture' Comes under Fire," IPS-Inter Press Service, May 12, 2005, http://www.lexis-nexis.com

58. For a report of British agents at Guantanamo, and European cooperation with the CIA, see Neil Mackay, "Torture Flights: The Inside Story," *The Sunday Herald*, October 16, 2005, 20.

59. Alan Cowell, "Diplomat Says Britain Used Data Gotten by Torture," *New York Times*, December 31, 2005, A4.

60. http://www.legalaffairs.org/issues/March-April-2006/review_Arimatsu-Marapro6.msp.

61. BBC news, February 23, 2006.

62. See also Katrin Benhold, "European Inquiry Points to the Illegal Transfer of Prisoners," *International Herald Tribune*, December 13, 2005.

63. On this and other relevant European developments see Ian Fisher, "Europe and the CIA: How Close?" *International Herald Tribune*, December 1, 2005.

64. See also the statements by British officials noted by Todd Landman in Chapter 5 of this volume. These statements are supportive of restrictions on human rights in a time of insecurity.

65. Richard Bernstein and Michael R. Gordon, "Berlin File Says Germany's Spies Aided U.S. In Iraq," *New York Times*, March 2. 2006, A1.

66. Mike Blanchfield, "Red Cross Condemns Handover of Insurgents," *Ottawa Citizen*, September 29, 2005, A15.

67. Tim Naftali, "Milan Snatch," *Slate Magazine*, June 30, 2005, http://www.lexis-nexis.com. The matter of U.S. kidnapping in Italy was exceedingly murky, as a newly elected government in Rome moved to indict an Italian security operative for violating Italian law by cooperating with the United States in the abduction. Ian Fisher and Elisabetta Povoledo, "Italy's Top Spy Is Expected to Be Indicted in Abduction Case," *New York Times*, October 24, 2006, A3.

68. See, for example, John H. Cushman, Jr., "U.N. Condemns Harsh Methods in Campaign against Terror," *New York Times*, October 28, 2004, A10. This refers to comments by Theo van Boven, a UN rapporteur on torture.

69. United Nations, Economic and Social Council, Commission on Human Rights, 2006.

70. Amnesty International 2004. This report, not terribly well organized, consists of 118 pages, with 771 reference notes.

71. Human Rights Watch 2005a. The report consists of 93 pages with 374 reference notes.

72. See Lelyveld 2005, covering a new U.S. military manual on interrogation, and a U.S. report to the UN Committee against Torture.

73. See Foot 2005: 291–310. There were reports that the CIA maintained a black site in Thailand.

74. The ICRC is a private Swiss association, part of Swiss civic society. But it is recognized in public international law, and given certain rights in IHL. It is treated by the Swiss government now, and by most governments, as if it were a public international organization or intergovernmental organization. See also Forsythe 2005.

75. "Action by the International Committee of the Red Cross in the event of violations of international humanitarian law or of other fundamental rules protecting persons in situations of violence," June 2005. *International Review of the Red Cross* 858: 393–400.

76. ICRC press release, February 9, 2002. Some of the Guantanamo detainees had no connection with Afghanistan and the armed conflict there, but rather were seized in places like Bosnia, Macedonia, etc.

77. GC IV, Article 143, stipulates that ICRC visits may be delayed for "military necessity," but this is supposed to be temporary. In some cases at Guantanamo the ICRC was denied visits to certain individuals for months.

78. In general, see Ratner and Ray 2004; in particular, see Neil A. Lewis, "Red Cross Finds Detainee Abuse in Guantanamo," *New York Times*, November 30, 2004, based on an ICRC report probably leaked by a U.S. source.

79. Agence France-Presse, June 17, 2005. See also for the Associated Press, Alexander G. Higgins, "International Red Cross says U.S. Cooperation Good on Guantanamo Despite Critics," June 17, 2005, http:lexis-nexis.com.

80. The Fay report said that U.S. military authorities did not always take ICRC reports seriously or investigate the allegations properly. AR 15-6 Investigation, p. 64, http://www.defenselink.mil/news/Aug 2004/d20040824fay.pdf.

81. Human Rights Watch interviewed a number of U.S. military personnel about Iraq and concluded that prisoner abuse was widespread there. BBC News, "Iraq Prisoner Abuse 'Was Routine,' " October 19, 2006, http://bbc.co.uk.

82. See especially the analysis by the conservative scholar Francis Fukuyama, "After Neoconservatism," *New York Times Magazine*, February 9, 2006.

83. Margulies 2006 is very convincing on this point.

84. Congress forced the executive to back away from internationally recognized human rights in the 1950s, then demanded more attention to at least civil and political rights in U.S. foreign policy in the 1970s. See Forsythe 1988.

85. See especially Tim Golden, "Detainee Memo Created Divide in White House," *New York Times*, October 1, 2006: "In the end, the White House pressed Republican senators to accept a broad definition of 'unlawful enemy combatants" whom the government can hold indefinitely, to maintain some of the

presidents control over C.I.A. interrogation methods and to allow the government to present some evidence in military tribunals that is based on hearsay or has been coerced from witnesses."

86. In the Arar decision, a U.S. court deferred to the executive and refused to allow a claim about U.S. responsibility for the torture of a Canadian in Syria, prioritizing U.S. relations with Canada rather than an individual right not to be tortured.

87. Shortly after the Hamdan decision, the U.S. government issued a new version of interrogation rules applicable to the military, and announced the transfer of fourteen persons previously held in secret detention to the facility at Guantanamo. These actions had the combined effect of placing "high value" detainees under the legal protection of part of the laws of war. This had been explicitly rejected by the Bush administration in 2002.

88. Neil MacFarquhar, "Lebanese Would-Be Suicide Bomber Tells How Volunteers Are Waging Jihad in Iraq," *New York Times*, November 2, 2004, A10.

89. According to many press reports, the Bush administration relied on a prisoner's "confession" that Iraq under Saddam Hussein had engaged in operational contacts with al Qaeda. According to these same reports, the confession was extracted under torture and later recanted. If true, the reports indicate one of the negatives about use of abusive interrogation. Saddam's purported links to al Qaeda were often mentioned by the administration, especially Vice President Cheney, as one of the primary justifications for the March 2003 invasion. No reliable proof has yet surfaced about these asserted contacts.

## 4. CAMPBELL, NORTHERN IRELAND

I am grateful to Professor Bill Bowring (London Metropolitan University) and to Gershon Shafir for helpful comments on drafts of this essay, and to my research associate, Ita Connolly (University of Ulster) for her ever-efficient assistance. The international law aspects of this essay draw upon Campbell 2005, the analysis of hegemony draws upon Bell, Campbell, and Ní Aoláin 2007, and analysis of the phases of the Northern Ireland conflict is based on Hadden, Boyle, and Campbell 1990.

1. Art. 1.4.

2. 25 Eur. Ct. H.R. (Ser. A) (1978).

3. 2 EHRR, p. 80.

4. *Donnelly and Others v. UK*, Application 5577, 5583/73, Decision of the Commission, April 5, 1973.

5. The *Greek* case (1969) 12 YB 1.

6. (1994) 19 EHRR 539.

7. Committee against Torture, Consideration of Reports Submitted by State Parties under Article 19 of the Convention, Initial State Reports Due in 1990, Addendum United Kingdom, para. 67, UN Doc. CAT/C/9/Add.6.

8. *Aksoy v. Turkey*, 23 EHRR 553 (1996)

9. See *Fox, Campbell and Hartley v. UK*, (1990) 13 EHRR 157, and more ambiguously in *Brogan v. UK* (1989) 11 EHRR 117.

10. Contrast *Fox, Campbell & Hartley v. UK* with the subsequent decision in *Margaret Murray v. UK* (1994) 19 EHRR 193. See also *O'Hara v. UK*, (2002) 34 EHRR 32.

11. *McCann and Others v. UK*, (1996) 21 EHRR 97; *John Murray v. UK*, (1996) 22 EHRR 29; *John Tinnelly & Sons Ltd. and Others and McElduff and Others v. UK*, (1999) 27 EHRR 249; *Averill v. UK*, (2001) 31 EHRR 36; *Magee v. UK*, (2001) 31 EHRR 35 ; *McKerr v. UK*, (2002) 34 EHRR 20; *Shanaghan v. UK*, Appl. no. 37715/97; *Kelly and Others v. UK*, Appl. no. 30054/96 (May 4, 2001); *McShane v. UK*, (2002) 35 EHRR 23; *O'Hara v. UK*, (2002) 34 EHRR 32; *Brennan v. UK*, (2002) 34 EHRR 18; *Finucane v. UK*, (2003) 37 EHRR 29, *Shannon v. UK*, (unreported) October 4, 2005.

12. See *Stewart v. UK*, (1985) 7 EHRR 453; *X. v. UK, Farrell v. UK*, (1983) 5 EHRR 466; and *Kelly v. UK*, (1993) 16 EHRR 20. In *McKay v. UK*, (unreported) October 3, 2006, no breach was found.

13. *Kaya v. Turkey*, (1999) 28 EHRR 1; *Salman v. Turkey*, (2002) 34 EHRR 17; *Cakici v. Turkey*, (2001) 31 EHRR 5; *Ertak v. Turkey*, Appl. no. 20764/92 (May 9, 2000); *Timurtas v. Turkey*, (2001) 33 EHRR 6; *Yasa v. Turkey*, (1999) 28 EHRR 408.

14. *Khashiyev and Akayeva v. Russia*, Appl. nos.57942/00 and 57945/00 (2006) 42 EHRR 20; *Isayeva v. Russia*, Appl. no. 57950/00 (2005) 41 EHRR 38, and *Isayeva, Bazayeva and Yusupova v. Russia*, Appl. nos. 57947/00, 57949/00, 57948/00 (2005) 41 EHRR 39.

15. UN Commission on Human Rights, "Report of the Working Group on Arbitrary Detention" (February 15, 2006), UN Doc. E/CN.4/2006/20; UN Committee Against Torture, "Conclusion and Recommendations of the Committee against Torture, United States of America" (July 25, 2006) UN Doc. CAT/C/USA/CO/2; UN Human Rights Committee, "Concluding Observations of the Human Rights Committee, United States of America" (September 15, 2006), UN Doc. CCPR/C/USA/CO/3.

## 5. LANDMAN, THE UNITED KINGDOM

1. Indeed, since the July bombing and increasingly so after the foiled plot to attack trans-Atlantic flights, Britain is struggling to understand how it has become a breeding ground for such radicalism, even though the level of public discourse has descended into offensive and defensive rhetoric about the clash of values, the use of the veil in public, and what is acceptable in a modern democracy.

2. British forces had initially used hooding in its military operations in Iraq to hide the identity of detainees, but then-Defence Secretary Geoff Hoon banned the reinstatement of such practices in late 2003.

3. The government has promised to establish a supreme court that would replace the House of Lords, but it has been unsuccessful in abolishing the position of lord chancellor, a medieval legal institution that has evolved to its modern role in having responsibility for constitutional affairs, royal affairs, and rela-

tions with the Church and Crown Dependencies (see http://www.dca.gov.uk). See Blom-Cooper 2005; Beetham et al. 2002; Quinn 2005.

4. In an ongoing case concerning the treatment of Iraqis, an appeals court ruled on December 21, 2005, that the full reach of the Human Rights Act extends to British military forces posted abroad and includes their actions inside and outside British controlled facilities (O'Hanlan 2006).

5. One of the most controversial uses of this power involved a House of Lords decision that allows the surviving partner in a homosexual couple tenancy rights and other benefits related to the deceased.

6. See http://www.parliament.uk/parliamentary_committees/joint_committee _on_human_rights.cfm.

7. For an act with 129 sections, the government timetabled just sixteen hours over three days for the House of Commons to consider the legislation, while giving the House of Lords nine days. See Haubrich 2003: 8–9.

8. Deportation to a country that tortures or engages in inhuman and degrading treatment would itself constitute a violation of Article 3 of the ECHR, which is why the government sought the power to detain those suspects who face such fate upon deportation. In the event, the Law Lords found that the attempt to create such a power was also incompatible with the ECHR. See Blom-Cooper 2005: 236–37; Parker 2005: 129.

9. It is arguable that this power itself is derogable under the ECHR since it is still a denial of liberty and may well be challenged (seeBlom-Cooper 2005: 236). Indeed, the Council of Europe's commissioner for human rights found that the control orders violate basic rights found in the ECHR and that the protection of judicial review in its current form over the use of such orders was simply too weak (Council of Europe 2005). Also see Blom-Cooper 2005: 236; and Amnesty International UK, "Proposed 'Control Orders' Would Violate Human Rights," press release, AI Index EUR 45/004/2005, February 22, London.

10. A. Gillan and F. al Yafari, "Control Order Flaws Exposed," *The Guardian*, March 24, 2005. http://www.guardian.co.uk/terrorism/story/0,12780,1444611,00 .html.

11. C. Clarke, "Response: I Welcome the Ban on Evidence Gained through Torture," *The Guardian*, December 13, 2005, 30.

12. Reported in M. Holden, "Judges Blamed as Terrorism Suspects Flee," Reuters, October 17, 2006.

13. *Countering International Terrorism: The United Kingdom's Strategy*, July 2006, Cm. 6888, Annex A, pp. 31–32; M. Campbell and J. Burns, "Blair Falls Short on Promised Counter-Terrorism Measures," *Financial Times*, July 7, 2006. See also Blick, Chowdury, and Weir 2006: 25.

14. In its November 10, 2005, edition, *The Sun* said that the MPs had "IGNORED the wishes of the vast majority of Britons and HUMILIATED Tony Blair by inflicting his first Commons defeat."

15. There are numerous press releases, briefing papers, and letters available on all their Web sites; see http://www.liberty-human-rights.org.uk, http://www .justice.org.uk, and http://www.amnesty.org.

16. Liberty UK, "Terrorism Bill: Liberty's Briefing for Second Reading in the House of Lords," November 2005; http://www.liberty-human-rights.org.uk. See also Parker 2005: 125–28.

## 6. SHAFIR, THE 'ISRAELI MODEL'

I wish to thank Gad Barzilai, Vivienne Bennett, Rachel Brenner, Lisa Hajjar, Joseph Klett, Lucy Mair, and Michael Schudson for their thoughtful comments and assistance.

1. The General Security Service is *Shin Beth* or *Shabak* in Hebrew; henceforth it will be abbreviated GSS.

2. Bybee to Gonzales, August 1, 2002, memo re: standards of conduct for interrogation, a.k.a. the "Torture Memo," reproduced in Greenberg 2006: 343–44. See also Lisa Hajjar, "In the Penal Colony," *The Nation,* February 7, 2005.

3. November 7, 2005; see David Bloom, "McCain, Israel and Torture," *Counterpunch,* November 8, 2005; http://www.counterpunch.org/bloom11082005.html.

4. See also "Let America Take Its Cues from Israel Regarding Torture," *Jewish World Review,* January 30, 2002.

5. Israel, Landau Commission, 1987 (henceforth LC).

6. There is an unexpected connection between the two cases: Nafsu identified (from a photo published in an Israeli newspaper) one of the security agents involved with the Bus 300 case as one of his interrogators. The exposure of that agent's lying in the Bus 300 case served as the major justification in Nafsu's appeal to reopen his case (Shelef 1990: 186 n. 3.).

7. "Shin Bet and IDF Paid 2.4 Million NIS to a Group of Palestinian Torture Victims," press release by Advocate Dan Assan.

8. A telling example is found in an interview with General Shlomo Goren, Israel's former chief military rabbi and chief rabbi. To the question, "Isn't torture of prisoners against the law?" he responded, "How so? Any law that serves the interests of the people of Israel is a good law. A law that's contrary to the interests of the people doesn't exist as far as I'm concerned. But I don't think anyone broke the law" ("Wrong Arm" 1991: 14).

9. Jon Elmer, "Israeli Terror Compensation Rules Treat Jews Victims Differently," *The New Standard,* August 31, 2005; http://newstandardnews.net/content/?action'show_item&itemid'2300.

10. Reuven Paz, "The Threat of Jewish Terrorism in Israel," August 30, 1998; http://www.ict.org.il/articles/articledet.cfm?articleid'45.

11. "Diskin: Shin Beth Softer on Jewish Terror Suspects," *Ha'aretz,* February 2, 2006.

12. See, for example, http://en.wikipedia.org/wiki/Operation_Phoenix. For a list of publications and memoirs, see http://users.skynet.be/terrorism/html/vietnam_phoenix.htm.

13. *Artzi v. Attorney General* 264/65, quoted in LC 4.2, p. 77; and also in SC 9.

14. http://outofkhiam.tripod.com/Haaretz100200.htm.

15. "To date, no cases of interrogation in which the 'defense of necessity' was pleaded have been brought for the approval of the Attorney General." Answer of Minister of Justice Meir Shitrit to parliamentary interpellation of Member of Knesset Zehava Gal'on, July 11, 2001; see PCATI 2001: 39.

16. In fact, when the court was ready to move, it did so disregarding the standing of the applicants, none of whom were subject to torture and some of whom have been released already.

17. http://www.hrw.org/reports/2002/isrl-pa/.

18. In fact, although forty-three legislators proposed a law permitting "physical pressure" in late 1999, it was never passed (Gross 2004: 375–77).

19. Amos Harel, "GSS Used 'Exceptional Interrogation Means' 90 Times since HCJ Ruling," *Ha'aretz*, July 25, 2002; PCATI 2003: 17.

20. Charlie Savage, "Bush Shuns Patriot Act Requirement: In Addendum to Law, He Says Oversight Rules Are Not Binding, *Boston Globe*, March 24, 2006; http://www.boston.com/news/nation/articles/2006/03/24/bush_shuns_patriot _act_requirement/.

21. "Bush Signs Military Commissions Act," October 17, 2006, *The Jurist*. http://jurist.law.pitt.edu/paperchase/2006/10/bush-signs-military-commissions-act.php.

## 7. MARTÍ, DOMINGO, AND IBARRA, COUNTERTERRORIST MEASURES IN SPAIN

1. Analyses of the scale of repression during the Franco dictatorship and the absence of any form of reparations (symbolic or material) only really began to emerge in Spain during the 1990s—indeed, when the numbers of those most affected were beginning to dwindle. See especially Aguilar Fernández (1996, 1997, 1998, 2002); Morán (1991); Preston (1995).

2. There is an abundant literature on Basque nationalism. For syntheses, see Bruni (1987); Domínguez Iribarren (1998); Douglass and Ibarra (2005); Egaña y Giacopucci (1992); Elorza (2000); Ibarra (2003, 2005); Letamendia (1994); Mata (1995); Onaindia (2000); Villanueva (2000); Zallo (2000); Wieviorka (1993); and Zulaika (1988).

3. There is limited academic work on the extreme right; notable exceptions include Rodríguez Jiménez (1992) and Casals (1998, 1999).

4. The literature on the extent of the repression under Franco is relatively recent but rapidly growing. Up to the end of the 1950s the similarities with Nazi ideology and Italian fascism were very evident; see, for instance, Marin, Molimero, and Ysás, (2001); Fontana (2005); and Vázquez Montalbán (2005). From 1959 on the regime began a process of economic liberalization, which had no impact on improving civil and political rights or relaxing the structures of social control. The last death sentences were signed as late as a few months before Franco's death in 1975.

5. To some extent this is also true regarding transitional justice. Only very recently have there begun to emerge some forms of reconstruction of historical memory in Spain regarding the Franco years, long after many other newer democracies have advanced farther down the path of truth, justice, and reparations—ironically, in some cases, with the help of the Spanish judicial system (most notably in the arrest of the Chilean dictator Augusto Pinochet, and in court cases against members of the Argentine military at the request of Spanish judge Baltasar Garzon).

6. Earlier the powers of civilian court judges had been extended with regard to acts of terrorism, which previously had been dealt with under military jurisdiction, with decree-law 2/1976 of February 18, 1976. The tribunal of law and order was eliminated and the Audiencia Nacional (National High Court) was created with the jurisdiction to deal with crimes related to terrorist activity.

7. It is worth highlighting the recent reports by the UN Special Rapporteur on torture, 2001 (E/CN.4/2002/76/Add.1), 2002 (E/CN.4/2003/68/Add.1) and 2003 (EC/CN.4/2004).

8. In 2004, 719 Basque prisoners were held in 88 different detention centers across six different countries. Of the 588 Basque prisoners held in Spain, only 11 were held within the Basque country. Of the 152 held in France, none were held in the French Basque region (Etxerat cited in Ubasart, 2005).

9. This position, Director General de Seguridad, is one of the more important within the ministry of the interior.

10. The MLNV combines the social and political organizations that form the core of radical Basque nationalism, in which Batasuna plays a dominant role.

11. In March 2002 Aznar refused to receive the leader of the PSOE because he was alleged to have spoken with the president of the Basque government, Ibarretxe.

12. For recent discussions on issues of human rights, democracy, multiculturalism, and violence in Spain, see, for instance, del Águila (2006), Sánchez Cuenca (2006), and Ibarra y Dougals (2005).

13. Elaine Sciolino, "Spanish Judge Calls for Closing U.S. Prison at Guantanamo," *New York Times*, June 4, 2006..

## 8. ADELMAN, CANADA'S BALANCING ACT

A NOTE ON SOURCES: In the text and notes to this chapter, references to some Canadian government documents will be given by the letter "C" followed by the abbreviation (e.g., "C, ATA"). These may be found in the Bibliography under the heading "Canadian Government Documents," with the abbreviation given in brackets.

1. McLellan and Cotler 2005. This statement has enhanced credibility because of the signature of Irwin Cotler, a former McGill University law professor and one of the foremost international lawyers who defended prisoners of conscience, including Nelson Mandela and Natan (Anatoly) Sharansky. Cotler is

both a thoughtful scholar and a committed activist on behalf of human rights (see, e.g., Cotler 2002).

2. This was identified prior to 9/11. Canada "has been a frequent destination for international terrorists and their supporters" (C, CSIS, 2000: para. 2). CSIS had a responsibility "to identify individuals and groups in Canada who are suspected of working with terrorists in support of their activities" (ibid., para. 7).

3. The MacDonald Commission revealed that the RCMP's agents had been responsible for planning and sometimes carrying out terrorist activities.

4. Though Canadians generally do not consider their country vulnerable, the Kelly Committee found that Canada is a "primary venue of opportunity to support, plan, or mount terrorist attacks" (C, Kelly, 1999, para. 9).

5. Singh Parmar was eventually shot by police in Punjab in 1992.

6. "The Terrorist Within: The Story behind One Man's Holy War against America," *The Seattle Times*, June 23–July 7, 2002, provides a Keystone Cops version of the RCMP's handling of Ressam's preparations.

7. Rod Mickleburgh, "Terrorism Suspect Deported from Canada," *The Globe and Mail*, January 13, 2006, A2.

8. "In essence, human security means safety for people from both violent and non-violent threats. It is a condition or state of being characterized by freedom from pervasive threats to people's rights, their safety, or even their lives" (C, *Human Security*, 1999: 3).

9. For insight into the debate prior to and after 9/11 with respect to the tension between human rights and security concerns, see *Promises to Keep* (C, *Promises*, 2001), published immediately after but prepared before 9/11, and the Senate Report on the human rights implications of the ATA legislation (C, Senate, 2005).

10. The formal title of the Arar Commission is the Commission of Inquiry into the Actions of Canadian Officials in Relation to Maher Arar.

11. http://www.psepc-sppcc.gc.ca/prg/ns/index-en.asp.

12. For various practices initiated with respect to border controls, see Adelman 2002.

13. The targets go beyond suspected terrorists to include those who have violated human or international rights or engaged in serious criminality.

14. Differential treatment of citizens versus noncitizens is an accepted principle of international law. Detention under security certificates is a matter that applies to foreigners on Canadian soil who are always free to leave the country. The issue of deportation to countries where the deportees are subject to torture is an issue applicable to both Canadian citizens and foreigners. Canada cannot take any action to deport an individual to a country to face torture. However, once a Canadian citizen is in that position, the Canadian government has a special responsibility to use all reasonable measures to extricate the Canadian citizen.

15. "In the national security context, the relevant exemptions [from the freedom to access information as spelled out in the Access to Information Act] include information obtained in confidence from a foreign government, foreign

institution, or international organization of states; international affairs and defence; law enforcement and investigations, and personal information" (C, Commission, 2004b: 8; cf. C, Access, 1985, sections 13, 15, 16 and 19).

16. Professor Stephen Toope noted with respect to his role in the Arar case (in determining Arar's credibility with respect to his claim that he was tortured) that "I was not refused access to any material that I requested to see," including "notes taken by the Canadian consular officer, Mr. Léo Martel, after his consular visits with Mr. Arar . . . and protected email communications amongst Canadian government officials during and after Arar's detention." Toope added, "I discovered no 'secret' material that caused me to re-evaluate that had been provided in public sources" (C, Toope, 2005: 2).

17. For example, in another case, Issam Al Yamani had two security certificates overturned, one because it relied on unconstitutional provisions, the other because the Security Intelligence Review Committee (SIRC) "failed to properly analyze the evidence before it in reaching the conclusion" (C, *Yamani*, 2002: 1).

18. In August 2002, fingerprints taken in 1996 of Jaballah were found to be those of Mahmoud Al Sayed Gaballah Said, who was wanted by Egypt as a member of a terrorist organization responsible for planning terrorist actions and supplying weapons and explosives to terrorists, and assisting in terrorist escapes. Second, Jaballah spent time in Afghanistan in 1993–94, a country he had denied visiting. Third, when Mohamed Zeki Mahjoub, who ran a "farm" in Sudan for Osama bin Laden and was a member of the Shura or governing body of al Jihad (AJ), was arrested in 2000, he carried a name which he admitted referred to Jaballah. Fourth, correspondence for Jaballah from Canada and abroad was received at a postal box up to June 1999; Jaballah testified that the box had not been used. In December 1999, a computer disk found in the possession of Khalil Said Deek, a member of the information committee of AJ, included Jaballah's post office box address. Information with respect to AJ and al Qaeda, not available prior to November 1, 1999, pointed to Jaballah's having been in contact with Ayman Al Zawaheri, the leader in integrating AJ with al Qaeda. In summer 1998, Jaballah was in contact with Ibrahim Eidarous and Abdel Al Bari, senior London operatives of AJ and al Qaeda who claimed responsibility for the bombings of the American embassies in Kenya and Tanzania in August 1998. Jaballah acknowledged contacts with Kassun Daher, a Canadian member of an extremist organization based in Lebanon. Jaballah had contact with Thirwat Salah Shehata, a member of a committee of three that was leading AJ, the head of the security committee, and a member of its governing body, the Majlis Shura. Jaballah admitted contact twenty times with the International Office for the Defence of the Egyptian People (IODEP), the front used as a communications center related to the 1998 bombing of the American embassies in Kenya and Tanzania. Anyone with access to and in contact with AJ–al Qaeda communication centers in Baku, Azerbaijan, and London would reasonably be considered to be high up in the organization. As Justice Mackay stated, "unless he (Jaballah) was a senior AJ–Al Qaida operative, he could not have had contact with so many others who were senior members and active in those organizations" (C, *Jaballah*, 2003: 85).

19. In *Mohamed Harkat v. Canada* (Minister of Citizenship and Immigration), 2005 FC1750, the guideline states: "Where removal of a foreign national is delayed so as to bring into play the reasonable time requirement, the judge . . . must consider the delay and look to the causes of such delay. Time and behaviour of the parties are the essence of subsection 84 (2) application for release from detention" (para. 76).

20. In balancing the risk to torture for a potential deportee and the risk to Canadian security, in accord with the *Suresh* decision by the Supreme Court of Canada (C, *Suresh*, 2002), the evidentiary process for making that determination of balance is crucial if the evidence for the person posing a risk was not adequately accessible, but the public evidence available pointed to a very high risk of torture upon return in spite of diplomatic assurances (Human Rights Watch 2004a). In the Suresh case, the judge questioned the reliability of diplomatic assurances, especially from countries that practiced systematic torture. "Where the Minister is relying on written assurances from a foreign government that a person would not be tortured, the refugee must be given an opportunity to present evidence and make submissions as to the value of such assurances" (C, *Suresh*, 2002: 123). Otherwise, the weight had to be cast in favor of the individual.

21. Amnesty International Canada 2005b: 1. See also Amnesty International Canada 2004a: 6, in which Amnesty deplored the Canadian bureaucratic culture of secrecy.

22. "The nature of intelligence is that we rarely, if ever, have complete information. Rather, intelligence reporting and assessments are based on fragmented and sometimes contradictory information. It is therefore essential to bring together information on threats to Canada from *all available sources* [my italics] and properly assess it in order to provide as accurate and complete a picture as possible (C, *Securing*, 2004: chapter 3). Proper assessment is critical. Recommendation 3 of the 2006 Arar Commission Report (C, Commission, 2006) pointed to the need to ensure that investigators are properly trained so that information is "analyzed with accuracy, precision and a sophisticated understanding of the context from which the information originates"; Recommendation 8 set the key standards as "relevance, reliability and accuracy."

23. After President Bush pledged "to protect the American people and their friends against future attacks," he admitted that "the USA arrests people and sends them back to their country of origin." In so doing, the United States seeks "assurances that nobody will be tortured when we render a person back to their country" (press conference, March 16, 2005; http:/www.whitehorse.gov/news/release2005/03/20050316–3.html). Was the request for assurances intended to ensure that torture would not be practiced? Were any measures used to assess the reliability of such assurances? What record was there of nontorture following the receipt of such assurances? Did the United States even track performance?

24. See the fact-finding report by Professor Stephen J. Toope (C, Toope, 2005).

25. The three-volume report providing the factual analysis of the case and twenty-three recommendations was finally released on September 18, 2006 (C, Commission, 2006).

26. For an in-depth chronological narrative of the Arar affair, see "CBC News In Depth: Maher Arar—Timeline" (http://www.cbc.ca/news/background/arar/index.html), from which my account partially draws.

27. See Amnesty International Canada 2005a: 13, exhibit P-42, tab 31, and the May 11, 2005, testimony by Consular Officer Maureen Girvan (transcript pp. 1850–51). The Arar Commission concluded in its 2006 report that there was "[n]o evidence that Canadian officials participated or acquiesced in the American authorities decision to detain and remove Mr. Arar to Syria . . . and there is no evidence that any Canadian authorities—Royal Canadian Mounted Police (RCMP), Canadian Security Intelligence Service (CSIS) or others—were complicit in those decisions" (C, Commission, 2006: 14). Further, by not informing the Canadian authorities, the American action breached the Vienna Convention on Consular Relations. Of course, deporting Arar to Syria also breached the UN Convention against Torture and Other Cruel, Inhuman, or Degrading Treatment or Punishment.

28. The Arar Commission concluded that while Arar was held and tortured in Syria, Canadian agencies used information about him received from the Syrians—which likely was obtained by torture—without performing any adequate reliability assessment to determine whether the information resulted from torture.

29. RCMP Superintendent Mike Cabana told the commission on June 30, 2005, that the RCMP had shared intelligence with Syrian officials in fall 2002 when Arar had been in prison.

30. According to the Arar Commission Report (C, Commission, 2006: p. 13, section 4.1), both before and after Arar's detention in the United States, the RCMP provided inaccurate information to American authorities that portrayed Arar in an unfair fashion.

31. C, CSIS, 2000: para. 2, 3.

32. However, the Arar Commission found otherwise, for the report concluded that the efforts lacked "a single, coherent approach to efforts to obtain his release" (C, Commission, 2006: 15).

33. The fact-finder report issued by the commission at the end of October 2005 (C, Toope, 2005) confirmed that Arar had been tortured in the Syrian prison. The report makes for very painful reading. Evidence by Arar indicated that early reports of his torture, horrendous enough, had been somewhat exaggerated—he was not bent in an automobile tire for many hours at a time.

34. Human Rights Watch, "Report to the Canadian Commission of Inquiry into the Actions of Canadian Officials in Relation to Maher Arar," June 7, 2005. http://hrw.org/backgrounder/eca/canada/arar/.

35. On the release of the Arar Commission's report, Lead Counsel Paul Cavalluzzo stated, "There are portions of the public report which have been redacted because of the government's assertion of a claim of national security confidentiality (NSC). However the Commissioner is of the opinion that this information should be disclosed to the public. The Commissioner urges the government to refer this dispute to the Federal Court for an expeditious resolution so that

the public might get maximum disclosure" (press release, Ottawa, September 18, 2006).

36. According to information filed with the commission, CSIS had handed the file over to the RCMP. Though the RCMP had received the information that Arar had been detained by the Americans before he was deported to Syria, and the RCMP had shared the information with CSIS, CSIS only attended to the fact that Arar had been detained after he had already been deported. However, the key issue is what the RCMP knew, for the RCMP then had charge of the file. And the RCMP need not have known of American *plans* to both arrest and deport Arar. The issue was whether the RCMP was aware that American authorities were very likely to question Arar and then should reasonably have expected the Americans to refuse admission to the United States, thus leading to Arar's return to Syria. On August 23, 2005, RCMP Sergeant Rick Flewelling admitted that he informed American officials that Arar had Syrian as well as Canadian citizenship, but the officer fell back on the RCMP litany that he did not know of American *plans* to deport Arar to Syria. He did not testify about what he could reasonably have expected to happen to Arar (C, Commission, 2006: p. 16, section 4.4).

37. The RCMP used an opposite model of total imbalance according to an unethical criterion—protect one's own institution, not the security of Canada—and damn the effects on the individual. The report shows that both before and after Arar's return to Canada, officials leaked confidential and inaccurate information to the media for the purpose of damaging Arar's reputation or protecting their self-interest or government interests even though there was no evidence to indicate that Arar had committed any offense or that his activities constituted a threat to the security of Canada.

38. CBC News, "Graham Sorry for Length of Arar's Prison Stay," April 23, 2005.

39. According to the commission's final report. "It is very likely that, in making the decisions to detain and remove Mr. Arar to Syria, the U.S. authorities relied on information about Mr. Arar provided by the RCMP . . . . [T]he evidence strongly supports this conclusion" (C, Commission, 2006).

40. Heyman was prescient in anticipating the outsourcing of intelligence collection to countries that use less scrupulous methods to collect information.


## 9. HEINZ, GERMANY

The following acronyms are used in the text and notes:

BfV      Bundesamt für Verfassungsschutz/ Federal Office for the Protection of the Constitution. Domestic intelligence, with individual autonomous agencies on the level of the sixteen German federal states.

BGS      Federal Border Police; renamed Federal Police in 2005 (powers are much more limited than those of, e.g., the FBI).

| BND | Bundesnachrichtendienst/Federal Intelligence Service. Foreign intelligence. |
| GG | Grundgesetz/German Constitution. Also called the Basic Law. |
| MAD | Militärischer Abschirmdienst. Military intelligence service. |
| PKG | Parlamentarisches Kontrollgremium. Parliamentary control committee for the three German intelligence agencies (BfV, BND and MAD). |
| RFA | Rote Armee Fraktion/Red Army Faction |
| StGB | Strafgesetzbuch/German Penal Code |
| StPO | Strafprozessordnung/German Code of Criminal Procedure |

1. I owe the following conceptualization to Todd Landman and fellow contributors.

2. As one federal ministry official told me some time ago regarding a Latin American country, "we would have liked to help professionalize the police, but politically this is not feasible at the moment because of the outcry of human rights groups and the media in view of human rights violations committed by the police."

3. For contributions to the debate see, among many others, Brugger 1995, 1996; Follmar, Heinz, and Schulz 2003; Bielefeldt 2004; Nitschke 2005; and Reemtsma 2005.

4. There are many publications on the RAF. In particular, see Schubert 1968; Becker 1977; Fetscher 1977; Funke 1977; Horchem 1987, 1990; Peters 1991, 2004; Hauser 1997; Wunschik 1997; Straßner 2001; Waldmann and Malthaner 2003; Oesterle 2003; Biesenbach 2005 (a volume with many newspaper articles that accompanied a Berlin exhibition about the RAF); and Kraushaar 2006.

The German government has published documentation including secret memos by RAF members (German Government 1978). Numerous government, academic, and journalistic contributions have been published on the origins and activities of, internal discussions about, and state reactions to the RAF, as well as debates within civil society. A large number of former RAF members, both those who still supporting its strategy as well as those who now dissent, have published their views in books and interviews.

5. See Schubert 1968 and collections of RAF political declarations in Bakker Schut, Pieter 1987; Germany, Bundesministerium des Innern, 1975; and ID-Verlag 1997.

6. Apart from the RAF there were two other violent left-wing phenomena. The 2nd of June Movement was a much smaller group founded in Berlin. "2nd of June" refers to the 1967 assassination attempt on the student leader Rudi Dutschke by a former policeman, which left Dutschke severely wounded and with chronic aftereffects. Part of the group merged with the RAF in 1980. There were also "revolutionary cells," highly decentralised groups that attacked symbolic buildings; they have hurt people only rarely, and killed no one (Horchem 1987:13).

7. In connection with the illegal wiretapping of the nuclear energy manager

Klaus Traube's phones, the chair of the Social Democratic Party, Herbert Wehner, suggested that the wiretapping of telephones in Stammheim prison should be suspended.

8. Author's observations. I served as chair of the German section of Amnesty International in 1977–79. Among many publications, see German Government 1975; and Bakker Schut 1987. Oesterle 2003 reports on the experience of the Stammheim prison official Bubeck during these years. He refutes criticisms of prison conditions.

9. See the decision of the European Commission on Human Rights of July 8, 1978, in the case of Ensslin, Baader, Raspe, DR 14,64 (84 ff.). *Europäische Grundrechte Zeitschrift* 1978, pp. 314 ff. (Applications 7572/76, 7586/76, and 7587/76 ).

10. Among the many contributions on Germany's post-9/11 climate, see Tolmein 2002; Prantl 2002; Hirschmann and Leggemann 2003; Stevenson 2003; Hein 2004; and Thamm 2004.

11. The German government has published an overview of antiterrorist measures (Bundesministerium des Innern 2004a) and a collection of academic contributions on radical Islamism (Germany, Bundesministerium des Innern, 2003). Annual reports on threats to internal security are being published every year by BfV (for 2004, see Germany, Bundesministerium des Innern, 2004b).

12. See Waldmann and Malthaner 2003: 120; Glaeßner 2003: 276; and Kant 2005. Brugger is quite positive regarding the legality and necessity of the dragnet (2004: 86–101).

13. "Die FDP ist ein Sicherheitsrisiko," interview with Federal Minster of the Interior Otto Schily, *Die Welt*, August 13, 2005; "Schily hält an Sicherungshaft fest," netzzeitung.de, August 8, 2005, http://www.netzeitung.de/spezial/kampfgegenterror/352090.html (accessed January 15, 2006).

14. Dana Priest, "CIA Holds Terror Suspects in Secret Prisons. Debate Is Growing within Agency about Legality and Morality of Overseas System Set Up after 9/11," *Washington Post*, November 2, 2005, A1.

15. See "Fahndung mit Fallstricken," *Süddeutsche Zeitung*, September 16, 2005; "Gravierender Folter-Fall," *Süddeutsche Zeitung*, December 17–18, 2005; "Verhöre auf Libanesisch" *Die Zeit*, January 19, 2006; and Germany, Federal Crime Office, 2005.

16. See "US-Regierung wollte 'Falsche Zeit, falscher Ort,' " *Der Spiegel*, February 24, 2007.

17. See "Der vergessene Gefangene," *Der Spiegel*, November 21, 2005; "Abgeordnete verlangen Aufklärung im Fall Zammar," *Der Spiegel*, November 24, 2005, and "Entführungsfall Zammar: Berlin frühzeitig von USA informiert," http://www.n24.de, March 4, 2006.

18. Under German law, BND is legally empowered to investigate leaks for the self-protection of the service, but this surveillance operation lasted way beyond what was permissible.

19. In February 2006 two BND operatives during the ongoing war had reported from Baghdad to the BND central office and had also passed on infor-

mation to the U.S. military. This raised the question of whether, despite Germany's neutral stance on the Iraq military intervention in 2003, German agents on the ground had supported the war effort, which the government denied ("German Intelligence Gave U.S. Iraqi Defense Plan, Report Says," *New York Times,* February 27, 2006).

20. See the interview with Schäuble in *Stuttgarter Zeitung,* December 16, 2005.

21. "Merkel: Guantanamo Mustn't Exist in Long Term," *Der Spiegel,* January 9, 2006; http://service.spiegel.de/cache/international/0,1518,394180,00 .html (accessed March 31, 2006).

# Bibliography

9/11 Commission Report. 2004. *Final Report of the National Commission on Terrorist Attacks upon the United States.* New York: W. W. Norton & Co.

9/11 Public Discourse Project. 2005. *Final Report on 9/11 Commission Recommendations.* December 5.

Abel, Richard. 1995. *Politics by Other Means: Law in the Struggle against Apartheid, 1980–1994.* New York: Routledge.

Adelman, Howard. 2002. "Canadian Borders and Immigration Post 9/11." *International Migration Review* 36(1): 15–28.

Aguilar Fernández, Paloma. 1996. *Memoria y olvido en la Guerra Civil española.* Madrid: Alianza.

———. 1997. "Collective Memory of the Spanish Civil War: The Case of Political Amnesty in the Spanish Transition to Democracy." *Democratization* 4(4): 88–109.

———. 1998. "The Memory of Civil War in the Transition to Democracy: The Peculiarity of the Basque Case." *West European Politics* 21(4): 5–25.

———. 2002. "Justicia, política y memoria: Los legados del franquismo en la Transición española." In A. Barahona de Brito et al., *Las políticas hacia el pasado: Juicios, depuraciones, perdón y olvido en las nuevas democracias.* Madrid: Istmo.

Albrecht, Ernst. 1976. *Der Staat, Idee und Wirklichkeit: Grundzüge einer Staatsphilosophie.* Stuttgart: Seewald.

Alleg, Henri. 1958. *The Question.* London: John Calder.

Allen, N. 2005. "A Restless Electorate: Stirrings in the Political System." In *Britain at the Polls 2005,* ed. John Bartle and Anthony King. Washington, D.C.: Congressional Quarterly Press, 54–77.

Amnesty International. 1979–82. *Annual Reports 1978–81.* London: Amnesty International Publications.

———. 1994. *Israel and the Occupied Territories: Torture and Ill-Treatment of Political Detainees.* April.

———. 2004. *USA: Human Dignity Denied: Torture and Accountability in the "War on Terror."* http://web.amnesty.org/library/index/ENGAMR511452004.

Amnesty International Canada (AIC). 2004a. *A Human Rights Approach to National Security Confidentiality.* May 28.

———. 2004b. *Securing a Commitment to Human Rights in Canada's Security Laws and Practices: Opening Submissions of Amnesty International Canada to the Commission of Enquiry into the Actions of Canadian Officials.* June 14.

———. 2005a. *Effective Oversight: Protecting Human Rights in the Context of Canadian National Security Investigations.* June 6.

———. 2005b. *Restoring His Rights, Addressing the Wrongs: Amnesty International's Closing Submissions to the Committee of Inquiry.* September 10.

———. 2005c. *Reply Submissions to the Commission of Inquiry into the Actions of Canadian Officials in Relation to Maher Arar.* November 2.

———. 2005d. "USA: 800 secret CIA flights into and out of Europe." Press release, May 12.

———. 2005e. "Was Maher Arar Detained and Interrogated as Part of a Canadian-Style Rendition Program? Press release, May 3.

Amnesty International Spain. 2004. *España. Acabar con la doble injusticia. Víctimas de tortura y malos tratos sin reparación.* http://www.es.amnesty.org/esp/docs_esp.htm.

Art, Robert J., and Louise Richardson, eds. 2006. *Democracy and Counterterrorism: Lessons from the Past.* Washington, D.C.: United States Institute of Peace Press.

Aussaresses, Paul. 2002. *The Battle for the Casbah: Terrorism and Counter-Terrorism in Algeria, 1955–1957.* New York: Enigma.

Aust, Stefan. 1998. *Der Baader-Meinhof-Komplex.* 2d ed. Munich: Goldmann.

B'Tselem. 1991. *The Interrogation of Palestinians During the Intifada: Ill-Treatment, "Moderate Physical Pressure" or Torture?* Jerusalem, March.

———. 1997. *Legitimizing Torture: The Israeli High Court of Justice Rulings in the Bilbeisi, Hamdan, and Mubarak Cases: An Annotated Sourcebook.* Jerusalem, January.

———. 1998. *Routine Torture: Interrogation Methods of the General Security Service.* Jerusalem, February.

———. 2000. *Legislation Allowing the Use of Physical Force and Mental Coercion in Interrogations by the General Security Service.* Jerusalem, January.

Baader-Meinhof-Report. 1972. *Der Baader-Meinhof-Report. Dokumente–Analysen-Zusammenhänge. Aus Akten des Bundeskriminalamtes, der "Sonderkommission Bonn" und des Bundesamts für Verfassungsschutz.* Mainz: v. Hase & Koehler.

Bakker Schut, Pieter, ed. 1987. *Das Info. Briefe von Gefangenen aus der Raf aus der Diskussion 1973–1977. Dokumente.* Hamburg: Neuer Malik Verlag.

Balbus, Isaac. 1977. *The Dialectics of Legal Repression: Black Rebels before the American Courts.* New Brunswick, N.J.: Transaction.

Barbalet, J. M. 1988. *Citizenship: Rights, Struggle, and Class Inequality.* Milton Keynes: Open University Press.

Bartholomew, Amy, ed. 2006. *Empire's Law: The American Imperial Project and the "War to Remake the World."* London: Pluto.

Barzilai, Gad. 1998. "The Argument of 'National Security' in Politics and Jurisprudence." In *Security Concerns: Insights from the Israeli Experience,* ed. Daniel Bar-Tal, Dan Jacobson, and Aharon Kleiman. Greenwich: JAI Press, 243–65.

Bästlein, Klaus. 2002. *Der Fall Mielke. Die Ermittlungen gegen den Minister für Staatssicherheit der DDR.* Baden-Baden: Nomos.

BBC. 2004. "Germany Probes Army Abuse Claims." November 29. http://news .bbc.co.uk/2/hi/europe/4051387.stm.

Becker, Julian. 1977. *Hitler's Children: The Story of the Baader-Meinhof Terrorist Gang.* London: Michael Joseph.

Beetham, D., et al. 2002. *Democracy under Blair.* 1st ed. London: Politico's.

Bell, Christine. 2003. "Dealing with the Past in Northern Ireland." *Fordham International Law Journal* 26: 1095–1147.

Bell, Christine, Colm Campbell, and Fionnuala Ní Aoláin. 2007. "The Battle for Transitional Justice: Hegemony, Iraq and International Law." In *Judges, Transition and Human Rights Cultures: Essays in Honour of Stephen Livingstone,* ed. K. McEvoy and J. Morrison. Oxford: Oxford University Press.

Benjamin, Daniel, and Steven Simon. 2004. *The Next Attack: The Failure of the War on Terror and a Strategy for Getting it Right.* New York: Simon and Schuster.

Berman, Nathaniel. 1997. "The International Law of Nationalism: Group Identity and Legal History." In *International Law and Ethnic Conflict,* ed. David Wippman. Ithaca, N.Y.: Cornell University Press.

Biesenbach, Klaus, ed. 2005. *Zur Vorstellung des Terrors: Die RAF-Ausstellung.* Vol. 1. Berlin: KW Institute for Contemporary Art.

Biggio, Frank A. 2002. "Neutralizing the Threat: Reconsidering Existing Doctrines in the Emerging War on Terrorism." *Case Western Reserve Journal of International Law* 34(1): 1–43.

Bilder, Richard B., and Detlev F. Vagts. 2004. "Speaking Law to Power: Lawyers and Torture." *American Journal of International Law* 98(4): 689–95. Republished in *The Torture Debate in America,* ed. by Karen J. Greenberg. New York: Cambridge University Press, 2006, 151–61.

Blick, A., T. Chowdury, and S. Weir. 2006. *The Rules of the Game: Terrrorism, Community and Human Rights.* Joseph Rowntree Reform Trust.

Blom-Cooper, L. 2005. "Government and Judiciary." In *The Blair Effect 2001– 2005,* ed. A. Seldon and D. Kavanagh. Cambridge: Cambridge University Press, 233–55.

Bolton, John R. 2000. "Is There Really 'Law' in International Affairs?" *Transnational Law and Contemporary Problems* 10: 1–48.

Bonner, D. 2000. "The United Kingdom's Response to Terrorism: The Impact of Decisions of European Judicial Institutions and the Northern Ireland 'Peace Process.' " In *European Democracies against Terrorism: Governmental Poli-*

cies and Intergovernmental Cooperation, ed. F. Reinares. Aldershot, UK: Ashgate, 40–47.

Bowden, Mark. 2003. "The Dark Art of Interrogation." Atlantic Monthly, October, 51–76.

Boyle, Kevin, and Hurst Hannum. 1972. "Ireland in Strasburg: An Analysis of the Northern Irish Proceedings before the European Commission on Human Rights." Irish Jurist 7.

———. 1976. "Ireland in Strasburg: Final Decisions in the Northern Irish Proceedings before the European Commission of Human Rights." Irish Jurist 6.

———. 1977. "The Donnelly Case: Administrative Practice and Domestic Remedies under the European Convention on Human Rights, One Step Forward and Two Steps Back." American Journal of International Law 71(2): 316–21.

Boyne, Shawn. 2005. "Preserving the Rule of Law in a Time of Terror: Germany's Response to Terrorism." In Law vs. War: Conference Report, ed. Shawn Boyne, Michael German, and Pillar R. Paul. Strategic Studies Institute, U.S. Army War College, 17–21. http://www.strategicinstitute.army .mil/pdffiles/PUB613.pdf.

Branche, Raphaëlle. 2001. La torture et l'armée pendant la guerre d'Algérie 1954–1962. Paris: Gallimard.

Brugger, Winfried. 1996. "Darf der Staat ausnahmsweise foltern?" Der Staat 35: 67–97.

———. 2000. "Vom unbedingten Verbot der Folter zum bedingten Recht auf Folter?" Juristenzeitung 55: 165–73.

———. 2004. Freiheit und Sicherheit. Eine staatstheoretische Skizze mit praktischen Beispielen. Baden-Baden: Nomos.

Bruni, Luigi. 1987. ETA. Historia política de una lucha armada. Bilbao: Txalaparta.

Bull, Melissa, and Mark Craig. 2006. "The Problem of Terrorism: Balancing Risk between State and Civil Responsibilities." Current Issues in Criminal Justice 18(2).

Bürgerrechte und Polizei. 2005. Special issue, Terrorismus. No. 1.

Byers, Michael. 2003. "Preemptive Self-Defense: Hegemony, Equality and Strategies of Legal Change." Journal of Political Philosophy 11: 171–90.

Byers, Michael, and Georg Nolte, eds. 2003. United States Hegemony and the Foundations of International Law. Cambridge: Cambridge University Press.

Calle, Ángel. 2005. Nuevos movimientos globales. Hacia la radicalidad democrática. Madrid: Editorial Popular.

Campbell, Colm. 1994. Emergency Law in Ireland, 1918–1925. Oxford: Oxford University Press.

———. 2005. " 'Wars on Terror' and Vicarious Hegemons: The UK, International Law, and the Northern Ireland Conflict." International and Comparative Law Quarterly 54: 321–56.

Campbell, Colm, and Ita Connolly. 2003. "A Model for the 'War against Terrorism'? Military Intervention and the 1970 Falls Curfew." *Journal of Law and Society* 30: 341–75.

———. 2006. "Making War on Terror? Global Lessons from Northern Ireland." *Modern Law Review* 69: 935–57.

Campbell, Colm, Fionnuala Ní Aoláin, and Colin Harvey. 2003. "The Frontiers of Legal Analysis: Reframing the Transition in Northern Ireland." *Modern Law Review* 66: 317–45.

CANADIAN GOVERNMENT DOCUMENTS. The following documents are cited in the text using the abbreviated titles given in brackets.

[Access.] 1985. Access to Information Act: An Act to Extend the Present Laws of Canada That Provides Access to Information under the Control of the Government of Canada. 1980-81-82-83, c. 111, Sch. 1 "1."

[Arrests.] 2006. *Use of Arrests without Warrant Pursuant to the Anti-Terrorism Act, Updated 2006-06-22.* http://www.ps-sp.gc.ca/abt/dpr/at/index-en.asp.

[ATA.] 2001. Anti-Terrorism Act Bill C-36: An Act to Amend the Criminal Code, the Official Secrets Act, the Canada Evidence Act, the Proceeds of Crime (Money Laundering) Act and Other Acts, and to Enact Measures Respecting the Registration of Charities, in Order to Combat Terrorism. December 18.

[———.] 2004–5. *The Anti-Terrorism Act—Annual Report concerning Investigative Hearings and Recognizance with Conditions.* http://www.doj.ca/en/anti_terr/reports.html.

[Backgrounder.] 2003. *Canada's Actions against Terrorism since September 11th—Backgrounder.* February 7.

Canada. 2002. Public Safety Act: An Act to Amend Certain Acts of Canada, and to Enact Measures for Implementing the Biological and Toxin Weapons Convention, in Order to Enhance Public Safety. C-15, P-31.5. May 6.

———. 2005a. *Canada's International Policy Statement—A Role of Pride and Influence in the World.* April 19.

———. 2005b. *Securing an Open Society: One Year Later.* April.

[Commission.] 2004a. Commission of Inquiry into the Actions of Canadian Officials in Relation to Maher Arar. *Accountability and Transparency: A Background Paper to the Commission's Consultation Paper.* December 10.

[———.] 2004b. Commission of Inquiry into the Actions of Canadian Officials in Relation to Maher Arar. *National Security and Rights and Freedoms: A Background Paper to the Commission's Consultation Paper.* December 10.

[———.] 2005a. Commission of Inquiry into the Actions of Canadian Officials in Relation to Maher Arar. *Summary of Information Received at In Camera Hearings.* December 20. http://www.ararcommission.ca/eng/window01.htm.

[———.] 2005b. Commission of Inquiry into the Actions of Canadian Officials in Relation to Maher Arar. *Commission Policy Review: Integrated National Security Review Committee: Further Option for Public Comment.* November 25.

[———.] 2006. Commission of Inquiry into the Actions of Canadian Officials in Relation to Maher Arar. *Final Report.* September.

[*Counter-Terrorism Measures.*] 2002. Department of Foreign Affairs and International Trade. *International Counter-Terrorism Measures since 9/11: Trends, Gaps and Challenges.* July.

[CSIS.] 2000. Canadian Security Intelligence Service. *International Terrorism: The Threat to Canada.* Report no. 2000/04, May 3. http://www.csis-scrs .gc.ca/en/publications/perspectives/200004.asp.

[———.] 2003. Canadian Security Intelligence Service. *Canadian Security Intelligence Service 2003 Public Report.* http://www.csis-scrs.gc.ca/en/ publications/annual_report/2003/report2003.asp.

[———.] 2005. Canadian Security Intelligence Service. *Control, Accountability and Review: The CSIS Experience.* Submission to the Commission of Inquiry into the Actions of Canadian Officials in Relation to Maher Arar. February 21. http://www.csis-scrs.gc.ca/en/newsroom/speeches/ speech21022005.asp.

[*Human Security.*] 1999. Department of Foreign Affairs and International Trade. *Human Security: Safety for People in a Changing World.* April. http://www.cpdsindia.org/global-humansecurity/changingworld.

[Intervenors.] 2005. Committee of Organizations with Intervenor Status at the Arar Inquiry. *Joint Intervenor's Submission to the Arar Commission Policy Review.* December 17.

[IRPA.] 2001. Immigration and Refugee Protection Act. C. 27, assented November 1. http://laws.justice.gc.ca/en/I-2.5/index.html.

[IRPR.] 2002. Immigration and Refugee Protection Regulations. SOR/2002-227. http://laws.justice.gc.ca/en/I-2.5/SOR-2002-227/index.html.

[*Jaballah.*] 2000. *Mahmoud Es Sayy Jaballah v. Canada* (Minister of Citizenship and Immigration). 196 F.T.R. 175 (F.C.T.D.).

[———.] 2003. Jaballah (Re) (T.D.), 2003 FCT 640, [2003] 4 F.C. 345. Trial Division, Mackay J. Toronto, December 17, 18, 2001; January 8, February 13, and March 11, 2002; Ottawa, May 23, 2003.

[*Keeping.*] 2001. *Keeping Canadians Safe.* http://www.psepc-sppcc.gc.ca/prg/ ns/seccert-en.asp. Reposted within *Enhancing Security for Canadians.* http://www.fin.gc.ca/budget01/mm/security/security_e.htm.

[Kelly.] 1999. *The Report of the Special Senate Committee on Security and Intelligence.* January. http://www.parl.gc.ca/36/1/parlbus/commbus/ senate/com-e/secu-e/rep-e/repsecintjan99-e.htm

[*Mahjoub.*] 2004. *Mohamed Zeki Mahjoub v. Canada (Minister of Citizenship and Immigration).* Federal Court, Dawson J. Toronto, December 17, 2004; Ottawa, January 31, 2005. http://reports.fja.gc.ca/en/2005/ 2005fc156/2005fc156.html.

[McDonald.] 1981. Commission of Inquiry into Certain Activities of the

Royal Canadian Mounted Police (McDonald Commission). *Freedom and Security under the Law.*

[*Minority Views of ATA.*] 2003. Department of Justice of Canada. *Minority Views on the Canadian Anti-Terrorism Act (Formerly Bill C-36): A Qualitative Study.* Ottawa, March 31. http://www.doj.ca/en/ps/rs/rep/2003/rr03-4a.html.

[*Promises.*] 2001. Standing Senate Committee on Human Rights. *Promises to Keep: Implementing Canada's Human Rights Obligations.* December.

[*Public Safety.*] 2003. Citizenship and Immigration Canada. *Public Safety and Anti-Terrorism: Final Report.* September.

[*Public Views of ATA.*] 2004. *Public Views of the Canadian Anti-Terrorism Act (formerly Bill C-36): A Qualitative Study* March 21. http://canada.justice.gc.ca/en/ps/rep/2005/n05-3/n05-3.pdf.

[*Scholars Views of ATA.*] 2004. *Canadian Scholars' Views of the Canadian Anti-Terrorism Act (formerly Bill C-36).* March 31. http://canada.justice.gc.ca/en/ps/rep/2005/n05–01/n05-1.pdf.

[*Securing.*] 2004. *Securing an Open Society: Canada's National Security Policy.* April.

[*Senate.*] 2005. Senate Legal and Constitutional Legislation Committee Inquiry into the Anti-Terrorism Bill (no. 2) 2005. Submission of the Human Rights and Equal Opportunity Commission. November 11.

[*SIRC.*] 2004. Security Intelligence Review Committee. *SIRC Report 2003–2004—An Operational Review of the Canadian Security Intelligence Service.* September 30.

[*Suresh.*] 2002. *Manickavasagam Suresh v. Canada (Minister of Citizenship and Immigration and the Attorney General).* 2002 SCC 1, File 27790, January 11. http://www.lexum.umontreal.ca/csc-scc/pub/2002/vol1/html/2002scr1_003.html.

[*Toope.*] 2005. Commission of Inquiry into the Actions of Canadian Officials in Relation to Maher Arar. *Report of Professor Stephen J. Toope, Fact Finder.* October 14. http://www.ararcommission.ca/eng/ToopeReport_final.pdf.

[*Yamani.*] 2002. *Issam Al Yamani v. The Minister of Citizenship and Immigration.* FCT 1162, IMM-5696-01 Trial Division, Kelen J. Toronto, October 23, 2002; Ottawa, November 8, 2002.

Carafano, James Jay, and Paul Rosenzweig. 2005. *Winning the Long War: Lessons from the Cold War for Defeating Terrorism and Preserving Freedom.* Washington, D.C.: Heritage Foundation.

Carothers, Thomas. 2006. "The Backlash against Democracy Promotion." *Foreign Affairs* 85(2): 55–68.

Casals, Xavier. 1998. *La tentación neofascista en España.* Barcelona: Plaza y Janés.

———. 1999. "La ultraderecha española, una presencia ausente (1975–1999)." *Historia y Política* 3: 147–72.

Cerdán, Manuel, and Antonio Rubio. 1997. *El origen del GAL.* Madrid: Temas de Hoy.

Chang, Nancy, and Alan Kabat. 2004. "A Summary of Recent Court Rulings on Terrorism-Related Matters Having Civil Liberties Implications." Center for Constitutional Rights, March 8.

Chesney, Robert M. 2003. "Terrorism and the Constitution: Sacrificing Civil Liberties in the Name of National Security & Enemy Aliens: Double Standards and Constitutional Freedoms in the War on Terrorism," *Michigan Law Journal* 101.

Cohen, Stanley. 1991. "Talking about Torture in Israel." *Tikkun,* November/December, 23–30, 89–90.

———. 2002. *Folk Devils and Moral Panics.* 3d ed. London: Routledge.

———. 2005. "Post-Moral Torture: From Guantanamo to Abu Ghraib." *Index on Censorship* 34(1): 24–30.

Cole, David. 2005. "All Power to the President—The Case of John Yoo." *New York Review of Books,* November 17, 8–12.

Cole, David, and James X. Dempsey. 2002. *Terrorism and the Constitution: Sacrificing Civil Liberties in the Name of National Security.* New York: New Press.

Conte, Alex. 2002. "Terror Meets Tyranny: The Interface Between Counter Terrorism and Human Rights." *Murdoch University Electronic Journal of Law* 9:3. http://www.murdoch.edu.au/elaw/issues/v9n3/conte93_text.html.

Cook, C., and J. Stevenson. 1996. *The Longman Companion to Britain since 1945.* New York: Longman.

Cotler, Irwin. 2002. "Terrorism, Security and Rights in the Post–September 11th Universe." *Windsor Year Book on Access to Justice* 21: 519.

Council of Europe. 2005. *Report by Mr. Alvaro Gil-Robles, Commissioner for Human Rights, On His Visit to the United Kingdom, 4–12 November 2004.* Strasbourg, June 8. CommDH(2005)6 (PDF document).

———. 2006. *Report by the Secretary General on the Use of His Powers under Article 52 of the European Convention on Human Rights.* Strasbourg, February 28.

Crewe, I. 2005. "New Labour's Hegemony: Erosion or Extension?" In *Britain at the Polls 2005,* ed. John Bartle and Anthony King. Washington D.C.: Congressional Quarterly Press, 200–220.

Daniels, N. 1996. *Justice and Justification: Reflective Equilibrium in Theory and Practice.* New York: Routledge.

Daniels, Ronald J., Patrick Macklem, and Kent Roach, eds. 2001. *The Security of Freedom: Essays on Canada's Anti-Terrorism Bill.* Toronto: University of Toronto Press.

Danner, Mark. 2004a. "Torture and Truth." *New York Review of Books,* June 10, 46–50.

———. 2004b. "The Logic of Torture." *New York Review of Books,* June 24, 70–74.

———. 2005. *Torture and Truth: America, Abu Ghraib, and the War on Terror.* New York: New York Review Books.

Daubney, David, et al., eds. 2002. *Terrorism, Law and Democracy: How Is Canada Changing following September 11?* Montreal: Canadian Institute for the Administration of Justice and Les Éditions Thémis.

Davenport, Christian. 2004. "The Promise of Democratic Pacification: An Empirical Assessment." *International Studies Quarterly* 48: 539–60.

Del Águila, Rafael. 2006. "Tolerancia y multiculturalismo: Instrucciones de uso." *Claves de Razón Práctica* 125.

DePaul, M. R. 1993. *Balance and Refinement: Beyond Coherence Methods of Moral Inquiry.* New York: Routledge.

Dershowitz, Alan. 1989. "Is It Necessary to Apply 'Physical Pressure' to Terrorists—and to Lie About It?" *Israel Law Review* 23(2–3): 193–200.

———. 2002. *Why Terrorism Works.* New Haven: Yale University Press.

———. 2004. "The Torture Warrant: A Response to Professor Strauss." *New York Law School Law Review* 48: 275–94.

Deutsche Welle. 2003. "Committee Says German Border Police Too Brutal." March 15. http://www.dw-world.de/dw/article/o,,807958,oo.html, accessed October 1, 2006.

———. 2004. "Germany Military Probes Torture Allegations." November 11. http://www.dw-world.de/dw/article/o,1564,1402837,oo.html, accessed October 1, 2006.

Dewitt, David B. 2004. "National Defence vs. Foreign Affairs: Culture Clash in Canada's International Security Policy?" *International Journal* 59(3): 579–95.

Diamond, Larry. 2005. *Squandered Victory: The American Occupation and the Bungled Effort to Bring Democracy to Iraq.* New York: Henry Holt.

Dionne, E. J., Jr. 2005. "America's Other President: The American Left, Right and Centre on Tony Blair and the Election of 2005." In *Britain at the Polls 2005,* ed. John Bartle and Anthony King. Washington D.C.: Congressional Quarterly Press, 185–99.

Domínguez Iribarren, Florencio. 1998. *De la negociación a la tregua. ¿El final de ETA?* Madrid: Taurus.

Donnelly, Jack. 1986. "International Human Rights: A Regime Analysis." *International Organisation* 40: 599–642.

———. 2003. *Universal Human Rights in Theory and Practice.* 2d ed. Ithaca, N.Y.: Cornell University Press.

Douglas, William A., and Pedro Ibarra. 2005. "A Basque Referendum: Resolution of Political Conflict or the Promised Land of Error?" In *Empire and Terror,* ed. Begoña Aretxaga et al. Reno: University of Nevada Press, 137–62.

Duve, Freimut, Heinrich Böll, and Klaus Staeck, eds. 1977. *Briefe zur Verteidigung der Republik.* Hamburg: Rowohlt.

Egaña, Iñaki, and Giovanni Giacopucci. 1992. *Los días de Argel.* Bilbao: Txalaparta.

Elkins, Caroline. 2005. *Imperial Reckoning: The Untold Story of Britain's Gulag in Kenya.* New York: Henry Holt.

222 / Bibliography

Elorza, Aantonio, ed. 2000. *La historia de ETA*. Madrid: Temas de Hoy.
European Commission on Human Rights. 1978. *Decision of 8 July 1978, G. Ensslin, A. Baader, J. Raspe v. Federal Republic of Germany (Applications 7572/76, 7586/76 et 7587/76), ECHR Decisions and Reports*. Strasbourg, 64–116.
Falk, Richard. 2003 *The Great Terror War*. Northampton, Mass.: Olive Branch Press.
—————. 2005a. "Demystifying Iraq?" *New Centennial Review* 5(1):43–62.
—————. 2005b. "Human Rights: A Descending Spiral." In *Human Rights in the "War on Terror,"* ed. Richard Ashby Wilson. Cambridge: Cambridge University Press, 225–41.
—————. 2007. "Regional War in the Middle East," *International Journal of Contemporary Iraqi Studies* 1(1): 77–92.
Falk, Richard, Robert Jay Lifton, and Gabriel Kolko, eds. 1971. *Crimes of War*. New York: Random House.
Feller, S. Z. 1989. "Not Actual 'Necessity' but Possible 'Justification'; Not 'Moderate' Pressure, but Either 'Unlimited' or 'None at All.'" *Israel Law Review* 23(2–3): 201–15.
Felner, Eitan. 2005. "Torture and Terrorism: Painful Lessons from Israel." In *Torture: Does It Make Us Safer? Is It Ever OK? A Human Rights Perspective*, ed. Kenneth Roth and Minky Worden. New York: New Press, 28–43.
Ferguson, Niall. 2004. *Empire: The Rise and Demise of the British World and the Lessons for Global Power*. New York: Basic Books.
Fetscher, Iring. 1977. *Terrorismus und Reaktion*. Köln: Europäische Verlagsanstalt.
Finkelstein, Norman G. 2005. *Beyond Chutzpah: On the Misuse of Anti-Semitism and the Abuse of History*. Berkeley and Los Angeles: University of California Press.
Fitzpatrick, Joan M. 1994. *Human Rights in Crisis: International System for Protecting Rights during States of Emergency*. Philadelphia: University of Pennsylvania Press.
—————. 2003. "Speaking Law to Power: The War against Terrorism and Human Rights." *European Journal of International Law* 14(2): 241–64.
Fleck, Dieter. 1995. *The Handbook of Humanitarian Law in Armed Conflicts*. Oxford: Oxford University Press.
Follmar, Petra, Wolfgang S. Heinz, and Benjamin Schulz. 2003. *Die deutsche Folterdebatte*. Berlin: German Institute for Human Rights.
Fontana, Josep. 2005. "Bases per una nova transició." *Revista HMiC*. http://seneca.uab.es/hmic.
Foot, Rosemary. 2005. "Human Rights and Counterterrorism in Global Governance: Reputation and Resistance." *Global Governance* 22: 291–310.
Forsythe, David P. 1988. *Human Rights and U.S. Foreign Policy: Congress Reconsidered*. Gainesville: University Presses of Florida.
—————. 2004. *Human Rights in International Relations*. Cambridge: Cambridge University Press.

———. 2005. *The Humanitarians: The ICRC.* Cambridge: Cambridge University Press.

Foweraker, J., and T. Landman. 1997. *Citizenship Rights and Social Movements: A Comparative and Statistical Analysis.* Oxford: Oxford University Press.

Fulbright, J. William. 1967. *The Arrogance of Power.* New York: Random House.

Funke, Manfred, ed. 1977. *Terrorismus. Untersuchungen zur Strategie und Struktur revolutionärer Gewaltpolitik.* Bonn: Bundeszentrale für Politische Bildung.

Galbraith, Peter W. 2005. *The End of Iraq: How American Incompetence Created a War Without End.* New York: Simon & Schuster.

Gavison, Ruth. 1997. "The Constitutional Revolution: A Reality or a Self-Fulfilling Prophecy." *Mishpatim* 28: 21–147 (in Hebrew).

Gearty, Conor. 2005. "11 September 2001, Counter-Terrorism, and the Human Rights Act." *Journal of Law and Society* 32: 18–33.

———. 2006. *Can Human Rights Survive?* Cambridge: Cambridge University Press.

Gerges, Fawaz A. 2005. *The Far Enemy: Why Jihad Went Global.* New York: Cambridge University Press.

German, Michael. 2005. "Squaring the Error." In *Law vs. War: Competing Approaches to Fighting Terrorism: Conference Report*, ed. Shawn Boyne, Michael German, and Pillar R. Paul. Strategic Studies Institute, U.S. Army War College, 11–16. http://www.strategicinstitute.army.mil/pdffiles/PUB613 .pdf.

Germany. 1977. *Dokumentation der Bundesregierung zur Entführung von Hanns Martin Schleyer.* Munich: Goldmann.

———. 2002. *Report of Germany to the UN Security Council's Counter-Terrorism Committee.* UN doc. S/2002/1193.

Germany. Bundesministerium des Innern [Ministry of the Interior]. 1975. *Dokumentation über Aktivitäten anarchistischer Gewalttäter in der Bundesrepublik Deutschland.* Bonn.

———. 2003. *Islamismus.* Berlin.

———. 2004a. *Nach dem 11. September 2001: Maßnahmen gegen den Terror.* Berlin.

———. 2004b. *Verfassungsschutzbericht 2004.* Berlin.

Germany. Bundesregierung [Federal Government]. 2006. *Bericht der Bundesregierung (offene Fassung) gemäß Anforderung des Parlamentarischen Kontrollgremiums vom 25.1.2006 zu Vorgängen im Zusammenhang mit dem Irakkrieg und der Bekämpfung des Terrorismus.* Berlin. February 15.

Germany. Federal Crime Office (BKA). 2005. *BKA weist Vorwürfe zurück.* Press release, December 23. http://www.bka.de/pressemitteilungen/2005/pm231205 .html.

Glaeßner, Gert-Joachim. 2003. *Sicherheit in Freiheit. Die Schutzfunktion des demokratischen Staates und die Freiheit der Bürger.* Opladen: Leske & Budrich.

Golden, Tim. 2006. "Senior Lawyer at Pentagon Broke Ranks on Detainees." *New York Times*, February 20, A8.

Goldsmith, Jack L., and Eric A. Posner. 2005. *The Limits of International Law.* New York: Oxford University Press.

Goldstone, Richard. 2005. "The Tension between Combating Terrorism and Protecting Civil Liberties." In *Human Rights in the "War on Terror,"* edited by Richard Ashby Wilson. Cambridge: Cambridge University Press, 157–68.

Goode, Erich, and Nachman Ben-Yehouda. 1994. *Moral Panics: The Social Construction of Deviance.* Oxford: Blackwell.

Gordon, Neva, and Ruchama Marton, eds. 1995. *Torture: Human Rights, Medical Ethics, and the Case of Israel.* London: Zed.

Govier, Trudy. 2002. *A Delicate Balance: What Philosophy Can Tell Us about Terrorism.* New York: Perseus.

Greenberg, Karen J., ed. 2006 *The Torture Debate in America.* New York: Cambridge University Press.

Greenberg, Karen J., and Joshua L. Dratel, eds. 2005. *The Torture Papers: The Road to Abu Ghraib.* Cambridge: Cambridge University Press.

Griffin, David Ray. 2004. *The New Pearl Harbor: Disturbing Questions about the Bush Administration and 9/11.* Northampton, Mass.: Olive Branch Press.

———. 2005. *The 9/11 Commission Report: Omissions and Distortions.* Northampton, Mass.: Olive Branch Press.

Gross, Michael L. 2001. "Just and Jewish Warfare." *Tikkun* 16(5): 31–36.

———. 2004. "Regulating Torture in a Democracy: Death and Indignity in Israel." *Polity* 34(3): 367–88.

Gross, Oren. 1998. "'Once More into the Breach': The Systemic Failure of Applying the European Convention on Human Rights to Entrenched Emergencies." *Yale Journal of International Law* 23: 437–501.

Gross, Oren, and Fionnuala Ní Aoláin. 2001. "From Discretion to Scrutiny: Revisiting the Application of the Margin of Appreciation Doctrine in the Context of Article 15 of the European Convention on Human Rights." *Human Rights Quarterly* 23: 625–49.

Hadden, Tom, Kevin Boyle, and Colm Campbell. 1990. "Emergency Law in Northern Ireland: The Context." In *Justice Under Fire*, ed. A. Jennings. 2d ed. (1st ed. 1988). London: Pluto Press, 1–26.

Hajjar, Lisa. 2000. "Sovereign Bodies, Sovereign States and the Problem of Torture." *Studies in Law, Politics, and Society* 21: 101–34.

———. 2004. "Torture and the Future." *Middle East Report Online.* May. http://www.merip.org/mero/interventions/hajjar_interv.html.

———. 2005. "An Army of Lawyers: From Disgruntled JAGs to Civil Libertarians, Legal Professionals Have Come Together against Torture." *The Nation*, December 26, 41–42.

Hampson, Fen. 2002. *Madness in the Multitude: Human Security and World Disorder.* Toronto: Oxford University Press.

Harris, David J., Michael O'Boyle, and Colin Warbrick. 2005. *Law of the European Convention on Human Rights.* Lexis-Nexis UK.

Harvey, Richard. 1990. "The Right of the People of the Whole of Ireland to Self Determination, Unity, Sovereignty and Independence." *New York Law School Journal of International Law and Comparative Law* 11: 167–206.

Haubrich, D. 2003. "September 11, Anti-Terror Laws and Civil Liberties: Britain, France, and Germany Compared." *Government and Opposition* 38: 3–28.

Hauser, Dorothea. 1997. *Baader und Herold—Beschreibung eines Kampfes.* Berlin: Alexander Fest Verlag.

Hein, Kirsten. 2004. "Die Anti-Terrorpolitik der rotgrünen Bundesregierung." In *Deutsche Sicherheitspolitik. Eine Bilanz der Regierung Schroeder,* ed. Sebastian Harnisch et al. Baden-Baden: Nomos, 145–71.

Heinz, Wolfgang S., and Jan-Michael Arend. 2005. *The International Fight against Terrorism and the Protection of Human Rights. With Recommendations to the German Government and Parliament.* Berlin: German Institute for Human Rights. http://www.institut-fuer-menschenrechte.de/webcom/show_shop.php/_c-488/_nr-38/i.html?PHPSESSID = 671c59109f300c2222d1a7979344fe18.

Hersh, Seymour. 2004. *Chain of Command: The Road from 9/11 to Abu Ghraib.* New York: Harper Collins.

Heymann, Philip B. 2002. "Civil Liberties and Human Rights in the Aftermath of September 11." *Harvard Journal of Law and Public Policy* 25(2): 441–56.

———. 2003. *Terrorism, Freedom, and Security.* Cambridge, Mass.: MIT Press.

Higgins, Rosalyn. 1994. *Problems and Process: International Law and How We Use It.* Oxford: Oxford University Press.

Hirschman, Albert O. 1991. *Retóricas de la intransigencia.* Mexico City: FCE. Spanish translation of *The Rhetoric of Reaction* (Cambridge, Mass.: Harvard University Press, 1991).

Hirschmann, Kai, and Christian Leggemann, eds. 2003. *Der Kampf gegen den Terrorismus: Strategien und Handlungserfordernisse in Deutschland.* Berlin: Berliner Wissenschafts-Verlag.

Hoffman, Paul. 2004. "Human Rights and Terrorism." *Human Rights Quarterly* 26(4): 932–55.

Holtzman, Elizabeth. 2005. "U.S. Detention: Torture and Accountability." *The Nation,* June 28.

Horchem, Hans Josef. 1987. "Fünfzehn Jahre Terrorismus in der Bundesrepublik Deutschland." *Aus Politik und Zeitgeschichte* 5: 3–15.

———. 1990. "Der Verfall der Roten Armee. *Aus Politik und Zeitgeschichte* 46/47: 54–61.

Hourani, Albert. 1989. Conclusion to *Suez 1956: The Crisis and Its Consequences,* ed. W. R. Louis and R. Owen. Oxford: Clarendon Press, 393–410.

*Human Rights Defenders on the Frontlines of Freedom.* 2003. Conference report. Atlanta, Ga.: The Carter Center. http://www.cartercenter.org/documents/1682.pdf.

Human Rights Watch. 1991. *Human Rights in Northern Ireland.* New York: Human Rights Watch.

———. 1992. "Israeli Interrogation Methods under Fire after Death of Detained

Palestinian: Israel's Supreme Court to Rule on Legality of Interrogation Guidelines." HRW Publications 4(6), Report E406, March 1. http://www.hrw.org/reports/1992/israel/.

———. 1994. *Torture and Ill-Treatment: Israel's Interrogation of Palestinians from the Occupied Territories.* New York: Human Rights Watch.

———. 1998. "Israel's Second Periodic Report to the Committee against Torture." Memorandum to the United Nations Committee against Torture. May. http://www.hrw.org/press98/may/isra0515.htm.

———. 2003. *In the Name of Counter-Terrorism: Human Rights Abuses Worldwide.* http://hrw.org/un/chr59/counter-terrorism-bck.htm.

———. 2004a. "Diplomatic Assurances and Their Use in North America." In *"Empty Promises": Diplomatic Assurances No Safeguard against Torture.* HRW Publications 16(4). http://hrw.org/reports/2004/un0404/4.htm.

———. 2004b. *Opportunism in the Face of Tragedy: Repression in the Name of Anti-Terrorism.* http://hrw.org/campaigns/september11/opportunismwatch.htm.

———. 2004c. "Timeline of Detainee Abuse Allegations and Responses." News release, May 7. http://www.hrw.org/english/docs/2004/05/07/usint8556.htm.

———. 2005a. *Getting Away with Torture? Command Responsibility for the U.S. Abuse of Detainees.* HRW Publications 17(1), April. http://www.hrw.org/reports/2005/us0405/.

———. 2005b. *Setting an Example? Counter-Terrorism Measures in Spain.* HRW Publications 17(1), January. http://hrw.org/reports/2005/spain0105/index.htm.

Ibarra, Pedro. 2003. "El impacto de ETA sobre el sistema político vasco." *Ecuador Debate* 60.

———. 2005. *Nacionalismo: Razón y pasión.* Barcelona: Ariel.

ID-Verlag, ed. 1997. *Rote Armee Fraktion. Texte und Materialien zur Geschichte der RAF.* Berlin.

Ignatieff, Michael. 2004. *The Lesser Evil: Political Ethics in an Age of Terror.* Princeton, N.J.: Princeton University Press.

———. 2005. "Moral Prohibition at a Price." In *Torture: Does It Make Us Safer? Is It Ever OK? A Human Rights Perspective,* ed. Kenneth Roth and Minky Worden. New York: New Press, 18–27.

———, ed. 2005. *American Exceptionalism and Human Rights.* Princeton, N.J.: Princeton University Press.

Imseis, Ardi. 2001. "'Moderate' Torture on Trial: Critical Reflections on the Israeli Supreme Court Judgment Concerning the Legality of General Security Service Interrogation Methods." *Berkeley Journal of International Law* 19(2): 328–49.

Ingram, A. 1994. *A Political Theory of Rights.* Oxford: Clarendon.

Ireland. Department of Foreign Affairs. 1969. *Ireland at the United Nations 1969.* Dublin.

Ishay, Micheline. 2004. *The History of Human Rights: From Ancient Times to the Globalization Era*. Berkeley and Los Angeles: University of California Press.

Israel. Attorney General [AGD]. 1999. *GSS Interrogations and the Necessity Defense—Framework for Attorney General's Deliberation (following the HCJ Ruling)*. Jerusalem. Memo, October 28 (in Hebrew).

Israel. Landau Commission [LC]. 1987. *Commission of Inquiry into the Methods of Investigation of the General Security Service regarding Hostile Terrorist Activity* (a.k.a. Landau Commission Report). Jerusalem, October.

Israel. Supreme Court [SC]. 1999. "Text of Israeli Supreme Court Decision on GSS Practices." September 6. http://www.totse.com/en/politics/foreign_military_intelligence_agencies/ua92170.html.

Jenkins, David. 2003. "In Support of Canada's Anti-Terrorism Act: A Comparison of Canadian, British and American Anti-Terrorism Law." *Saskatchewan Law Review* 66: 419–54.

Jones, P. 1994. *Rights*. London: Macmillan.

Kagan, Robert. 2003. *Of Paradise and Power: America and Europe in the New World Order*. New York: Knopf.

Kaldor, Mary. 1999. *New & Old Wars: Organized Violence in a Global Era*. Cambridge: Polity.

Kant, Martina. 2005. "Außer Spesen nichts gewesen? Eine Bilanz der Rasterfahndung nach dem 11.9.2001." *Bürgerrechte und Polizei* 1: 13–20.

Karpinski, Janis. 2005. *One Woman's Army: The Commanding General of Abu Ghraib Tells Her Story*. New York: Mirimax Books.

Katzenstein, Peter. 2001. "September 11th in Comparative Perspective: The Anti-Terrorism Campaigns of Germany and Japan." Unpublished ms. http://www.einaudi.cornell.edu/9-11/content/pdf/pkatzenstein.pdf.

———. 2003. "Same War—Different Views: Germany, Japan, and Counterterrorism." *International Organization* 57: 731–60.

Kelley, Matt. 2006. "Abu Ghraib Ended Career, a Top General Says." *USA Today*, November 3, 8A.

Keohane, Robert O. 1984. *After Hegemony: Cooperation and Discord in the World Political Economy*. Princeton, N.J.: Princeton University Press.

Kirby, Michael. 2001. "Australian Law—After 11 September 2001." *Australian Bar Review* 21.

Kraushaar, Wolfgang, ed. 2006. *Die RAF und der linke Terrorismus*. 2 vols. Hamburg: Hamburger Edition.

Kremnitzer, Mordechai. 1989. "The Landau Commission Report—Was the Security Service Subordinated to the Law or the Law to the 'Needs' of the Security Service?" *Israel Law Review* 23(2–3): 216–79.

Kretzmer, David. 1992. "The New Basic Laws on Human Rights: A Mini-Revolution in Israeli Constitutional Law?" *Israel Law Review* 26: 238–49.

———. 2005. "Targeted Killing of Suspected Terrorists: Extra-Judicial Executions or Legitimate Means of Defence?" *European Journal of International Law* 16: 171–212.

Krisch, Nico. 2005 "International Law in Times of Hegemony: Unequal Power and the Shaping of the International Legal Order." *European Journal of International Law* 16: 369–408.

Langer, Felicia. 1995. "The History of the Legal Struggle against Torture in Israel." In *Torture: Human Rights, Medical Ethics, and the Case of Israel,* ed. Neva Gordon and Ruchama Marton. London: Zed, 75–80.

Large, J. 2005. "Democracy and Terrorism: The Impact of the Anti." *International IDEA Policy Paper.* Stockholm: International IDEA. March.

Lelyveld, Joseph. 2005. "Interrogating Ourselves." *The New York Times Magazine,* June 12, 36–43, 60, 66–69.

Letamendia, Francisco. 1994. *Historia del nacionalismo vasco y de ETA.* 3 vols. San Sebastián: R&B Ediciones.

Levinson, Sanford. 2003a. " 'Precommitment' and 'Postcommitment': The Ban on Torture in the Wake of September 11." *Texas Law Review* 81(7): 2013–53.

———. 2003b. "The Debate on Torture: War against Virtual States," and "Reply." *Dissent* 50(3): 79–85.

———, ed. 2004. *Torture: A Collection.* Oxford: Oxford University Press.

Luban, David. 2005. "Eight Fallacies about Liberty and Security." In *Human Rights in the "War on Terror,"* ed. Richard Ashby Wilson. Cambridge: Cambridge University Press, 242–57.

———. 2006. "Liberalism, Torture, and the Ticking Bomb." In *The Torture Debate in America,* ed. Karen J. Greenberg. New York: Cambridge University Press, 35–83.

MacMaster, Neil. 2000. "The Torture Controversy (1998–2002): Towards a New History of the Algerian War." *Modern and Contemporary France* 10 (4): 449–59.

———. 2004. "Torture: From Algiers to Abu Ghraib." *Race & Class* 46(2): 1–21.

Mandelbaum, Michael. 2003. *The Ideas that Conquered the World: Peace, Democracy, and Free Markets in the Twenty-First Century.* New York: Public Affairs.

Mann, James. 2004. *Rise of the Vulcans: The History of Bush's War Cabinet.* London: Penguin.

Margulies, Joseph. 2006. *Guantanamo and the Abuse of Presidential Power.* New York: Simon and Schuster.

Marín, José M., Carmen Molinero, and Pere Ysàs. 2001. *Historia política. 1939–2000.* Madrid: Istmo.

Marks, Susan. 1995. "Civil Liberties in the Margin: The UK Derogation and the European Court of Human Rights." *Oxford Journal of Legal Studies* 15: 69–95.

Marshall, T. H. 1950. *Citizenship and Social Class, and Other Essays.* Cambridge: Cambridge University Press.

Marton, Ruchama. 1995. "The White Coat Passes Like a Shadow: The Health Profession and Torture in Israel." In *Torture: Human Rights, Medical Ethics, and the Case of Israel,* ed. Neva Gordon and Ruchama Marton. London: Zed, 33–40.

Massimino, Elisa. 2004. "Leading by Example? U.S. Interrogation of Prisoners in the War on Terror." *Criminal Justice Ethics* 23 (1): 74–76.

Mata, José M. 1995. *El nacionalismo vasco radical: Discurso, organización y expresiones.* Bilbao: Servicio Editorial UPV-EHU.

Mayer, Jane. 2005a. "Outsourcing Torture" *The New Yorker,* February 14 & 21, 106–23.

———. 2005b. "The Experiment." *The New Yorker,* July 11 & 18, 60–71.

———. 2006. "The Memo: A Hidden History of Torture Policy." *The New Yorker,* February 27.

McCoy, Alfred W. 2006. *A Question of Torture: CIA Interrogation from the Cold War to the War on Terror.* New York: Metropolitan.

McDougal, Myres S., et al. 1960. *Studies in World Public Order.* New Haven, Conn.: Yale University Press.

McGarry, John, and Brendan O'Leary. 1995. *Explaining Northern Ireland: Broken Images.* Oxford: Blackwell.

McLellan, Anne, and Irwin Cotler. 2005. Joint Statement by the Hon. Anne McLellan, Deputy Prime Minister and Minister of Public Safety and Emergency Preparedness, and the Hon. Irwin Cotler, Minister of Justice and Attorney General of Canada, on the occasion of appearances before the Canadian Senate Special Committee on the Anti-Terrorism Act and the House of Commons Subcommittee on Public Safety and National Security. November 14.

McRae, Rob and Don Hubert, eds. 2001. *Human Security and the New Diplomacy,* Montreal: Queen's University Press.

Merillat, H. C. L., ed. 1964. *Legal Advisors and Foreign Affairs.* Dobbs Ferry, N.Y.: Oceana.

Mertus, Julie. 2005. "Human Rights and Civil Society in a New Age of American Exceptionalism." In *Human Rights in the "War on Terror,"* ed. Richard Ashby Wilson. New York: Cambridge University Press, 317–35.

Millett, Kate. 1994. *The Politics of Cruelty: An Essay on the Literature of Political Imprisonment.* New York: W. W. Norton.

Moir, Lindsay. 2002. *The Law of Internal Armed Conflict.* Cambridge: Cambridge University Press.

Moore, John Norton, Frederick S. Tipson, and Robert F. Turner, eds. 1990. *National Security Law.* Durham, N.C.: Carolina Academic Press.

Morán, Gregorio. 1991. *El precio de la transición.* Barcelona: Planeta.

Moravcsik, A. 2000. "The Origins of Human Rights Regimes: Democratic Delegation in Postwar Europe." *International Organization* 54: 217–52.

Mosley, Richard G. 2002. "Preventing Terrorism Bill C-36: The Anti-Terrorism Act 2001." In *Terrorism, Law & Democracy: How Is Canada Changing following September 11?* ed. David Daubney. Montreal: Les Éditions Thémis.

Mueller, John. 2005. "Simplicity and Spook: Terrorism and the Dynamics of Threat Exaggeration." *International Studies Perspective* 6: 208–34.

Ní Aoláin, Fionnuala. 2000. *The Politics of Force: Conflict Management and State Violence in Northern Ireland.* Belfast: Blackstaff Press.

Nitschke, Peter, ed. 2005. *Rettungsfolter im modernen Rechtsstaat? Eine Verortung.* Bochum: Kamp.

O'Brien, Justin. 2005. *Killing Finucane.* Dublin: Gill & Macmillan.

O'Brien, Martin. 1996. "Northern Ireland at the United Nations, 1960–1996." Unpublished LL.M. thesis, Queen's University Belfast.

O'Donnell, Pierce. 2005 *In Time of War: Hitler's Terrorist Attack on America.* New York: New Press.

Oesterle, Kurt. 2003. *Stammheim—Die Geschichte des Vollzugsbeamten Horst Bubeck.* Tübingen: Klöpfer & Meyer

Office of the High Commission for Human Rights (OHCHR). 2000. *Terrorism and Human Rights.*

O'Hanlan, K. 2006. "Application of Human Rights Act to Civilian Deaths in Occupied Iraq." *The Independent,* January 17.

Onaindia, Mario. 2000. *Guía para orientarse en el laberinto vasco.* Madrid: Temas de Hoy.

Orend, Brian. 2002. *Human Rights: Concept and Context.* Toronto: Broadview Press.

Ornstein, Norman J., and Thomas E. Mann. 2006. "When Congress Checks Out." *Foreign Affairs* 85(6): 67–82.

OSPDH (Observatori del Sistema Penal i els Drets Humans). 2005. *El populismo punitiu. Anàlisi de les reformes i contra-reformes del sistema penal espanyol.* Barcelona: Ajuntament de Barcelona.

OVDH (Observatorio Vasco de Derechos Humanos/Giza Eskubideen Euskal Herriko Behatokia). 2003. "Medidas antiterroristas: Panorama internacional y Euskal Herria." http://www.behatokia.info.

PACE (Parliamentary Assembly of the Council of Europe). 2006. Committee on Legal Affairs and Human Rights. "Alleged Secret Detentions and Unlawful Inter-State Transfers Involving Council of Europe Member States." Draft report, part II. Explanatory memorandum by Dick Marty, rapporteur. Strasbourg, AS/Jur (2006) 16 Part II, June 7.

Pacheco, Allegra. 2001. "U.N. and International Law—Possibilities and Limitations in Palestine." *Guild Practitioner* 58(1): 20–26.

———, ed. 1999. "The Case against Torture in Israel: A Compilation of Petitions, Briefs and Other Documents Submitted to the Israeli High Court of Justice." Jerusalem: Public Committee against Torture in Israel. May.

Parker, T. 2005. "Appendix A: Counterterrorism Policies in the United Kingdom." In *Protecting Liberty in an Age of Terror,* ed. P. B. Heymann and J. M. Kayyem. Cambridge, Mass.: MIT Press, 119–48.

PCATI (Public Committee against Torture in Israel). 2001. *Flawed Defense: Torture and Ill-Treatment in GSS Interrogations following the Supreme Court Ruling, 6 September 1999–6 September 2001.* Jerusalem, September.

———. 2003. *Back to a Routine of Torture: Torture and Ill-Treatment of Palestinian Detainees during Arrest, Detention and Interrogation, September 2001–April 2003.* Jerusalem.

Pelzer, Marei. 2005. "Zurück zum Fremden-Polizeirecht? Anti-Terror-Gesetzgebung im Zuwanderungsgesetz." *Bürgerrechte und Polizei* 1: 21–26.

Peters, Butz. 1991. *RAF. Terrorismus in Deutschland*. Stuttgart: Deutsche Verlags-Anstalt.

———. 2004. *Tödlicher Irrtum. Die Geschichte der RAF*. Frankfurt am Main: Scherz.

Peters, Edward. 1985. *Torture*. New York: Basil Blackwell.

Pfaff, William. 2005. "What We've Lost: George W. Bush and the Price of Torture." *Harper's*, November, 50–56.

Pictet, Jean S., ed. 1960. *Commentary: Geneva Convention III*. Geneva: ICRC.

PNAC (Project for a New American Century). 2000. Rebuilding America's Defenses: Strategy, Forces and Resources for a New Century. Report, Thomas Donnelly, principal author. September. http://www.newamericancentury.org/RebuildingAmericasDefenses.pdf.

Porch, Douglas. 1995. *The French Secret Services: From the Dreyfus Affair to the Gulf War*. New York: Farrar, Straus and Giroux.

Posner, Richard. 2004. "Torture, Terrorism, and Interrogation." In *Torture: A Collection*, ed. Sanford Levinson. Oxford: Oxford University Press, 291–98.

Power, Samantha. 2002. *"A Problem from Hell:" America and the Age of Genocide*. New York: Perennial.

Prantl, Heribert. 2002. *Verdächtig. Der starke Staat und die Politik der inneren Sicherheit*. Hamburg: Europa-Verlag.

Preston, Paul. 1995. *La política de la venganza. El fascismo y el militarismo en la España del siglo XX*. Barcelona: Península.

Quinn, T. 2005. "Tony Blair's Second Term." In *Britain at the Polls 2005* ed. John Bartle and Anthony King. Washington, D.C.: Congressional Quarterly Press, 1–30.

Rasch, Wilfried. 1976. "Die Gestaltung der Haftbedingungen für politisch motivierte Täter in der Bundesrepublik Deutschland." *Monatszeitschrift für Kriminologie und Strafrechtsreform* 59: 61–69.

Ratner, Michael, and Ellen Ray. 2004. *Guantanamo: What the World Should Know*. White River Junction, Vt.: Chelsea Green.

Reemtsma, Jan-Philipp. 2005. *Folter im Rechtsstaat?* Hamburg: Hamburg Ed.

Rejali, Darius. 2004a. "Torture's Dark Allure." June 18. http://dir.salon.com/story/opinion/feature/2004/06/18/torture_1/index.html.

———. 2004b. "Does Torture Work?" June 21. http://dir.salon.com/story/opinion/feature/2004/06/21/torture_algiers/index.html.

Rieff, David. 2002. "The Bureaucrat of Torture." *World Policy Journal* 19(1): 105–10.

Roach, Kent. 2002. "Did September 11 Change Everything? Struggling to Preserve Canadian Values in the Face of Terrorism." *McGill Law Journal* 47(4): 893–947.

Roberts, Adam, and Richard Guelff, eds. 1989. *Documents on the Laws of War*. Oxford: Clarendon Press.

Roberts, Anthea. 2004. "Righting Wrongs or Wronging Rights? The United

States and Human Rights Post-September 11." *European Journal of International Law* 15(4): 721–49.

Robertson, G. 2005. "Fair Trials for Terrorists?" In *Human Rights in the "War on Terror,"* ed. Richard Ashby Wilson. Cambridge: Cambridge University Press, 169–83.

Robin, Marie-Monique. 2005. "Counterinsurgency and Torture: Exporting Torture Tactics from Indochina and Algeria to Latin America." In *Torture: Does It Make Us Safer? Is It Ever OK? A Human Rights Perspective*, ed. Kenneth Roth and Minky Worden. New York: New Press, 44–54.

Rodríguez Jiménez, José Luís. 1992. "La extrema derecha en España: Del tardofranquismo a la transición democrática (1967–1982)." Diss., Universidad Complutense de Madrid.

Rosenberg, Morris. 2002. "An Effective Canadian Legal Framework to Meet Emerging Threats to National Security." Address to Canadian Association for Intelligence and Security Studies, September 26. http://canada.justice.gc .ca/en/news/sp/2002/doc_30694.html.

Ross, James. 2005. "A History of Torture." In *Torture: Does It Make Us Safer? Is It Ever OK? A Human Rights Perspective*, ed. Kenneth Roth and Minky Worden. New York: New Press, 3–17.

Roth, Kenneth, and Minky Worden, eds. 2005. *Torture: Does It Make Us Safer? Is It Ever OK? A Human Rights Perspective.* New York: New Press.

Rowe, Peter, and Michael A. Meyer. 1996. "The Geneva Conventions (Amendment) Act 1995: A Generally Minimalist Approach." *International and Comparative Law Quarterly* 45: 476–84.

Roxin, Claus, ed. 2005. *Strafprozessordnung.* 39th ed. Munich: C. H. Beck.

Ruthven, Malise. 1978. *Torture: The Grand Conspiracy.* London: Weidenfeld & Nicolson.

Saar, Erik, with Viveca Novak. 2005. *Inside the Wire.* New York: Penguin.

Sampedro, Víctor, ed. 2005. *13-M. Multitudes on line.* Madrid: Libros de la Catarata.

Sánchez Cuenca, Ignacio. 2006. "Los hechos confirman la derrota del terrorismo." *El País*, September 7.

Sands, Philippe. 2005. *Lawless World: America and the Making and Breaking of Global Rules.* London: Penguin.

Scanlon, T. M. 2002. "Rawls on Justification," In *The Cambridge Companion to Rawls*, ed. S. Freeman. Cambridge: Cambridge University Press, 139–67.

Scarry, Elaine. 1985. *The Body in Pain: The Making and Unmaking of the World.* Oxford: Oxford University Press.

Scheppele, Kim. 2004. "Law in a Time of Emergency: States of Exception and the Temptations of 9/11." *Journal of Constitutional Law* 6(5): 1001–83.

———. 2005. "Hypothetical Torture in the 'War on Terrorism.'" *Journal of National Security Law* 1(2): 285–340.

Schily, Otto, and Christian Ströbele. 1973. *Plädoyers einer politischen Verteidigung. Reden und Mitschriften aus dem Mahler-Prozeß.* Berlin: Merve Verlag.

Schlesinger, Arthur M., Jr. 1973. *The Imperial Presidency.* Boston, Mass.: Houghton-Mifflin.

Schubert, Alex. 1968. *Stadtguerilla Tupamaros in Uruguay—Rote Armee Fraktion in der BRD.* Berlin: Wagenbach.

Schulz, William F. 2001. *In Our Own Interest.* Boston: Beacon Press.

———. 2003. *Tainted Legacy: 9/11 and the Ruin of Human Rights.* New York: Nation Books.

Sciolino, Elaine. 2006. "Spanish Judge Calls for Closing U.S. Prison at Guantanamo." *New York Times,* June 4, A16.

Sellars, Kristen. 2002. *The Rise and Rise of Human Rights.* Stroud: Sutton.

Serrano-Piedecasas, José R. 1988. *Emergencia y crisis del Estado social. Análisis de la excepcionalidad penal y motivos de su perpetuación.* Barcelona: PPU.

Shafir, Gershon, and Yoav Peled. 2002. *Being Israeli: The Dynamics of Multiple Citizenship.* Cambridge: Cambridge University Press.

Shane, Scott, and Lowell Bergman. 2006. "Adding Up the Ounces of Prevention." *New York Times,* September 10.

Shank, Gregory. 2001. "Limitation of War and the Pursuit of Justice." *Social Justice* 28(3): 5–30.

Shelef, Leon. 1990. "The Lesser Evil and the Greater Good—On the Landau Commission Report, Terror and Torture." *Plilim: Israel Journal of Criminal Justice* 1: 185–219 (in Hebrew).

Sherry, Virginia N. 1999. "Torture in Khiam Prison: Responsibility and Accountability." *al-Hayat,* October 28. English translation at http://www.hrw.org/editorials/1999/khiam-prison.htm.

Shue, Henry. 1978. "Torture." *Philosophy and Public Affairs* 7(2): 124–43.

Sidel, Mark. 2004. *More Secure, Less Free? Antiterrorism Policy and Civil Liberties after September 11.* Ann Arbor: University of Michigan Press.

Siegel, H. 1992. "Justification by Balance." *Philosophy and Phenomenological Research* 52(1): 27–46.

Silveira, Héctor. 1998. *El modelo político italiano. Una laboratorio: de la tercera vía a la globalización.* Barcelona: Ed. Universidad de Barcelona.

Simpson, A. W. B. 2001. *Human Rights and the End of Empire: Britain and the Genesis of the European Convention.* Oxford: Oxford University Press.

Sinnar, Shirin. 2003. "Patriotic or Unconstitutional? The Mandatory Detention of Aliens under the US Patriot Act." *Stanford Law Review* 55(4): 1419–38.

Stevenson, Jonathan. 2003. "How Europe and America Defend Themselves." *Foreign Affairs* 82: 75–90.

Steyn, Johan. 2004. "Guantanamo Bay: The Legal Black Hole." *International and Comparative Law Quarterly* 53: 1–15.

Strasser, Steven, ed. 2004. *The Abu Ghraib Investigations: The Official Reports of the Independent Panel and Pentagon on the Shocking Prisoner Abuse in Iraq.* New York: Public Affairs.

Straßner, Alexander 2001. "Die dritte Generation der "Roten Armee Fraktion." In *Jahrbuch Extremismus und Demokratie,* ed. Uwe Backes and Eckhard Jesse. Baden-Baden: Nomos, 49–71.

Sullivan, Andrew. 2005. "Atrocities in Plain Sight." *The New York Times Book Review*, January 23, 1–11.

Taylor, T. 2002. "United Kingdom." In *Combating Terrorism: Strategies of Ten Countries*, ed. Y. Alexander. Ann Arbor: University of Michigan Press, 187–223.

Tesón, Fernando R. 2005. "Liberal Security." In *Human Rights in the "War on Terror,"* ed. Richard Ashby Wilson. Cambridge: Cambridge University Press, 57–77.

Thamm, Berndt Georg. 2004. *Terrorbasis Deutschland. Die islamistische Gefahr in unserer Mitte.* Munich: Diederichs.

Tilly, Charles. 2003. *The Politics of Collective Violence.* Cambridge: Cambridge University Press.

Tolmein, Oliver 2002. *Vom Deutschen Herbst zum 11. September.* Hamburg: Konkret Verlag.

Tucker, Robert W. 1960. *The Just War: A Study in Contemporary American Doctrine.* Baltimore, Md.: Johns Hopkins University Press.

Tucker, Robert W., and David C. Hendrickson. 2004. "The Sources of American Legitimacy." *Foreign Affairs* 83(6): 18–32.

"Turkey Seeks Tougher Anti-Terror Measures." 2005. *Southern European Times*, October 10. http://www.setimes.com/cocoon/setimes/xhtml/en_GB/features/setimes/features/2005/10/10/feature-03.

Ubasart, Gemma. 2005. "Cap a una nova cultura de l'emergència. Conseqüències de la guerra global a Europa." Master's thesis, Universitat de Barcelona.

Uildriks, Niels. 2000. "Torture in Israel." *Human Rights Review* 1(4): 85–105.

United Nations. Economic and Social Council. Commission on Human Rights. 2006. "Situation of Detainees at Guantanamo Bay." Future E/CN.4/2006/120.

United Nations. General Assembly (UNGA). 2005a. *Human Rights and Terrorism: Report of the Secretary-General.* 1 September.

———. 2005b. *Protecting Human Rights and Fundamental Freedoms While Countering Terrorism.* 22 September.

United Nations. Human Rights Committee (UNHRC). 2005. *Review of Canada's Record of Compliance with the International Covenant on Civil and Political Rights.*

United Nations. Office of the UN High Commissioner for Human Rights (UNHCHR). 2002. *Digest of Jurisprudence of the UN and Regional Organizations on the Protection of Human Rights while Countering Terrorism,* 107 pp, June 3–4.

United Nations. Special Rapporteur on Torture. 2001. Country visit document. E/CN.4/2002/76/Add.1.

———. 2002. Country visit document. E/CN.4/2003/68/Add.1.

———. 2003. Country visit document. EC/CN.4/2004.

United States. 2005. "Second Periodic Report of the United States of America to the Committee against Torture." May 6.

United States. Department of State. 2003. *Country Report on Human Rights Practices (USHR)—Syria (2003)*.

Urban, Mark. 1993. *Big Boys' Rules: The Secret Struggle against the IRA*. London: Faber.

Vagts, Detlev F. 2001. "Hegemonic International Law." *American Journal of International Law* 95: 843–48.

Vidal-Naquet, Pierre. 1963. *Torture: Cancer of Democracy: France and Algeria 1954–62*. Baltimore: Penguin Books.

Villanueva, Javier. 2000. *Nacionalismos y conflicto nacional*. Donosita: Gakoa.

Waldmann, Peter, and Stefan Malthaner. 2003. "Terrorism in Germany: Old and New Problems." In *Confronting Terrorism: European Experiences, Threat Perceptions and Policies*, ed. Marianne van Leeuwen. The Hague: Kluwer Law International, 111–28.

Walker, C. 2003. "Policy Options and Priorities: British Perspectives." In *Confronting Terrorism: European Experiences, Threat Perceptions and Policies*, ed. Marianne van Leeuwen. The Hague: Kluwer Law International, 11–35.

Walker, Clive. 1986. "Irish Republican Prisoners: Political Detainees, Prisoners of War or Common Criminals." *Irish Jurist* 19: 189–225.

Wallace, Donald H., and Betsy Kreisel. 2003. "Martial Law as a Counter-Terrorism Response to Terrorist Attacks: Domestic and International Legal Dimensions." *International Criminal Justice Review* 13: 50–75.

Warbrick, Colin. 2004. "The European Response to Terrorism in an Age of Human Rights." *European Journal of International Law* 15(5): 989–1018.

Waxman, Dov. 2000. "Terrorizing Democracies." *Washington Quarterly* 23(1): 15–19.

Weigend, Thomas, ed. 2005. *Strafgesetzbuch*. 41st ed. Munich: C. H. Beck.

Wiewiorka, Michel. 1993. *ETA et la violence politique au pays basque espagnol*. DP 40. New York: United Nations Research Institute for Social Development.

Wiktorowicz, Quintan. 2006. "A Genealogy of Radical Islam." In *Terrorism and Counterterrorism: Understanding the New Security Environment*, 2d ed., ed. Russell D. Howard and Reid L. Sawyer. Dubuque, Ia.: McGraw Hill, 207–29.

Wilson, Richard Ashby. 2005. "Human Rights in the War on Terror." In *Human Rights in the "War on Terror,"* ed. Richard Ashby Wilson. Cambridge: Cambridge University Press.

Wilson, Richard Ashby, ed. 2005. *Human Rights in the "War on Terror."* Cambridge: Cambridge University Press.

Woodworth, Paddy. 2002. *Dirty War, Clean Hands: ETA, the GAL and Spanish Democracy*. New Haven: Yale University Press.

Woodworth, Paddy. 2004. "The War against Terrorism: The Spanish Experience from ETA to al-Qaeda." *International Journal of Iberian Studies* 17(3): 169–82.

"The Wrong Arm of the Law: Torture Disclosed and Deflected in Israeli Politics." 1991. *Tikkun* 6(5): 13–14, 86–88.

Wunschik, Tobias. 1997. *Baader-Meinhofs Kinder. Die zweite Generation der RAF*. Opladen: Westdeutscher Verlag.

Yee, James. 2005. *For God and Country: Faith and Patriotism under Fire*. New York: Public Affairs.

Yizhar, S. 1962. "The Prisoner." In *Israeli Stories: A Selection of the Best Contemporary Hebrew Writing*, ed. Joel Blocker. New York: Schocken, 151–74.

Yoo, John. 2005. *The Powers of War and Peace: The Constitution and Foreign Affairs after 9/11*. Chicago: University of Chicago Press.

Zallo, Ramón. 2001. *El país de los vascos*. Madrid: Fundamentos.

Zamir, Itzhak. 1989. "Human Rights and National Security." *Israel Law Review* 23(2–3): 375–406.

Zulaika, Joseba. 1988. *Basque Violence: Metaphors and Sacrament*. Reno: University of Nevada Press.

# Contributors

HOWARD ADELMAN is Professor Emeritus at York University, Canada, and is currently Research Professor at the Key Centre for Ethics, Justice, Law and Governance, Griffith University, Brisbane, Australia.

ALISON BRYSK is Professor of Political Science and International Studies at the University of California, Irvine.

COLM CAMPBELL is Professor of Law and Director of the Transitional Justice Institute, University of Ulster, Northern Ireland.

PILAR DOMINGO is Professor of Political Science at the University of Salamanca, Spain.

RICHARD FALK is Professor Emeritus of International Law and Politics at Princeton University, and Distinguished Professor of Global Studies at the University of California, Santa Barbara.

DAVID P. FORSYTHE is Charles J. Mach Distinguished Professor of Political Science, University of Nebraska.

WOLFGANG S. HEINZ is Senior Lecturer at the Free University of Berlin and Senior Research Fellow of the German Institute for Human Rights.

PEDRO IBARRA is Professor of Political Science at the University of the Basque Country, Spain.

TODD LANDMAN is Reader in the Department of Government and Human Rights Centre, University of Essex, United Kingdom.

SALVADOR MARTÍ is Professor of Political Science, University of Salamanca, Spain.

GERSHON SHAFIR is Director of the Institute for International, Comparative and Area Studies and Professor of Sociology at the University of California, San Diego.

DANIEL WEHRENFENNIG is a doctoral candidate in political science at the University of California, Irvine.

# Index

9 780520 098602